SPEAKING WITH CONFIDENCE AND SKILL

Lynne Kelly
The University of Hartford

Arden K. Watson
The Pennsylvania State University

UNIVERSITY
PRESS OF
AMERICA

Lanham • New York • London

Copyright © 1986 by
Harper & Row, Publishers, Inc.

University Press of America,® Inc.
4720 Boston Way
Lanham, MD 20706

3 Henrietta Street
London WC2E 8LU England

British Cataloging in Publication Information Available

This edition was reprinted in 1989 by arrangement with
Harper & Row, Publishers, Inc., New York, New York

Library of Congress Cataloging-in-Publication Data

Kelly, Lynne.
Speaking with confidence and skill / Lynne Kelly, Arden K. Watson.
p.   cm.
Reprint. Originally published: New York : Harper & Row, ©1986.
(Speech communication series)
Bibliography: p.
Includes index.
1. Oral communication. I. Watson, Arden K. II. Title.
[P95.K45 1989]   88–33322 CIP
001.54'2– –dc19

ISBN: 978-0-8191-7278-5

To Gerald M. Phillips, mentor and friend—Your original work on reticence and your concern for the reticent individual have served as an inspiration to both my research and my teaching. Because of you, this book was written.

—Lynne Kelly

Contents

Preface **xi**

Part One

Understanding Yourself as a Communicator   1

1   THE PROCESS OF COMMUNICATION   3

Introduction   3

Understanding the Process of Communication   4

The Value of Communication   11

Aspects of the Individual That Affect
    Communication   12

Becoming a More Skilled and Confident
    Communicator   17

Summary   17

2   ASSESSING YOURSELF AS A COMMUNICATOR   19

Introduction   19

Four Communicators   20

A Guide to Self-assessment   27

Your Personal Communicator Profile   44

Your Personal Improvement Program   45

Summary   46

Part Two

Improving Yourself as a Communicator   49

3   IMPROVING ATTITUDES AND REDUCING APPREHENSION   51

Introduction   51

Improving Attitudes   52

Controlling Communication Apprehension   62

Controlling Situational Apprehension   66

Summary   69

4   **SETTING PERSONAL COMMUNICATION GOALS**   71

Introduction   71

What Is Goal Setting?   72

The Importance of Goal Setting   73

The Steps of Goal Setting   75

Summary   87

5   **ASSESSING THE COMMUNICATION SITUATION
AND LISTENERS**   89

Introduction   89

What Is Situation and Listener Assessment?   90

The Importance of Situation and Listener
    Assessment   92

How to Assess a Communication Situation   93

How to Assess Your Listeners   102

Summary   113

Part Three

Understanding Communication Contexts   *115*

6   **COMMUNICATION IN SOCIAL RELATIONSHIPS**   117

Introduction   117

Functions of Our Relationships   118

Types of Relationships   119

Improving Attitudes in Social Relationships   120

Reducing Apprehension in Social Relationships   126

Improving the Skills of Relating   130

Summary   142

7   **GROUP DISCUSSION**   143

Introduction   143

What Is a Group?   144

The Group Discussion Process   145

Improving Attitudes and Reducing Apprehension   153

Improving Skills in Group Discussion   155

Summary   165

8   PREPARING A PUBLIC SPEECH   167

Introduction   167

Public Speaking as Extended Conversation   168

Types of Speeches   170

Improving Public Speaking Skills   174

Summary   196

9   DELIVERING A PUBLIC SPEECH   199

Introduction   199

Improving Attitudes and Reducing Apprehension   200

Preparing to Deliver and Delivering the Speech   204

Summary   223

Notes   *225*

Glossary   *231*

Index   *235*

Preface

On the basis of a survey of 5000 people, psychologist Philip Zimbardo discovered that over 80 percent considered themselves to be shy at some point in their lives.[1] Of those people, about 40 percent considered themselves shy at present.[2] Findings such as these argue quite convincingly that feelings of nervousness and tension about communication are very common. When we consider that *The Book of Lists* reports public speaking as the number one fear of those surveyed,[3] the urgency of this issue for speech communication professionals becomes readily apparent. The authors believe that nearly all students in a beginning performance course, as well as novice speakers, experience apprehension about speaking in one or more contexts, particularly in public speaking. For too long we either ignored that issue or assumed that practice speaking would alleviate apprehension. After years of working with apprehensive students in special programs, the authors have discovered that more than practice is needed to reduce apprehension. There are many techniques that can be used to help overcome apprehension in performance skills.

We have incorporated those techniques into this book, intended primarily for a basic speech communication course. Performance in three areas—public speaking, small group discussion, and interpersonal interaction—is emphasized, but the most original feature is the weaving of cognitive restructuring (or attitude change), relaxation techniques, and skills training techniques through the fabric of the basic book. All three of these techniques have been found to be very effective in alleviating apprehension about speaking. Although special programs using these techniques have been instituted around the country to help more severely apprehensive students and other beginning speakers, little has been done for those in regular performance courses who also experience tension. The techniques included here can help speakers to be more relaxed, confident, and effective communicators.

The content of the book is divided into three parts and nine chapters. Part One, "Understanding Yourself as a Communicator," focuses on the process of communication and on the communicator. Chapter 1, "The Process of Communication," discusses what communication is; the importance of communication to the individual, to relationships, and to society; the contexts of communication;

[1]Philip G. Zimbardo, *Shyness: What It Is, What to Do About It* (Reading, Mass.: Addison-Wesley, 1977), p. 13.
[2]Ibid., p. 14.
[3]David Wallechinsky, Irving Wallace, and Amy Wallace, *The Book of Lists* (New York: Bantam Books, 1978), p. 469.

and the dynamics that affect communication. These include attitudes toward self, others, and communication; apprehension about speaking; and the skill level of the speaker. The notion that all people experience communication apprehension in at least some situations is introduced, as is the idea that techniques are available that can help people become more confident, effective speakers.

Chapter 2, "Assessing Yourself as a Communicator," stresses the importance of understanding personal strengths and weaknesses as a first step toward becoming a more effective communicator. A number of self-assessment activities are included to help readers assess their attitudes toward self, others, and communication; their level of apprehension about communication; and their skills in the three areas of public speaking, group discussion, and interpersonal communication. By the end of the chapter readers will have identified their communication strengths and areas in which they need improvement.

Part Two, "Improving Yourself as a Communicator," comprises three chapters that focus on techniques for improving attitudes, reducing apprehension, and improving communication skills necessary for any communication situation. Chapter 3, "Improving Attitudes and Reducing Apprehension," presents techniques for improving attitudes toward self, others, and communication. In particular, it presents the technique of reasonable thinking, designed to change unreasonable thinking into more productive, reasonable thinking. Chapter 3 also describes a relaxation procedure and systematic desensitization, which help people learn to relax in situations that provoke anxiety.

Chapter 4, "Setting Personal Communication Goals," presents the technique of goal setting, which has been found to be very effective in helping people alleviate communication apprehension and become more effective speakers. The technique is described, and its importance as a general communication skill for all types of situations is emphasized.

Chapter 5, "Assessing the Communication Situation and Listeners," illustrates that the most effective communicators are able to adapt to various communication situations and to their listeners. This general communication skill can be developed by learning the systematic procedure for analyzing situations and listeners that is described in this chapter.

Part Three, "Understanding Communication Contexts," examines communication in dyadic, small group, and public speaking contexts. Chapter 6, "Communication in Social Relationships," discusses why we need relationships and types of relationships and provides techniques for improving attitudes and alleviating apprehension in one-to-one communication situations. Chapter 6 also teaches skills that are of importance in the development of relationships, such as building trust, expressing ideas effectively, communicating confirmation, self-disclosure, social conversation skills, and listener and situation adaptation.

Chapter 7, "Group Discussion," looks at the group discussion process to provide an understanding of its complexity due to the interaction of many factors, both internal and external to the group. Techniques for controlling apprehension and improving attitudes about group discussion are offered. Six skills important for becoming an effective group member are examined.

Chapters 8 and 9 focus on the public speaking context. Chapter 8, "Preparing a Public Speech," examines the concept of public speaking as extended conversation in three types of speeches. This chapter emphasizes how to prepare a public speech by presenting nine stages of speech preparation: choosing a speech topic, writing a specific speech purpose, assessing the listeners and the situation, writing the residual message, generating ideas and researching the topic, organizing the speech, preparing supporting materials, planning the introduction and the conclusion, and inserting transitions.

Chapter 9, "Delivering a Public Speech," focuses on preparing to deliver and delivering the public speech by presenting six steps in speech delivery. These steps include choosing the type of delivery; controlling what the audience hears by thinking about word choice, speech patterns, and use of the voice; controlling what the audience sees by being aware of body movement and gestures, facial expression, and eye contact, and by effective use of visual aids; controlling the environment; rehearsing the speech; and delivering the speech. Chapter 9 also provides techniques for improving attitudes and reducing apprehension about public speaking.

We wish to thank the panel of reviewers, which included Phillip Backlund, Central Washington University; Dan B. Curtis, Central Missouri State University; Joe Martinez, El Paso County Community College; Gerald M. Phillips, The Pennsylvania State University; and Douglas M. Trank, University of Iowa.

Lynne Kelly
Arden K. Watson

one

UNDERSTANDING YOURSELF AS A COMMUNICATOR

chapter 1

The Process of Communication

CHAPTER OBJECTIVES

1. To understand the process of communication and the components of that process.
2. To examine three major types of communication: dyadic, small group, and public.
3. To understand the ways in which the process of communication is important in our lives.
4. To understand personal qualities that affect the communication process, including attitudes toward self and others, apprehension, and skill level.

INTRODUCTION

Think of a situation you have faced with a great deal of confidence. Remember how terrific you felt? You knew just what to do and performed skillfully. We all can remember situations like that, but we can also recall situations we encountered that made us feel uncertain and afraid. For many of us, those situations involved speaking. Perhaps it was a conference with a teacher, a public speech, or a conversation with an attractive stranger at a party.

One of the main reasons we feel confident in some situations is that we know we have the skills to perform the behaviors that are important in the situation. If you know what to do and also know that you are capable of doing it, you are likely to feel confident. If you are sure about how to prepare and deliver a speech, for example, you will probably feel confident about public speaking.

This is a book about becoming more confident in speaking situations, not just public speaking but also dyadic (one-to-one) and small group situations. It is a "how-to" book designed to help you develop the skills you need to be a more effective communicator. It is based on a method called *goal setting*. Goal setting is a step-by-step procedure for formulating your goals in a communication situation, developing a flexible plan for your behavior, and identifying concrete indicators of goal achievement. We will describe the method in detail in Chapter 4 and show you how to use it. We have chosen the goal-setting method as the basis for this book because it has been found to be very successful at helping students improve their communication skills and increase their confidence.[1] We have used it successfully with students in high school and college classes designed specifically for those who report feeling very uneasy about speaking. Both of the authors of this book have considerable experience working with students who feel very nervous about a variety of communication situations. Through the goal-setting method and the other techniques in this book, we have seen such students make tremendous strides in developing confidence and skill as communicators.

We hope that you will find these techniques helpful to you. They are designed to help you develop your skills in communication situations. You may discover that as you acquire greater skill, your confidence will grow. And as you become more confident in your ability to speak, you will take advantage of new opportunities to speak, which will help you gain greater skill. Confidence and skill are interdependent, and you will see improvement in both areas if you are willing to work to improve your ability to communicate.

UNDERSTANDING THE PROCESS OF COMMUNICATION

Communication may be one of the most overused words in our society. To many people, *communication* simply means talk. How many times have you heard someone say, "We need more communication"? When they say this, they mean that if they talk, problems will be solved or understanding will occur. This is not necessarily so. We need not only communication, but *effective* communication. And sometimes we need less communication. In order to decide when you need more communication, when you need less, and when you need better communication, you must understand the process of communication. This book, and particularly this chapter, will introduce you to the process of communication.

We will begin by discussing the process of communication and its importance to you. Then we'll take a look at various types of communication and how the process is influenced by the type of situation. We'll then consider how the three areas of attitude, apprehension, and skill level affect the communication process.

There is no simple definition of communication. In fact, Dance and Larson list 126 different definitions of communication that have been published.[2] Dance and Larson published their book in 1976, so there are probably many more definitions that could be added to their list.

We define communication as *a process through which people create meaning by exchanging verbal and nonverbal symbols*. In order for this definition to be useful to you, we need to explain each of the major terms in the definition.

First, communication is a *process* because as people talk to one another, they are changed by the interaction. As they change, their interaction changes, this in turn changes them, and so on. Think of the ways in which the act of communicating with another person changes us. First, it changes the way we perceive the other person. We may like the person more or less; we may see the person as more or less kind, witty, interesting, or fun. Our perceptions change continually as we communicate. Sometimes the changes are drastic, as when you discover you really like someone that you previously didn't care for. Sometimes the changes are more subtle and may not be noticeable to you at all.

Second, as we communicate, what we say and how we say it will be affected by our changing perceptions. Suppose you begin feeling closer to someone as you talk to him or her. You may decide to tell that person something very personal about yourself, even though you did not originally plan to disclose that information. The act of communicating has changed your perception of the other person, and this has changed your talk. Keep in mind that changes are happening to the other person too. Perhaps because you revealed a secret, your partner will share some secret with you. This will alter how you see that person, which will influence what you say and do, and so on. The process is one of continual change.

Third, the act of communicating can change the way we see ourselves. Remember when you were a child and some other child made fun of you? And then the soothing words of some teacher made you feel better about yourself. When you talk with someone who tells you that you are attractive or intelligent, how you see yourself may be changed. This will influence how you communicate and how you see the other person. Notice how the changes that occur through the process of communication are interrelated.

Finally, communication can change our feelings or mood, our attitudes, beliefs, and values, how we view the world, and how we view people in general. By someone's words you may be made to feel sad, such as when a friend confides in you about some personal troubles. You may decide to try a new food because of someone's persuasion, or you may be convinced not to waste food. You may view the world with greater optimism or people in general with increased suspicion. All of these changes can occur because of the act of communication. And it is because of all these changes that we describe communication as a process. It is not a static, predictable event. You cannot plan exactly what you will say, say it without being influenced in any way by the other person, and produce a result exactly as you had planned.

In our definition of communication we stated that it is a process *through which people create meaning*. We sometimes think of words as having a specific meaning that is the same for everyone. As we will explain in more detail shortly, words are symbols that represent things and ideas. When two people communicate, each one interprets the words and actions of the other based on a host of factors such as their experiences, their values, attitudes, and beliefs, their knowledge of the other person and the situation, and so forth. Thus, as people communicate, each one assigns meaning to the words and actions of the other. Sometimes we assign a meaning that is similar to what the other person intended, but not always. And most of the time we don't even know if the meaning that we assume is what the other person intended. In fact, people do not always know precisely what they intend to communicate.

Thus communication is a process through which people create meaning. Both people involved assign meaning to each other's words and actions and to their own. And as each person is influenced by the process of communication in the ways that we have discussed, the meanings that they assign may be changed. For example, suppose you meet a stranger at a party who makes remarks that you interpret as sarcastic. As you talk with that person, you may find yourself liking him or her. As you begin liking the other, you may interpret his or her comments as funny or witty instead of sarcastic. The meaning you assign to the comments has changed because your perception of the other person has changed.

The final component of our definition of communication is that it is a process through which people create meaning *by exchanging verbal and nonverbal symbols.* A symbol is something that represents a thing or an idea. The word *love* is a symbol in that it stands for some idea, whereas the word *chair* stands for an object. Notice that in both cases, people may have different interpretations for these symbols. When we mentioned the word *love,* some of you may have thought of a romantic love, some may have thought of the love of a close friend, and others may have thought of familial love. And although the word *chair* represents a tangible object, different individuals will assign very different meanings to the word. You may have immediately thought of your favorite chair at home. Other people may have had the image of the chair they are sitting in as they read this book. And the image of a classroom chair may have appeared in other readers' minds.

Thus, although symbols represent ideas or things, they can be interpreted in many ways. This is true not only of word symbols but of nonverbal symbols as well. Nonverbal symbols include dress, gestures, posture, facial expressions, distance between people as they interact, and the manner in which words are spoken. We may not intend to send a message by what we wear or how we stand, but people may assign meaning to our clothing and our posture. And different people are likely to assign different meanings to our clothes and our posture.

Another way to understand the communication process is to examine the components of the process and their relationships to one another. So in addition to our definition of communication, we will discuss the components of the communication process and explain how they are related.

The Components of the Communication Process

Participants   The participants are the people involved in the process. There can be two or more individuals involved. Clearly, the participants have a tremendous impact on the act of communication by what they say and do. And, of course, what they say and do is affected by what they bring to the situation and by the other participants. By "what they bring to the situation" we mean the sum of their experiences, their knowledge, their attitudes, beliefs, and values, their expectations, their goals for the encounter, and other goals. These are added to and altered as the participants interact, but they clearly have an effect on the interaction. Let's look at a simple example.

Suppose you have a date with a person of the opposite sex, and the plan is to go to the movies and then grab a bite to eat. Suppose the interaction begins when the other person picks you up at your apartment. Consider all of the things that you bring to the situation. First, you bring your expectations for the encounter. Do you expect to have a good time, or do you expect it to be boring? Are you unsure about what to expect? Second, what other experiences have you had with dates of this kind? How do those experiences affect how you perceive this date? Third, how do you feel, mentally and physically? Fourth, how do you perceive the other person? Do you think he or she is nice, intelligent, fun, attractive? How well do you feel you know this other person? What are your feelings for the person as you enter the situation? What are your goals for the date? Do you have other goals that are affecting your feelings about the date? We could go on with these questions, but the point is that who you are and what you have experienced will influence your communication with another. You cannot set your past aside and start with a clean slate each time you interact with someone. Neither can the other participant. Furthermore, you will both be changed, even if ever so slightly, as you communicate with each other.

Situation　　Communication occurs at a specific time in a particular place when participants get together. The situation in which people communicate is an important part of the process because it affects what people say and how they say it, how they see one another, their expectations, their goals, and so forth. If we return to our dating example, think about how a change in situation could change your feelings and expectations. Instead of going to the movies with someone that you know, suppose the situation is a blind date to a party. How would the change in situation affect you and your communication?

Many important aspects of a communication situation influence the participants and their communication. First, and one of the most obvious, is the physical location. Where we talk with someone influences the encounter. For example, consider a conversation with one of your professors at his or her office. Now move the conversation to the cafeteria on campus. Finally, move it to a grocery store, where you happen to run into each other. You may be more formal in your speech at the professor's office, somewhat formal in the cafeteria, and less formal in the grocery store. What you talk about will probably also change somewhat, as will how you feel, what you expect, what your goals are, how you perceive the professor, and so forth.

A second aspect of the situation is the presence or absence of other people, who may or may not be involved in the actual interaction. When you run into your professor at the grocery store, there will be other people there shopping, or at least there will be a cashier, and there will probably be other people in line who can overhear what you say. Notice how this will affect what you say and how you say it.

Third, the nature of your relationship with the other participant influences your communication. If you have been in several classes with this professor and are on friendly terms, you might call him or her by first name or be able to talk about a wider variety of topics. The type of relationship we have with another affects how we feel, what we say, what we expect, our goals, and more.

A fourth aspect is the nature of the event at which the communication takes place. Is the event a date? Is it a small group discussion in a classroom? Is it a conference or a party? Note that the type of event is closely tied to the location of the encounter, but it is a different aspect of the situation. For example, you can be in a classroom working with a group of your peers while class is being conducted. You could be in the same classroom before class begins, talking with a friend. The location is the same, but the nature of the event is different. Another way to describe this aspect of the situation is to talk about the purpose of the interaction. Is the purpose to engage in social conversation? Is it to participate in class?

A final aspect that we will consider is the set of norms or private "rules" that govern the situation. Let's look at social norms first. Every social situation occurring in a public place is governed by norms, which are expectations for behavior. For instance, one norm that operates in a job interview situation is that we let the interviewer lead. If we violated that norm by walking into the interview and saying, "Let me begin this interview by asking the questions I have, and then I'll let you talk about whatever you'd like," we would probably not get the job unless the interviewer likes people who violate social norms. These norms affect our communication with others. They affect the topics we talk about, whom we talk to, the language we use, and how we behave.

When you develop a close relationship with another, such as with a friend, you often find yourself interacting in private locations, like an apartment or dorm room. In these private situations, social norms do not have as great an impact and may actually have no impact at all. Instead, the participants have worked out private rules for behavior that supersede social norms.[3] For instance, although it is not acceptable in most public situations to use foul language, it may be perfectly acceptable to two people in private situations if both agree that it is. If one person does not want to hear bad language and the other uses it, it is bound to lead to relational conflict. In that case, the two people need to negotiate what is appropriate and what is not. Sometimes this happens explicitly, when the individuals talk about the rules for a relationship. At other times the people involved in a relationship don't verbalize the rules; the rules evolve out of the interaction over time. For instance, when you are eating dinner with your family, there may be certain topics that are fine to talk about and certain behaviors that are expected. Your parents may never have explicitly stated the rules for dinner table conversation, but you learned about them over time by observing the topics your parents brought up and their reactions to topics you or your family members brought up. It is often only when a violation of the private rules occurs that the rules are made explicit. So, for example, you may not have known that it was not acceptable to talk about what you did in biology lab until you did. At that time, your parents or siblings may have made it explicit that such topics were not appropriate at the dinner table.

Thus the second component of the communication process, the situation in which communication occurs, is a complex component consisting of the location, the nature or purpose of the event, the presence or absence of other people, the nature of your relationship with the other participants, and the social norms or privately transacted rules governing the interaction. We will discuss all of these aspects of the situation in greater detail in Chapter 5.

Message The message refers to the verbal and nonverbal communication exchanges that occur, that is, what is said and done by the participants. As participants attempt to achieve their goals, they create messages that are meant to influence one another. Your message may be "Let's go to the movies" or "I'm going to vote Democratic in the next election." Your nonverbal message could be a smile or a wink that signals that you like the other.

When we discussed what we mean by communication as a process, we stressed the idea that all participants create messages and are influenced by their own messages and those of others. Watzlawick, Beavin, and Jackson claim that in an interactional setting, all behavior has message value, and so it is impossible not to communicate.[4] This means that everything we say and do when we are interacting with another can be interpreted by the other as having some meaning, even if we did not intend it to have meaning. So, for instance, when you are talking to a friend and you yawn, your friend may interpret your yawn as a message that you are bored with the conversation, when in fact your yawn may be the result of studying all night.

In summary, the participants, the situation, and the messages are the three major components of the communication process. We have shown how complex these components are and how they influence each other. You can see that the messages sent are influenced by both the situation and the participants; the participants are affected by the messages and the situation; and, finally, the situation is influenced by the participants and the messages. Think about two different sessions of the same course. In one class there may have been a lively, stimulating discussion, with many people participating. You left that class feeling very excited about the course. In another session, even though the participants were the same people, the discussion was very dull, with few participating. Notice how the situation was altered by the messages and the participants from one class to the next. In the next section of this chapter, we'll examine various types of communication situations and how the process of communication operates within those situations.

Types of Communication Situations

In most of the examples we have given so far, communication has occurred between two people in what is commonly called a conversation. That is not the only type of situation in which communication takes place. There are three major types of communication situations in which face-to-face talk occurs: one-to-one, group, and one-to-many.

One-to-One (Dyadic)   Dyadic communication refers to talk between two participants. A casual conversation with a friend, a job interview, a conference with your teacher, and a meeting with a physician are all examples of dyadic communication. In dyadic communication both participants are free to create and send messages, and there is typically a fairly rapid exchange of messages. Although one person may talk more than the other, and in a few special circumstances one participant may do all of the talking, typically the amount of time each participant talks is about equal. And regardless of how much each person talks, keep in mind that nonverbal messages are also being conveyed through facial expressions, eye movement, posture, gestures, physical distance between participants, and so on.

Group   Group communication takes place among a fairly small number of participants who interact both verbally and nonverbally. You are participating in group communication when you are working on a class project with other students, when you are carrying on a conversation with a group of friends at the dinner table, and when you meet with the other officers of your club or organization. In each case, everyone typically has a chance to talk, although each person probably talks less than he or she would if involved in a dyadic situation. As in dyadic communication, messages are exchanged fairly rapidly. Notice, however, how the addition of participants complicates the situation. Now we have several participants who bring different experiences, interests, knowledge, goals, and general background to the situation and all of whom are influencing one another. Just think about how much more difficult it is to keep a group like this focused on a common topic of talk. Typically, it is also harder to get a chance to be heard, simply because there are more people trying to talk. Often there are competing or differing goals. This is not to say that in dyadic communication there are never competing goals but simply that with an increasing number of participants, the chances for competing goals goes up, and the difficulty associated with everyone trying to achieve their goals also increases.

One-to-Many (Public)   Public communication refers to a situation in which one person does most or all of the talking to two or more others. A speech is an example of public communication. So is a sales presentation, a sermon by a preacher, and an oral report you make to your class about a project you did. The crucial difference between this situation and dyadic and group situations is that one person has responsibility for most of the talking, if not all of it. Of course, there are times when the listeners have the opportunity to ask questions, but those questions are directed to the speaker, who then has the responsibility of answering them. Essentially, in public communication, if the speaker didn't show up, either nothing would happen or another speaker would fill the void. The speaker controls the communication by deciding what is to be talked about and what is not to be discussed.

That does not mean that the listeners don't communicate. Remember what Watzlawick, Beavin, and Jackson said: "One cannot not communicate."[5] The listeners' reactions may be observed and interpreted by the speaker; in fact, a good speaker will attempt to adjust to the responses of the listeners. For instance, a good speaker will look for signs that the audience members are confused or bored or uncomfortable and will alter the speech to accommodate to that audience. That does not mean that the speaker is wishy-washy and says whatever the listeners want to hear, but it means that the speaker changes *the way ideas are presented* to suit the audience better. This idea will be discussed at length in Chapters 8 and 9, which focus on public communication.

THE VALUE OF COMMUNICATION

We have examined the process of communication and its major components. We have also discussed the three basic types of communication situations. A topic we have not yet considered is the importance of communication. Sometimes things that we take for granted are actually very important to us. We certainly take air for granted most of the time, but it is crucial for our survival. At times we take people for granted, perhaps our families or closest friends, when in fact these people are very important to us. Communication is a process that is vital to all of us, yet like air and people, we often take it for granted. Let's look at some of the ways in which communication is important.

First, communication is important to our self-concepts and our identities as individuals. The way we see ourselves is affected by our communication with others. Whether you see yourself as witty or dull, outgoing or quiet is affected by your communication with others. Whenever you communicate with others, they provide verbal and nonverbal messages to you and about you, as we have already explained. If those messages are negative messages about you, and if people consistently send you negative messages, you will probably begin to see yourself in a negative light. Suppose that when you talk to others, they constantly send you the message that you are stupid. Sometimes people tell you directly that you aren't very smart, but most of the time they ignore your attempts to display your intelligence, or they kid you about being a "space case" or an "airhead." After a while you are bound to see yourself as not very intelligent, particularly if the people who have been sending you those messages about yourself are important to you.

Our point is that how we see ourselves and feel about ourselves can be very strongly influenced by our communication with others. Zimbardo argues that one reason people may have trouble with shyness is that they have been labeled as shy and have accepted the label.[6] This is exactly what we are talking about. If you can become a more effective communicator, people will respond to you in more positive ways and will apply positive labels to you. And their positive labels and responses will produce good feelings about yourself.

The second value of communication is that it is the principal means by which we form and maintain our relationships. When you first spoke to another person in a class or started a conversation with a stranger at a party your communication helped to initiate a relationship or to get to know the other person better so that you could decide whether or not you wanted to start a friendship. Talk allows us to know what's inside another person, what that person thinks, believes, and feels. It is difficult to feel close to people about whom we know very little. Several communication scholars have examined stages of relationships, the stages people go through as a relationship progresses and as a relationship deteriorates.[7] What they have found is that the nature of the communication changes as people become closer and as people break up. Thus it is clear that communication plays an important role in our relationships. The more effectively we can communicate, the more likely we are to be able to initiate and maintain satisfying relationships.

The third way in which communication is important to all of us is that it is a means by which we are able to influence others to accept our ideas, to do what we would like, and to understand our feelings. Communication is therefore important to us as community members within a larger, democratic society. We can influence decisions that are made in our communities, such as whether or not a shopping area should be built. Through communication we can influence our local, state, and federal governments. We can call or write to our representatives, letting them know how we think they should vote on a proposed tax increase or the proposed cutting of student loans and grants. Clearly, this does not mean that every time you voice your opinions and ideas people will automatically accept them. But there is no chance of their being accepted if your ideas remain unspoken. If we can communicate effectively, we will be better equipped to influence others.

ASPECTS OF THE INDIVIDUAL THAT AFFECT COMMUNICATION

We have already emphasized the importance and complexity of communication. In fact, by discussing the components of communication—the participants, the situation, and the message—we have begun to consider factors that affect communication. In this section we will focus on aspects of the individual that influence the communication process. There are personal aspects or areas that *you can control* so that you can become a more effective communicator. It is not always possible to control the situation (the time of day or place where we communicate), and we cannot control the other participants or the messages they send. Thus to become better communicators, we must concentrate on controlling those aspects of ourselves that we are indeed capable of controlling. The three personal aspects that will be introduced here and developed throughout the book are your attitudes, your apprehension level, and your skill level.

Attitudes

There are three types of attitudes that can influence your communication: your attitude toward yourself, your attitude toward others, and your attitude toward communication. In this section we will discuss all three sets of attitudes and how they influence the communication process. In the next chapter we will be asking you to evaluate your attitudes, but you should begin thinking about them as we explain them here.

Attitude Toward Self   How we feel about ourselves can influence our communication. If we feel good about ourselves, we are likely to convey that as we speak. In fact, we may be more inclined to try more opportunities to speak. Perhaps a goal that we should all strive for is self-acceptance. Self-acceptance is the ability to accept ourselves without any requirements or conditions. We don't have to achieve goals or possess particular talents in order to accept ourselves. People who accept themselves don't rate themselves as good or bad, worthy or unworthy. They simply accept themselves for what they are and what they can and cannot do.

An attitude of self-acceptance has many advantages to the individual. There is some research available that suggests that self-accepting people have a high level of personal adjustment, see themselves in a realistic manner, and have a healthy view of the world.[8] Furthermore, those who accept themselves tend to expect to be accepted by others and will tend to accept other people as well.

People who accept themselves realize that failures and inadequacies in communication do not mean that they are bad people. They realize that these failures indicate that they need to improve their skills.

We do not mean to suggest that self-accepting people do not ever make judgments about their abilities. They most certainly do. But it is their abilities and their behavior that they judge, not themselves as people. So when we advocate that you accept yourself, we are advocating that you begin rating your behavior and skills, not yourself. We want you to take a close look at your communication behavior and determine your strengths and weaknesses so that you can identify the areas in which you need improvement. By accepting yourself, you may find it easier to work on your communication skills. You will be more willing to try new opportunities to speak, and you will not consider yourself a bad person when you encounter some failures.

Attitude Toward Others   How we perceive another person and evaluate that person affects our communication with that individual. This does not mean that our attitude toward another is constant; we have already discussed how the process of communication influences our perceptions of other people. So as we discuss the ways in which our attitude toward others affects our communication, keep in mind that our attitudes can change as we interact.

There is plenty of research evidence that suggests that when we perceive someone as similar to us, we are more likely to find that person attractive.[9] This may increase the likelihood that we will choose that person as an interaction partner. In addition, we may engage in what some call a self-fulfilling prophecy.[10] That is, we see the person as attractive and therefore as someone we like, so we treat that person in such a way that he or she will act in very likable ways. We are pleasant and kind to that person, who is then very likely to be pleasant and kind to us, increasing our liking and feelings of attraction. What has happened in this situation is that we have helped to get the person to act in ways that reinforce our initial perception of the person's behavior. This is a positive self-fulfilling prophecy in that the result was a pleasant interaction and increased liking. Self-fulfilling prophecies can be negative too. Consider the example of someone who is described by a close friend of yours as nasty or hard to get along with. What happens when you meet that person? Unless you are aware of what you are doing, your verbal and nonverbal behavior are likely to communicate disdain or lack of interest. There is a good chance, then, that the other person will treat you in a similar manner, and you'll leave thinking that your friend was right about this "creep."

We don't want to give you the impression from this description that we control the behavior of other people. But there is a tendency for people to act in a reciprocal manner with one another. That is, if you treat someone kindly, that person is likely to treat you kindly. If you speak defensively to another person, that person is probably going to attack you verbally. Timothy Leary developed a theory of interpersonal behavior that posited that behaviors tend to evoke counterpart behaviors, such that submissive behavior in one tends to produce dominant behavior in the other.[11] Watzlawick, Beavin, and Jackson talked about symmetrical escalation, which is a term that means that a behavior produced by one interactant is followed by a similar but more intense behavior from the other, and so on.[12] Both of these theories support our claim that the behavior of one person tends to evoke certain types of behavior in the other.

Just as we can accept ourselves, we can accept others. When we accept ourselves, we don't judge ourselves as people. We evaluate our behaviors instead. To accept others means that we evaluate their *behavior* and don't rate them as good or bad people. This is difficult to achieve because we have a tendency to judge people rather than their behaviors. If someone makes a mistake, we are inclined to say, "That person is stupid," rather than to say, "What that person did is stupid." But if we strive for other-acceptance, we may find that we feel more tolerant of others. This will undoubtedly have a positive effect on our communication. Another person will probably respond less defensively if we say, "I am unhappy with what you just did," rather than, "I am unhappy with you."

Thus our attitude toward another person affects our communication with that person, and this in turn affects the other participant's behavior. We cannot advocate that you have a positive attitude toward everyone because that would be unrealistic. We do, however, want you to be aware of how your attitude toward another can affect the interaction so that you are better able to understand what occurs in a particular interaction. If, for example, you find that another person acts very defensively when you are interacting, examine your own behavior and attitude to determine how you may have been provoking that defensiveness.

Attitude Toward Communication   Our attitudes toward communication in general and toward particular communication situations will have an effect on our behavior. There is a large body of research on the shy individual that indicates that one of the problems shy people experience involves their attitude toward communication.[13] For instance, the shy (also called "reticent") person has a tendency to evaluate communication situations as threatening.[14] Shy people also may devalue communication and feel that they have more to lose than to gain by communicating.[15] The result of these negative attitudes is often avoidance of communication situations. And if we avoid communication, we will not have sufficient opportunities to develop our communication skills. Then when we are forced to communicate, we will probably not be as effective as someone with more experience. This can then contribute to a negative attitude toward communication, and the cycle continues.

Thus a more positive attitude toward communication can help you develop as a communicator. Just as self-acceptance may lead you to taking more risks, a positive attitude toward communication may do the same. And by taking more risks, you take advantage of more opportunities in which to practice and improve your communication skills. In the next chapter, we will ask you to examine your attitude toward communication to determine if this is an aspect of yourself that you need to change.

In addition to our attitude toward communication in general, our attitude toward a particular communication situation can influence our behavior in that situation. If you perceive a situation as being too difficult for you to handle, you may avoid that situation or present yourself as lacking in confidence. If you perceive a situation as boring, you will probably act bored, and your talk may reflect your boredom. Some scholars argue that one of the problems that shy people have is that they make negative self-statements about situations and other participants.[16] They tell themselves that they can't possibly do well in that type of situation, such as a public speaking situation. Or they tell themselves that the other person will be bored by them or think them stupid. These attitudes, of course, affect how they communicate in those situations and with those people.

In summary, our attitudes toward ourselves, toward others with whom we interact, and toward communication situations influence our communication behavior. Attitudes constitute one aspect of yourself that you can change. In Chapter 3 we will provide you with information and activities to help you develop more positive attitudes that will allow you to improve as a communicator.

Apprehension Level

There are a variety of terms that can be used to denote a feeling of uneasiness about communication. These include *apprehension, anxiety, nervousness,* and *fear.* Because scholars are not in agreement over the precise meanings of these words and how they differ from one another, we will use them interchangeably. Thus when we refer to apprehension about communicating, we mean feelings of uneasiness about it.

People vary in the degree to which they feel apprehension about communicating. Some people have a tendency to feel anxiety about communication most of the time.[17] Other people report feeling anxious about communication in particular types of situations, and still others say that they occasionally feel anxious about communication.[18] Apprehension about communication may affect our communication in several ways.

First, if we feel anxious about communication, we may have a tendency to avoid it, particularly those situations that are the most anxiety-provoking. We have already explained that we need to take advantage of communication situations so that we can practice our communication skills. Avoiding difficult situations will not help us become more skillful at handling them.

Second, apprehension about communication may cause us to withdraw in communication situations. In other words, we may not be able to avoid certain situations, but we may talk very little in them. The unfortunate consequence of this is that we cannot influence others to accept our ideas. We cannot achieve our communication goals, and we do not allow others to get to know us.

Finally, if we feel anxious about communication, we may behave awkwardly and less effectively than we would if we were not quite so anxious. People who feel a great deal of anxiety about public speaking, for example, claim to have trouble remembering what they want to say and report that they tremble, stumble over words, and are very disorganized in their speech.[19]

However, thus far there is very little research that has found apprehension to be associated with ineffective behavior. In fact, some research has found no qualitative differences in the behavior of people who are very apprehensive and those who are not.[20] Thus reducing your apprehension level may not necessarily make you a more effective communicator. It may, however, make you feel better and feel freer to try new speaking opportunities. We believe that apprehension can actually help us perform more effectively. It can give us extra energy that adds a spark to our delivery. Our goal in this book, then, is not to help you eliminate all tension about speaking. It is to help you relax enough that you will feel freer to try new speaking experiences.

In Chapter 2 you will be asked to assess your apprehension about communication; then, in Chapter 3, we will teach you a technique that has been successful in reducing anxiety about communication. We will also introduce you to other ways that you can reduce your anxiety as a communicator. The most important of these is to develop your communication skills.

Skill Level

The third personal aspect that we can control to become more effective communicators is our skill level. As you will see as you read this book, many skills are necessary to be an effective communicator. There are some general skills, and there are skills specific to different contexts. Chapters 4 and 5 will present the communication skills that are important regardless of the communication situation, and Chapters 6 through 9 will examine the specific skills needed in dyadic, group, and public speaking situations.

Unlike attitudes and apprehension, it is easy to see how our basic skill level affects our communication. Keep in mind that the issue is not that some people lack skills in all situations and other people are very skillful in every context. Even shy people, who are described by some scholars as lacking adequate communication skills,[21] are not deficient in all communication skills or in all situations. Everyone has some skill deficiencies, either in terms of general skills, such as listening or goal setting, or in terms of specific skills, such as how to introduce someone or how to use visual aids in a public speech. In the next chapter we will help you to determine the specific and general communication skills that you need to develop. Then you will have the opportunity to develop and practice those skills as you read the remainder of the book.

BECOMING A MORE SKILLED AND CONFIDENT COMMUNICATOR

This book is designed to help you become a more *skilled* and more *confident* speaker in dyadic, group, and public communication contexts. Our approach is to teach you the skills you need to be a more effective communicator, so that as you become more skillful, your confidence will increase. We will also try to show you how to improve your attitudes toward yourself, toward others, and toward communication and how to reduce your apprehension so that your confidence grows and you are more willing to practice your communication skills. Note that we intend to help you work on all three aspects of yourself that affect communication: attitudes, apprehension, and skill.

We take the position that all people can improve in these three areas. We also believe that all people experience some problems in all three areas. All of us can improve our attitudes toward ourselves, others, and communication. We all have some difficulty with apprehension about communication. For many students taking their first and perhaps only speech communication course, there is a great deal of tension, particularly surrounding the public speech. We will help you deal with that anxiety, incorporating the techniques that have been developed by theorists and practitioners who have worked with people who typically experience a great deal of anxiety about communication. Their techniques work, and we will share them with you. Finally, all of us can afford to brush up on our communication skills, and we will provide information and exercises to help you do that.

So whether you describe yourself as shy, quiet, talkative, confident, tense, or any other label you can think of, this book is designed to help you become a better, more confident communicator. To help us help you, you need to be willing to discover yourself as a communicator, to work to improve, and to practice the skills that we teach you.

SUMMARY

Although there are many definitions of communication, we have defined it as a process through which people create meaning by exchanging verbal and nonverbal symbols. It is a process because as people communicate, they are changed, and this affects what they say and how they say it. People create meaning by interpreting their own and the other participants' behavior and speech. Specifically, they interpret the verbal and nonverbal symbols that they exchange.

There are three main components of the communication process. First, there are the participants, whose values, attitudes, experiences, and background affect their communication and how they interpret each other's verbal and non-verbal symbols. Second, there is the situation, the specific time and place in which communication occurs. This also influences the interaction. The actual messages that are exchanged constitute the third component of the process.

The communication process occurs in three major types of situations. Communication may be dyadic, involving a one-to-one situation. It may take place in a small group, or it may take the form of a public (one-to-many) speech. This book will discuss each of these three types of communication situations in detail.

There are three major ways in which communication is important to us as individuals. First, it is a process that influences how we see ourselves, affecting our self-concepts. Second, communication is the process through which we initiate and maintain our relationships with others. Finally, communication is the principal means by which we influence others and the world around us.

This book is designed to help you to improve your skills and increase your confidence as a communicator. It will help you to improve in three specific areas. First, your attitudes toward yourself, toward others, and toward communication can influence your effectiveness as a communicator. We feel that people need to accept themselves, accept others, and have realistic ideas about communication in order to be most effective in communication. Second, the level of apprehension or nervousness we feel may affect our communication. Our goal is not to eliminate apprehension but to reduce it if it is causing you to feel distressed or preventing you from participating in speaking situations. Finally, our skill level affects our communication. If we are weak in the skills necessary to be effective communicators, we need to develop those skills. You may find that as you become more skillful, your confidence will grow.

chapter 2

Assessing Yourself as a Communicator

CHAPTER OBJECTIVES

1. To complete a set of self-assessment activities to determine your strengths and weaknesses as a communicator
2. To plan a self-improvement program geared toward the specific weaknesses identified through the assessment activities.

INTRODUCTION

In the first chapter we explored the process of communication and its importance to you. We also looked at how our attitudes toward self, others, and communication, our apprehension level, and our skill level influence our communication. Now that you are acquainted with these aspects of yourself that affect communication, it is time to examine yourself in each area. Remember, these are personal aspects that you can change to enhance your effectiveness as a communicator. But the first step in improvement is to understand your strengths and weaknesses in each of the three areas: attitude, apprehension, and skill.

This chapter, then, will ask you to look carefully at yourself as a communicator to discover the specific areas in which you need improvement. You may find that this will make the job of trying to better yourself as a communicator much easier because you'll know where to start. And don't worry if you discover that there are a lot of areas in which you need to improve. You don't have to tackle all of them by the end of the course. You have a lifetime to work on them.

FOUR COMMUNICATORS

Before you take a look at yourself as a communicator, let's examine four communicators to identify their strengths and weaknesses. As you read about each one, think about which person seems most like you. This may help you as you assess yourself as a communicator.

Pat   Pat tends to be more of a listener than a speaker in most situations. When she is at parties and other social events, she finds herself letting others initiate and dominate conversations. She says that she prefers to be the listener because she doesn't want to bore people. She feels that they are much more interesting and are more skillful at communicating. Pat reports that she feels depressed when she makes mistakes in communicating—or in anything, for that matter. She says that she loses confidence in herself every time she is unsuccessful at something. Since she considers herself a good listener, she is willing to take on that role.

Pat's quietness is apparent in other types of situations too. In the classroom, she does not volunteer and will speak only if called on. She claims that she is afraid people will think she is stupid if she gives a wrong answer or offers an observation that others don't like. She hates public speaking, claiming that it makes her very nervous. When she gets nervous, she can't remember what she wants to say and makes a lot of mistakes. She says that when she has to prepare for a speech, she spends most of her time worrying about it. She is glad that as soon as she graduates from college she'll "never have to give another speech again" because she "just can't do it and will never be able to."

Now that you have read this description of Pat, answer the following questions.

1. Does Pat sound like you? If so, in what ways? _Yes, I_
act the same way in social
situations and in the classroom. I also
feel the same emotions

2. What are Pat's weaknesses as a communicator? _She is not_
confident + doesn't take iniative

_____

_____

3.   What are Pat's strengths as a communicator? ___Listens___

_____

_____

_____

Let's discuss questions 2 and 3. Although the strengths and weaknesses you listed may not match ours completely, you should not feel concerned. In assessing strengths and weaknesses you are using your judgment just as we are, so there may be some differences in our answers. Pat's major weaknesses as a communicator center around her attitudes toward herself, others, and communication. She does not appear to be very self-accepting because she judges herself as a person on the basis of her performance. When she performs well, she feels good about herself, but when she is unsuccessful, she feels depressed.

In addition to not accepting herself, Pat seems to have an overinflated view of others. She sees them as better communicators and as more interesting people than herself. Because of this attitude toward others in combination with her lack of self-acceptance, she defers to others and lets them dominate interactions.

Finally, Pat has a poor attitude toward communication. She has what we call "unreasonable beliefs" about the act of communicating, a concept that we will develop in Chapter 3. She believes that every time she participates in class she must be right or she will appear stupid. This is an unreasonable belief because no one can be right every time, and to be wrong occasionally will probably not win her the label "stupid." She also has the unreasonable belief that she will never have to give another speech again after college and that she will never be good at public speaking. Many jobs required public communication of some sort, and people can be trained to be more effective public speakers. Pat's attitudes toward communication are preventing her from trying to improve herself as a communicator. She believes that she cannot improve, so instead of attempting to change, she has accepted the role of listener in most situations.

What are Pat's strengths as a communicator? You probably listed that she is a good listener. Yes, Pat does appear to be effective in the role as listener, which is an important strength. Many people are weak in this area because they would rather talk than listen. But many misunderstandings can occur and mistakes made because people do not listen to one another.

It is difficult to determine Pat's other strengths as a communicator because she avoids taking an active role most of the time. She may possess good communication skills, but because she rarely uses them, it is difficult to tell.

By examining Pat's strengths and weaknesses as a communicator, we could make some recommendations as to what areas she needs to begin working on. Above all, Pat needs to change her attitudes toward herself, others, and communication. She needs to develop greater self-acceptance so that she can begin to judge her behavior, not her worth as a person. By accepting herself, she can begin to identify successful and unsuccessful behaviors so that she knows what to try to change. By concentrating on altering unsuccessful behaviors, she can stop feeling so demoralized when she is unsuccessful. She will realize that failure at performing means that she needs to change her behavior, not that she is a failure as a person.

Pat also needs to change her attitudes toward others. She feels that others are more interesting and more skilled, so she allows them to take the lead in conversations. She will never get a chance to try on a new role as speaker if she continues to allow others to dominate the interaction.

Finally, Pat should change her attitudes toward communication. She has several unreasonable beliefs about communication that need to be altered. She needs to change her belief that public speaking is done only in college classrooms and that she can't possibly ever be good at it. She should try to alter her belief that she needs to give a correct answer every time that she answers in class.

Chris   Our second communicator is Chris. Chris tends to avoid talking in most situations and regards himself as shy. At parties and other social situations he talks only with his friends and makes few attempts to initiate conversations with strangers. He says that he feels very nervous when he talks to people he doesn't know well. He worries that they will see his nervousness because he blushes easily and his voice trembles.

Chris rarely speaks out in classes. He reports that he gets very tense when the teacher is calling on students because he is afraid the teacher will call on him. He says he usually knows the answer but he doesn't like to "show off."

In small group discussions Chris is also tense. He tends not to say much, but when he does, it is usually a valuable contribution. He has good ideas and he knows it, but he reports that he gets too nervous to say them.

Chris has never had to give a speech or speak in front of a group but says that the thought of it scares him. He says he'd probably drop a course in which he had to give a speech.

1.   Does Chris sound like you? If so, in what ways? _____

yes nervous to talk to strangers

_____

_____

2.   What are Chris's strengths as a communicator? *can talk*

to friends

_____

_____

3.   What are Chris's weaknesses as a communicator? ___*Shy*___

nervous

_____

_____

As you have probably answered, Chris's strength as a communicator is that he generally has things to say that are worthwhile. He has good ideas during group discussions, and he often has answers to questions asked in class. Chris may have fairly good communication skills, but he does not exercise them enough.

Chris's major weakness is his apprehension about communication. He feels tense and nervous in most situations including social conversation, small groups, and class participation. He has never given a speech but feels nervous at the thought of presenting one.

The anxiety Chris feels about communicating is preventing him from participating when he wants to. As a result, Chris is not developing his communication skills to the maximum, and he is losing opportunities to share his good ideas and information with others.

It would appear that for Chris the ideal training program would involve helping him overcome his apprehension about communication and develop skills in areas such as public speaking where he has not gotten enough practice. If Chris can learn to be more relaxed about communication, he may begin taking advantage of more opportunities to speak. This will help him develop greater skill and confidence as a communicator.

Jackie   Jackie talks quite easily in most social situations and enjoys meeting new people. At parties she often takes the initiative in conversations and has little trouble maintaining them.

When it comes to class participation, however, Jackie rarely speaks out. Jackie says that she would like to speak out in classes, but she doesn't know when to make a contribution. If the teacher asks a specific question, she frequently answers, but she does not volunteer thoughts or observations she has.

In small group discussions Jackie doesn't like to speak much either because she does not want to be seen as too dominant. When she speaks, she speaks easily and clearly and offers good ideas. She says she doesn't know how to tell if she is contributing too much. She says that if people would just tell her to be quiet when she is talking too much, it would make everything a lot easier.

Jackie reports that she is very nervous about public speaking. She says she tries to spend a lot of time preparing for a presentation but just doesn't know how to give a good speech. She says that she'd like to be able to plan an attention-getting introduction so that she could get people interested in her talk, but she doesn't know what to do. She claims that she is not very good at telling jokes, and there is no other way that she can really gain attention. Jackie reports that she can write a speech out and read it, but she would like to be able to speak from an outline rather than reading her speech.

1.   Does Jackie sound like you? If so, in what ways? _____

Kinda. I also don't know how to construct speechs or gain attention

2.   What are Jackie's weaknesses as a communicator? _She_

doesn't grab attention and doesn't utilize queues in class.

3.   What are Jackie's strengths as a communicator? _She is_

Somewhat outgoing + has a desire to speak

In terms of Jackie's weaknesses as a communicator, there appear to be some situations in which she lacks the skills necessary to be effective. Notice, for example, that she doesn't know when to add contributions in class. She lacks a skill that we will discuss in detail in Chapter 5. That skill is situation analysis, which essentially refers to the ability to size up situations in order to determine what is appropriate communication behavior. If Jackie were more skilled in situation analysis, she might be able to determine when it is appropriate to speak in class and when it is not. She also has this trouble with regard to small group discussions. She would like people to tell her when she is dominating the discussion. But if she were more skilled at situation analysis, she would be able to determine for herself when it was time to let others take over the discussion.

Jackie reports that she is nervous about public speaking. In this case it appears that her feelings are caused by her deficient public speaking skills. She needs to learn how to prepare a speech, including the introduction. She has the idea that the only good attention-getter is a joke, but actually there are many techniques for gaining an audience's attention. You will be reading about those techniques in Chapter 8. Jackie also lacks the skills of extemporaneous speaking, or speaking from notes rather than reading. This is also something that she can learn to do. In fact, in Chapter 9, we will discuss how to deliver a speech.

In terms of Jackie's strengths as a communicator, she is skillful at social conversation. She seems to be fairly confident and has a good attitude toward herself, others, and communication. And she does not appear to experience much apprehension about communicating.

An improvement program for Jackie should involve skills training. She needs to develop skills in class participation, small group discussion, and public speaking. A particular skill area in which she could use some work is situation assessment, so that she could monitor herself as she communicates. This would help her know when to speak and how much to speak.

Terry   Terry is an effective communicator in nearly all situations. There is no one type of situation in which Terry needs improvement. Terry seems to experience the occasional failures that all effective communicators experience. For example, sometimes when he gives a speech, it is not quite as good as it could be. And on occasion, when he tries to communicate a point in conversation or class discussion, he does not make himself clear. Once in a while Terry will remain fairly quiet in a social situation, but he claims that this is just because of his mood.

Terry is about as close to an ideal communicator as one can get. In spite of occasional failures, Terry feels very good about himself as a communicator. He knows that failures are sometimes his fault and sometimes the fault of circumstances. And he does not consider himself a failure as a person because of poor performances.

Terry is skilled at social conversations. He is able to initiate and maintain conversations with a wide variety of people. In social situations he moves easily from person to person, able to enjoy conversations with each of them.

In class discussion Terry participates on a regular basis but does not dominate the discussion. He seems to be able to know when to speak and when not to. This is also true in group discussions, as when working on a class project. Other students like working with him because he has good ideas and can usually communicate them clearly. He has leadership abilities but does not dominate the group.

Most of Terry's speeches are very well prepared and organized. He is able to use a variety of techniques to gain attention and make his points. Occasionally, he gets lazy and does not spend sufficient time preparing. On those occasions the quality of his speech usually suffers.

1.   Does Terry sound like you? If so, in what ways? _Only in_

Knowing when my communication

skills feel off

2.   What are Terry's strengths as a communicator? _____

___Pretty much everything___

_____

_____

3.   What are Terry's weaknesses as a communicator? _____

___None___

_____

_____

_____

You probably listed many strengths for Terry, as we did. Terry is generally a very strong communicator in one-to-one, small group, and public speaking situations. Terry appears to be confident and self-accepting. He seems to have very reasonable beliefs about himself, others, and communication. He also is skillful in most communication situations. As we stated, he is about as close to the ideal communicator as one can get.

As far as weaknesses go, Terry has few. His only weakness is that he sometimes fails to prepare for communication situations and so does not participate as effectively as he could. Notice that Terry is not weak in a particular type of communication context. He sometimes has trouble with situations, but so does anyone, regardless of how effective the person is as a communicator.

In terms of an improvement program, Terry could probably just use some brushing up on his skills in all three types of situations: one-to-one, small group, and public speaking. He certainly is a fine communicator, but everyone can always stand some improvement.

After reading the four descriptions, take some time to think about and answer each of the following questions. This will help you as you begin to assess yourself as a communicator.

1. Of the four communicators, which one are you most like: Pat, Chris, Jackie, or Terry? Why?
2. Do you see yourself as a composite of two or more of these communicators? If so, which ones and in what ways?
3. Try writing a brief description of yourself as a communicator, as we did for these people. Then list your own strengths and weaknesses.

The answers you write are for your own use, although your teacher may ask to read them so that he or she can help you throughout the course. Keep these answers in your notebook. You can refer to them at the end of the course to see how you have changed, and you can look at them from time to time to remind yourself of the areas on which you should concentrate during the course.

A GUIDE TO SELF-ASSESSMENT

You now have a preliminary assessment of yourself as a communicator. The remainder of this chapter will take you through a systematic self-assessment procedure so that you can take a more thorough look at yourself as a communicator.

Assessing Strong and Weak Situations

As a first step, we need to begin thinking about the types of situations in which we are generally effective and those in which we are generally ineffective (if there are any). This gives us an initial idea of where we need improvement.

Rate yourself on each type of situation in Table 2.1 by checking whether you are typically effective or typically ineffective. By effective we mean any or all of the following: (1) You feel confident, (2) you think you are skillful, (3) you don't have a negative attitude, and (4) you don't feel apprehension. After you rate yourself, in the cases where you have rated yourself as generally ineffective, write why you rated yourself as ineffective.

You may have found it difficult to judge whether you are generally effective or ineffective. If you found yourself saying, "It depends," it may mean that you are most like Terry, our fourth communicator, who was generally effective in all types of situations but who occasionally had trouble. If that is the case, go back and try to identify when it is that you sometimes have trouble in that type of situation. For example, for the first situation, perhaps you have trouble only at

Table 2.1 SITUATIONS IN WHICH I AM GENERALLY EFFECTIVE OR INEFFECTIVE

Type of situation	Effective	Ineffective	Reason for ineffectiveness
1. Carrying on a conversation with strangers	✓	✓	awkward, no flow
2. Carrying on a conversation with people I know	✓		confidence
3. Volunteering answers and opinions in class		✓	don't want to be wrong
4. Participating in small group discussions	✓		
5. Being interviewed		✓	nervous, don't know answers
6. Presenting a speech or an oral report		✓	blackout
7. Speaking with a person in authority such as a teacher, adviser, or employer		✓	nervous, don't want to disappoint

large parties or only with the opposite sex. Write those answers under "Reason for ineffectiveness." As we have said, this rating is for your information, but your teacher may ask to see your ratings in order to help you throughout the course.

Assessing Your Attitudes

In this section you will be assessing your attitude toward yourself, or what has been called self-acceptance. Since it has been found that people who are self-accepting usually accept others,[1] we will not ask you to assess your attitude toward others. If you find that you are self-accepting, you can assume that you also tend to be accepting of others. After you complete the self-acceptance instrument, you will examine your attitudes about communication. In that section you will be assessing how you feel about communication and whether or not you hold any unreasonable beliefs about communication.

Assessing Your Self-acceptance   Complete the following scale to assess your self-acceptance.[2] When you have finished answering the items, follow the directions to compute your final score.

> DIRECTIONS: Please give your reaction to these statements concerning your feelings about yourself and others. There are no right or wrong answers. Work quickly and record your first reactions. Put the number that is most like your feelings in the blank before the statement: 1 = completely false, 2 = somewhat false, 3 = half true, half false, 4 = somewhat false, and 5 = completely true.

3   1.   I'd like it if I could find someone who would tell me how to solve my personal problems.

   2.   I don't question my worth as a person, even if I think others do.

3   3.   When people say nice things about me, I find it difficult to believe they really mean it. I think maybe they're kidding me or just aren't being sincere.

   4.   If there is any criticism or anyone says anything about me, I just can't take it.

2   5.   I don't say much at social affairs because I'm afraid that people will criticize me or laugh if I say the wrong thing.

   6.   I look on most of the feelings and impulses I have toward people as being quite natural and acceptable.

   7.   I realize that I'm not living very effectively, but I just don't believe I've got it in me to use my energies in better ways.

_2_   **8.**   Something inside me just won't let me be satisfied with any job I've done—if it turns out well, I get a very smug feeling that this is beneath me, I shouldn't be satisfied with this, this isn't a fair test.

_2_   **9.**   I feel different from other people. I'd like to have the feeling of security that comes from knowing I'm not too different from others.

_2_   **10.**   I'm afraid for people that I like to find out what I'm really like, for fear they'd be disappointed in me.

_3_   **11.**   I am frequently bothered by feelings of inferiority.

_2_   **12.**   Because of other people, I haven't been able to achieve as much as I should have.

_4_   **13.**   I am quite shy and self-conscious in social situations.

_3_   **14.**   In order to get along and be liked, I tend to be what people expect me to be rather than anything else.

_4_   **15.**   I seem to have a real inner strength in handling things. I'm on a pretty solid foundation and it makes me pretty sure of myself.

_4_   **16.**   I feel self-conscious when I'm with people who have a superior position to mine in business or at school.

_1_   **17.**   I think I'm neurotic or something.

_2_   **18.**   Very often, I don't try to be friendly with people because I think they won't like me.

_4_   **19.**   I feel that I'm a person of worth, on an equal plane with others.

_1_   **20.**   I can't avoid feeling guilty about the way I feel toward certain people in my life.

_4_   **21.**   I'm not afraid of meeting new people. I feel that I'm a worthwhile person and there's no reason why they should dislike me.

_3_   **22.**   I sort of only half-believe in myself.

_3_   **23.**   I'm very sensitive. People say things and I have a tendency to think they're criticizing me or insulting me in some way, and later when I think of it, they may not have meant anything like that at all.

_3_ **24.** I think I have certain abilities and other people say so too. I wonder if I'm not giving them an importance way beyond what they deserve.

_4_ **25.** I feel confident that I can do something about the problems that may arise in the future.

_1_ **26.** I guess I put on a show to impress people. I know I'm not the person I pretend to be.

_4_ **27.** I do not worry or condemn myself if other people pass judgment against me.

_2_ **28.** I don't feel very normal, but I want to feel normal.

_3_ **29.** When I'm in a group I usually don't say much for fear of saying the wrong thing.

_4_ **30.** I have a tendency to sidestep my problems.

_1_ **31.** Even when people do think well of me, I feel sort of guilty because I know I must be fooling them—that if I were really to be myself, they wouldn't think well of me.

_4_ **32.** I feel that I'm on the same level as other people and that helps to establish good relations with them.

_3_ **33.** I feel that people are apt to react differently to me than they would normally react to other people.

_2_ **34.** I live too much by other people's standards.

_5_ **35.** When I have to address a group, I get self-conscious and have difficulty saying things well.

_2_ **36.** If I didn't always have such hard luck, I'd accomplish much more than I have.

To determine how self-accepting you are, take a look at items 2, 6, 15, 19, 21, 24, 25, 27, and 32. Add your responses on these items and write the sum of your scores here: _36_. Your score on these items can range from a low of 9 to a high of 45. The _higher_ your score on these items, the greater your level of self-acceptance because agreement with these items indicates self-acceptance.

Now add your responses on the remaining items. Write that score here: _74_. Your score on these items can range from a low of 27 to a high of 135.

On these items, the *lower* your score, the greater your level of self-acceptance because agreement with these items indicates a lack of self-acceptance.

Use both of these scores to determine your level of self-acceptance. Then refer to the following chart:

First score	Second score	Level of self-acceptance
High (33–45)	Low (27–62)	High
Moderate (21–32)	Moderate (63–99)	Moderate
Low (9–20)	High (100–135)	Low

By looking at this chart, you can determine if your level of self-acceptance is high, moderate, or low. For example, if your first score is 35 and your second score is 30, your level of self-acceptance is high. You determine this by locating your first score, which in this example is a high score because it falls between 33 and 45. Your second score of 30 falls between 27 and 62 and is in the low category. By reading across the chart, you can see that your level of self-acceptance is high. If you have any questions about your scores, be sure to talk to your instructor, who can help you interpret them.

Assessing Your Attitudes Toward Communication   Sometimes people avoid communication or feel apprehensive about it because they have a poor attitude about communication. They evaluate communication as a negative experience because their beliefs about communication are unreasonable. Unreasonable beliefs are beliefs that require us to be perfect or to do the impossible. For example, sometimes people believe that if they stumble over one word in a speech, they will be seen as poor speakers and everyone will notice. This is an unreasonable belief because everyone stumbles over a word occasionally, even professional speakers such as newscasters. It is also an unreasonable belief because it assumes that *everyone* will notice the mistake. We would be very lucky indeed if we could get everyone in our audience to pay that much attention to us when we speak. If we possess unreasonable beliefs about communication, we are likely to have a poor attitude about it.

Perhaps you have some unreasonable beliefs that are causing you to feel negatively toward communication and even apprehensive about it. To assess your beliefs about communication, read the statements that follow. If you agree with the statement, check "yes." If you do not agree with the statement, check "no."

Beliefs about communication

	Yes	No
1. I always bore people when I speak.		
2. People usually don't notice when I make a small mistake.		

	Yes	No
3. If everyone in the audience does not like my speech, I have done a poor job as a speaker.	✓	✓
4. I must maintain 100 percent eye contact in all speaking situations.		✓
5. It is all right to speak about mundane topics like the weather.	✓	✓
6. People are constantly evaluating me when I speak.	✓	
7. If I give a wrong answer, people will think I am stupid.	✓	
8. It doesn't matter if people don't agree with my opinions.	✓	
9. Not everyone that I talk with will like me, and that is OK.	✓	
10. It is my fault if a conversation doesn't go smoothly and there are long pauses in it.	✓	

To determine your score, you need to know which statements represent unreasonable beliefs about communication. The statements that reflect unreasonable beliefs are 1, 3, 4, 6, 7, and 10. Check your answers to those items. You should have checked "no." Put a 1 next to each of those items that you checked "yes." Count the number of 1s you just gave yourself and write the number here:

Number of "yes" responses that should have been "no" responses:

Items 2, 5, 8, and 9 represent reasonable beliefs about communication, so you should have checked "yes" for these. Give yourself a 1 for each of those that you checked "no." Count the number of these 1s and write the total here:

Number of "no" responses that should have been "yes" responses:

Add these two totals together to determine your total number of unreasonable beliefs about communication. The lower your score, the fewer unrealistic ideas you have about the act of communication. Your score can range from 0 to 10. If your score is anything other than 0, go back through the list of statements to determine which ones represent your unreasonable beliefs about communication. If you do not understand why they are unreasonable beliefs, be sure to talk with your instructor. Also, read Chapter 3, which explains more about unreasonable beliefs and how to improve them.

Assessing Your Apprehension Level

One of the reasons that we sometimes think we are ineffective in a particular type of communication situation is that we feel nervous about that type of situation. For instance, many people claim to be very apprehensive about public speeches and job interviews. They say that they would perform much more effectively if they weren't so nervous. It may be true that their nervousness gets in the way of their ability to perform, although keep in mind that they also need public speaking and job interviewing skills to be effective. Reduction of their apprehension isn't enough to make them effective. They also need skills.

Perhaps you feel nervous in some or all types of communication situations. By "nervous" we mean tense and uneasy. This feeling is usually accompanied by physical symptoms such as trembling, perspiring, dryness in the mouth, and butterflies in the stomach. If you feel nervous and it doesn't bother you, don't try to change anything because there are many situations in which it is perfectly appropriate to feel nervous. Who wouldn't feel nervous standing in front of an audience or sitting across from a recruiter in an employment interview? Just about everybody does, so if you feel satisfied with yourself in those situations and aren't concerned about your apprehension, you are in good shape. If you do feel some concern about your nervousness, you may decide to work on trying to reduce that tension by applying the techniques we describe in this book.

Before you concern yourself with whether or not you want to reduce apprehension about speaking, you need to assess your level of apprehension and figure out in which situations your apprehension level is high. James McCroskey has been working for years on developing a reliable method for assessing levels of communication apprehension.[3] The scales he has developed are here for your self-assessment.

The scale that you should complete is the Personal Report of Communication Apprehension (PRCA-24).[4] It is designed to give you five scores. One score you will receive is a general measure of your overall level of apprehension across various types of communication situations. You will also receive a score for four types of communication situations: (1) your level of apprehension in group situations, (2) your level of apprehension in meetings and class discussions, (3) your level of apprehension in dyadic or one-to-one situations, and (4) your level of apprehension in public speaking situations.

Complete the following instrument and then compute each of your five scores as you are instructed.

DIRECTIONS: This instrument is composed of 24 statements concerning your feelings about communication with other people. Please indicate in the space provided the degree to which each statement applies to you by marking whether you (1) strongly agree, (2) agree, (3) are undecided, (4) disagree, or

(5) strongly disagree with each statement. There are no right or wrong answers. Many of the statements are similar to other statements. Do not be concerned about this. Work quickly; just record your first impression.

_4_   1. I dislike participating in group discussions.

_2_   2. Generally, I am comfortable while participating in a group discussion.

_3_   3. I am tense and nervous while participating in group discussions.

_3_   4. I like to get involved in group discussions.

_2_   5. Engaging in group discussion with new people makes me tense and nervous.

_4_   6. I am calm and relaxed while participating in group discussions.

_2_   7. Generally, I am nervous when I have to participate in a meeting.

_4_   8. Usually I am calm and relaxed while participating in meetings.

_4_   9. I am very calm and relaxed when I am called upon to express an opinion at a meeting.

_3_   10. I am not afraid to express myself at meetings.

_2_   11. Communicating at meetings usually makes me uncomfortable.

_4_   12. I am very relaxed when answering questions at a meeting.

_2_   13. While participating in a conversation with a new acquaintance, I feel very nervous.

_4_   14. I have no fear of speaking up in conversations.

_3_   15. Ordinarily I am very tense and nervous in conversations.

_3_   16. Ordinarily I am very calm and relaxed in conversations.

_4_   17. While conversing with a new acquaintance, I feel very relaxed.

_3_   18. I'm afraid to speak up in conversations.

_5_   19. I have no fear of giving a speech.

___1___ 20. Certain parts of my body feel very tense and rigid while giving a speech.

___5___ 21. I feel relaxed while giving a speech.

___1___ 22. My thoughts become confused and jumbled when I am giving a speech.

___5___ 23. I face the prospect of giving a speech with confidence.

___1___ 24. While giving a speech I get so nervous, I forget facts I really know.

Scoring: The numbers in parentheses are the numbers of the questions you should use to compute that particular score. For example, to compute your score for *group* situations, you would take 18 minus the number you filled in next to item 1 plus the number you filled in next to item 2 minus the number you filled in next to item 3 plus the number you filled in next to item 4 and so forth until you complete the entire formula.

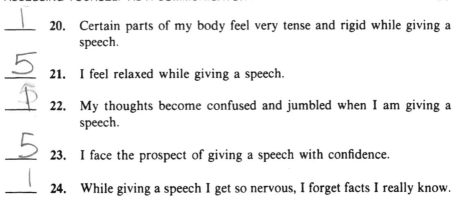

Group = 18 − (1) + (2) − (3) + (4) − (5) + (6)
Meeting = 18 − (7) + (8) + (9) − (10) − (11) + (12)
Dyad = 18 − (13) + (14) − (15) + (16) + (17) − (18)
Public Speaking = 18 + (19) − (20) + (21) − (22) + (23) − (24)
Overall communication apprehension = Group + Meeting + Dyad + Public speaking

Using the scoring formulas, compute your five scores and write them here:

Overall score: ___93___

Group score: ___19___

Meeting score: ___23___

Dyad score: ___21___

Public speaking score: ___30___

To interpret those scores it is necessary to know how you compare to other people. Perhaps your teacher will begin a discussion in class in which students compare their scores so that you can see how you scored in comparison to the other students in your class. You can also compare yourself to the thousands of people who have completed the PRCA-24. McCroskey reports that the average overall score on the PRCA-24 is 65.6.[5] If your score is close to that, it is about average. This means that you do not have a high level of communication apprehension overall. If your score fell below 65.6, this means that you have a lower level of overall communication apprehension than many of the people tested. If you received a score above 65.6, you have a higher level of apprehension than many of the people tested. Before you conclude that you have a high level of communication apprehension, look at how much higher your score is than 65.6. McCroskey uses one standard deviation above the mean as a cutoff point. It is not necessary that you understand what a standard deviation is, but the value that McCroskey has obtained for one standard deviation is 15.3.[6] What this means is that your score must be 80.9 or higher in order for you to conclude that you have a higher level of communication apprehension than most people that have been tested. It also means that you have to have a score of 50.3 or lower in order to conclude that you have a lower level of apprehension than most people tested.

When you are interpreting your score, also keep in mind that your level of apprehension is not a problem unless you consider it to be. In other words, if you received a high overall score on the PRCA-24 but find that you are not bothered by your apprehension, move on. On the other hand, you may have received an average score but feel very concerned about your apprehension. We want you to see how you compare numerically to the other people who have completed the PRCA-24, but don't interpret your score rigidly.

Let's look at how your score compares to other scores on the four subscales of the PRCA-24. Here are the average scores and the standard deviations:[7]

Subscale	Average score	Standard deviation
Public speaking	19.3	5.1
Meeting	16.4	4.8
Group	15.4	4.8
Dyad	14.5	4.2

For the public speaking subscale, your score would have to be 24.4 or higher to conclude that you have a higher level of apprehension about public speaking than many people tested. You would also have to have a score of 14.2 or lower to conclude that you are less apprehensive about public speaking than most people tested. Notice, though, that the average score for public speaking is higher than all the other averages listed. What this means is that people tend to be more apprehensive about public speaking than about any of the other types of situations that the PRCA-24 tests.

Your score would have to be 21.2 or higher to conclude that you have higher apprehension about meetings than most people tested. You would also have to have received a score of 11.6 or lower to conclude that you have less apprehension than many people tested. If your score falls between 11.6 and 21.2, you have an average level of apprehension about meetings.

For group situations, a score of 20.2 or higher represents a higher level of apprehension about groups, and a score of 10.6 or lower represents a lower level of apprehension than most people tested.

Finally, if your score on the dyad subscale is between 10.3 and 18.7, your level of apprehension is about average. Again, we urge you to use caution and your best judgment in interpreting your scores. If you received a high score but feel you have no problem, forget about it and move on. Scales like the PRCA-24 are very useful, but they are not infallible. They may be very good at accurately measuring a person's level of apprehension some of the time, but not in every case. If you have any questions concerning your scores, you should talk with your teacher, who can help you.

According to James McCroskey, the PRCA-24 is designed to assess "trait-like" apprehension about communication.[8] "Traitlike" means that you would generally experience apprehension about communication in most situations. "Situational" apprehension means that in a specific situation you experience anxiety. For example, if you occasionally feel nervous about presenting a speech, you are situationally apprehensive.

Thus your overall PRCA-24 score assesses the extent to which you experience "traitlike" apprehension about communication. If you received a high score, as we discussed, you may be a person who usually feels anxiety about communicating. Table 2.3 at the end of this chapter summarizes the improvement program you should follow. If your overall communication apprehension score is high, you should concentrate on learning the relaxation technique we present in Chapter 3.

Your scores on the dyad, meeting, group, and public speaking scales also represent your general tendency to feel apprehension in those types of situations. If you received a high score on any of these types of situations, you probably generally experience apprehension in those situations. Someone who received a low score on these situations may still experience occasional anxiety in them. A person with a low score then experiences more situational apprehension. That is, the individual may have difficulty giving public speeches sometimes, but not usually. Perhaps when that person is not completely prepared or in an unfamiliar situation, he or she feels apprehension about public speaking. If you experience situational apprehension, you may want to practice using the relaxation method explained in Chapter 3. You may find, however, that by working to improve your skills, some of that occasional apprehension may be alleviated.

Assessing Your Skill Level

So far in this chapter you have made a general rating of your effectiveness as a communicator in various types of situations, you have assessed your attitudes, and you have assessed your level of communication apprehension. Now it is time to take a look at how skillful you are as a communicator. To be skillful means that you can perform the necessary behaviors in a given communication situation. For example, in a social conversation situation, you can consider yourself skillful if you are able to initiate a conversation or respond to someone else's attempt at initiation, if you are able to ask and answer questions about the topic of conversation, if you are able to bring up new topics, if you are able to maintain eye contact, if you are able to speak clearly and loudly enough to be heard by the other person, if you are able to end the conversation in a socially appropriate manner, and so forth. From this example you can see that being skillful in social conversation involves many small behaviors. We may be skillful at some but not at others. In this section you'll assess how skillful you are in three types of situations: dyadic communication, group discussion, and public speaking.

Assessing Your Skill in Dyadic Communication   For each of the skills listed, rate yourself using the scale 1 = poor, 2 = fair, 3 = good, 4 = very good, and 5 = excellent. As you rate your skill level, think about how you generally perform that skill. We all have good days and bad days, so assess your skill level in general.

Skills for dyadic communication

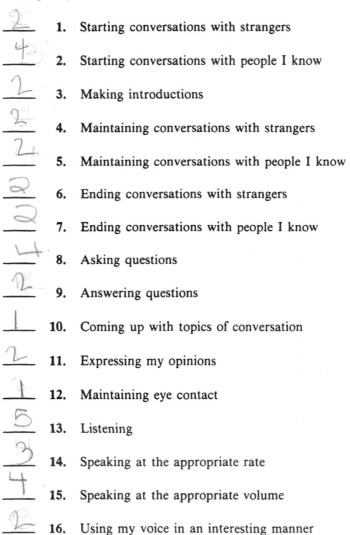

 2   1. Starting conversations with strangers

 4   2. Starting conversations with people I know

 2   3. Making introductions

 2   4. Maintaining conversations with strangers

 2   5. Maintaining conversations with people I know

 2   6. Ending conversations with strangers

 2   7. Ending conversations with people I know

 4   8. Asking questions

 2   9. Answering questions

 1   10. Coming up with topics of conversation

 2   11. Expressing my opinions

 1   12. Maintaining eye contact

 5   13. Listening

 3   14. Speaking at the appropriate rate

 4   15. Speaking at the appropriate volume

 2   16. Using my voice in an interesting manner

_3_ 17. Using gestures appropriately

_3_ 18. Using facial expressions appropriately

_1_ 19. Speaking fluently (without many *um*s, *OK*s, etc.)

_23_ 20. Speaking clearly and concisely

To determine your skill level, go back through your ratings and count how many 1s you gave yourself, how many 2s, and so on, and list those here:

Ratings of 1: ___3+___

Ratings of 2: ___10___

Ratings of 3: ___3___

Ratings of 4: ___3___

Ratings of 5: ___1___

Now look at where the majority of your ratings fell. Did you give yourself mostly 1s and 2s? How about 2s and 3s? Use the following as a guideline to make a general assessment of your dyadic communication skills, but be sure to note in which specific skill areas you are weakest so that you can work to improve them.

If you scored mostly 1s and 2s: *low* development of skills
If you scored mostly 2s and 3s: *slightly below average to average*
If you scored mostly 3s and 4s: *average* to *slightly above average*
If you scored mostly 4s and 5s: *high* development of skills

Regardless of your general skill level, go back through the checklist and determine your strong areas and your weak areas in dyadic communication. This will help you determine where to start working to improve yourself and also where your strengths are so that you can continue to use and build your strong points.

My three strongest skills in dyadic communication

1. _listening_

2. _conversing w/ people I know_

3. _asking question_

My three weakest skills in dyadic communication

1. __intros__

2. __strangup__

3. __topics__

Assessing Your Skill in Group Discussion   As you know from your experience, there are many types of groups. You may be involved in task groups such as those that work on class projects or the student council, or you may participate in social or counseling groups. In this section you will be assessing your skills in task-oriented group discussions. If you have never been in such a group, use your best judgment in making your ratings, and skip items if necessary. Use the following scale to rate yourself: 1 = poor, 2 = fair, 3 = good, 4 = very good, and 5 = excellent.

Skills for group discussion

____ 1. Preparing for meetings

____ 2. Expressing my opinions and ideas

____ 3. Supporting my opinions and ideas

____ 4. Listening

____ 5. Following the planned agenda

____ 6. Expressing disagreement appropriately

____ 7. Accepting criticism

____ 8. Expressing criticism appropriately

____ 9. Asking questions

____ 10. Answering questions

____ 11. Speaking clearly and concisely

____ 12. Allowing others to speak without interrupting them

____ 13. Taking leadership when necessary

____ 14. Following the leadership of others

_2_ **15.** Encouraging others to speak

_3_ **16.** Speaking at an appropriate rate

_3_ **17.** Speaking at an appropriate volume

_2_ **18.** Using my voice in an interesting manner

_5_ **19.** Following group norms (for example, doing what is expected, such as arriving on time)

_4_ **20.** Summarizing at the end of meetings

Count the number of ratings that you gave yourself in each of the five categories, and write them here:

Ratings of 1: _____0_____

Ratings of 2: _____6_____

Ratings of 3: _____6_____

Ratings of 4: _____5_____

Ratings of 5: _____3_____

Look at where the majority of your ratings fell, and determine your overall skill level in group discussion by using the following guidelines:

If you scored mostly 1s and 2s: _low_ development of skills

If you scored mostly 2s and 3s: _slightly below average_ to _average_

If you scored mostly 3s and 4s: _average_ to _slightly above average_

If you scored mostly 4s and 5s: _high_ development of skills

For any of these sections in which you are assessing your skill level, if you have any doubts about interpreting your ratings, be sure to talk with your teacher. Also keep in mind that these are general guidelines, so use your best judgment.

Now examine your ratings to determine your strongest and weakest skill areas and list them here:

My three strongest skills in group discussion

1. listening

2. following norms / agenda

3. allowing others to speak

My three weakest skills in group discussion

1. <u>explessins opinius</u>
2. <u>answerins questives</u>
3. <u>taking leadership.</u>

Assessing Your Skill in Public Speaking   The last type of communication situation in which you will assess your skills is public speaking. You may never have presented a public speech, but you may have done some sort of oral report in front of the class. Use this experience as your guide in rating yourself. If you have never had to stand in front of any group to speak, think about how skillful you are at answering questions or asking them in class. That may help you in making your ratings. Again, use the scale 1 = poor, 2 = fair, 3 = good, 4 = very good, and 5 = excellent.

Skills for public speaking

3 1. Choosing an appropriate topic

3 2. Preparing an outline

4 3. Finding information on my topic

4 4. Rehearsing my speech

2 5. Providing an effective introduction to my speech

4 6. Sticking to my outline while I speak

3 7. Expressing my opinions

3 8. Supporting my opinions

2 9. Speaking at an appropriate rate

2 10. Speaking at an appropriate volume

1 11. Maintaining eye contact with audience members

2 12. Using my voice in an interesting manner

2 13. Using facial expressions appropriately

1   **14.**   Using gestures appropriately

2   **15.**   Speaking fluently (without many *um*s, *OK*s, etc.)

2   **16.**   Speaking clearly and concisely

3   **17.**   Remaining within the allotted time

3   **18.**   Answering questions after my speech

3   **19.**   Providing an effective conclusion to my speech

4   **20.**   Accepting criticism appropriately

Now count how many ratings you gave yourself in each category, and write the numbers here:

Ratings of 1: _____ IIII

Ratings of 2: __9__ HHT '

Ratings of 3: __7__ III I

Ratings of 4: __3__ III

Ratings of 5: __0__ III

Examine where the majority of your ratings fell to determine your overall level of skill development in public speaking. Use the following guideline to help you.

If you scored mostly 1s and 2s: *low* skill development

If you scored mostly 2s and 3s: *slightly below average* to *average*

If you scored mostly 3s and 4s: *average* to *slightly above average*

If you scored mostly 4s and 5s: *high* skill development

You may have found that your skill level is lowest in public speaking. This may be true for two reasons: You may lack experience, and you may lack training in this area. For instance, you may have never been taught how to prepare an effective introduction and conclusion for a speech. Because you don't know how to do that and you have had little experience, you probably lack the skills. Regardless of your skill level, examine your strongest and weakest skills and list them here:

My three strongest skills in public speaking

1. ~~preparation~~ researching
2. ~~time~~ rehearsing
3. receiving criticism

My three weakest skills in public speaking

1. eye contact
2. Sticking to outline
3. speaking fluently

You have just completed your assessment of your level of skill in dyadic communication, group discussion, and public speaking. You now have a good idea of which are your strongest and weakest skills in each area. You can probably also determine which type of situation is your weakest, which is your strongest, and which is in the middle. For instance, you may have discovered that you are strongest in dyadic communication, then group discussion, then public speaking. Or you may be strongest in group discussion, then dyadic communication, then public speaking. Take a minute now to list the three situations *from strongest overall to weakest overall.* This will be useful to you in Chapter 4, when you begin trying to set your personal communication goals.

My skill level from strongest to weakest type of situation

1. Group
2. Public speaking
3. Dyadic

YOUR PERSONAL COMMUNICATOR PROFILE

You have assessed yourself as a communicator in many ways. Now to complete your personal profile as a communicator, you need to go back through this chapter to find your scores. Then complete the profile form in Table 2.2. This will summarize your strong and weak points as a communicator. You can use this form to help you as you get started improving as a communicator. You may want to go over this form with your teacher so that he or she is aware of your strengths and areas in which you need improvement and can give you guidance.

Table 2.2 PERSONAL COMMUNICATOR PROFILE FORM

Instrument name	Score	Level: Low	Level: Average	Level: High
I. Self-acceptance	34, 74		X	
II. Beliefs About Communication	5		X	
III. PRCA-24				
A. Overall	93			X
B. Group	19		X	
C. Meeting	23			X
D. Dyad	21			X
E. Public speaking	30			X
IV. Skill Level				
A. Dyadic communication	2.45		X	
B. Group discussion	3.25		X	
C. Public speaking	2.6		X	

To determine your score on each of the three skill areas in Part IV of the form, take an average of the ratings you gave yourself. Add your ratings in each skill area and then divide by the number of items on each skill development subscale. Since each skill area subscale has 20 items, you would add your ratings and divide by 20 to obtain your average rating. For example, add the ratings you gave yourself on the dyadic communication skills form. Divide that total by 20 to obtain your score for dyadic communication. Use these average ratings as your score on the communicator profile form.

YOUR PERSONAL IMPROVEMENT PROGRAM

Self-assessment is very important in helping you to pinpoint your strengths and weaknesses as a communicator. Now that you have completed your self-assessment and filled out the personal communicator profile form, you are ready to examine the chart in Table 2.3 to set up your personal improvement program. To read the chart, look at the list of instruments you have completed, at the left. If you discovered that you have a particular area in which you need improvement as determined by your scores on the various instruments you have filled out, look to the right to see what techniques are recommended for improvement. These techniques have not yet been explained, but they will be explained in the remaining chapters of the book. In the fourth column, put a check (✓) next to those that apply to you. For example, if your self-acceptance score was low, you should put a check on the line that corresponds to "Self-acceptance." By determining which techniques of improvement are most likely to benefit you, you can pay particular attention to those techniques when they are discussed.

If you have more than one type of communication weakness as indicated by the various instruments you completed in this chapter, you should use the appropriate improvement techniques listed. For instance, if you have a problem of poor skill development in public speaking and traitlike anxiety about public

Table 2.3 PERSONAL IMPROVEMENT PROGRAM

Instrument name	Communication weakness identified	Improvement technique	Areas I need to improve
I. Self-acceptance	Poor attitude toward self	Improve attitudes	_____
II. Beliefs About Communication	Unreasonable beliefs	Improve attitudes	_____
III. PRCA-24			
A. Overall	Traitlike apprehension	Relaxation	⤫
B. Group[a]	Traitlike apprehension	Relaxation	⤫
C. Meeting[a]	Traitlike apprehension	Relaxation	⤫
D. Dyad[a]	Traitlike apprehension	Relaxation	_____
E. Public speaking[a]	Traitlike apprehension	Relaxation	⤫
IV. Skill Level			
A. Dyadic communication	Poor skill development	Improve skills	_____
B. Group discussion	Poor skill development	Improve skills	_____
C. Public speaking	Poor skill development	Improve skills	_____

[a] If your scores on the various subscales of the PRCA-24 were not very high but you occasionally experience apprehension in any of these types of communication situations, you are situationally apprehensive. You should stress skill development in your improvement program and learn the relaxation technique presented in Chapter 3.

speaking, you should work to develop your skills and practice the relaxation techniques that we describe. However, it is important to realize that improvement techniques can address more than one problem. By developing your skills, your apprehension level may drop and your attitudes improve. Thus the more you try to work with all three improvement techniques, the greater your improvement should be.

SUMMARY

In this chapter we have taken you through a thorough assessment of yourself as a communicator. We believe that before people can begin to improve themselves as communicators, they need to determine their strengths and weaknesses in the three areas of attitude, apprehension, and skill. By identifying our strengths and weaknesses, we can see more specifically how to begin trying to improve.

We introduced four communicators and pointed out their strengths and weaknesses as communicators. This was designed to illustrate the point that all people have strong and weak points in communication, no matter how effective or ineffective they appear to be.

Next we asked you to assess your strong and weak communication situations. These situations included social conversation, class participation, small group discussion, interviews, public speeches, and meetings with people in authority.

Then we asked you to assess your attitude about yourself, using the self-acceptance scale. We asked you to determine your attitude about communication by determining if you have any unreasonable beliefs about communication.

The next assessment tool we presented was the Personal Report of Communication Apprehension (PRCA-24). This scale was designed to help you determine your apprehension level overall and in meetings, groups, one-to-one situations, and public speeches.

The fourth assessment instrument we provided was designed to help you determine whether you have low, average, or high skill development. You completed this for three situations: dyadic communication, group discussion, and public speaking.

Finally, we presented a personal communicator profile form to assist you in summarizing your strengths and weaknesses as a communicator. Moreover, we included a chart illustrating which improvement techniques to use, depending on your specific areas of improvement. However, we have found that each improvement technique may address more than one weakness. Using relaxation, for example, may not only reduce your apprehension but also improve your attitude. Your attitude may improve because you feel more relaxed.

two

IMPROVING YOURSELF AS A COMMUNICATOR

chapter 3

Improving Attitudes and Reducing Apprehension

CHAPTER OBJECTIVES

1. To learn techniques for improving self-acceptance and acceptance of others.
2. To learn techniques for developing realistic attitudes toward communication.
3. To learn techniques for reducing apprehension about communication.

INTRODUCTION

In the first chapter we discussed how the personal aspects of attitude toward self, toward others, and toward communication; apprehension level; and skill level affect our communication behavior. In Chapter 2 you completed a thorough self-assessment of these personal aspects that influence you as a communicator and developed a personal communicator profile to help you identify your specific strengths and areas for improvement.

This chapter is designed to teach you techniques for developing more positive attitudes toward yourself, toward others, and toward communication. In addition, the purpose of this chapter is to provide you with methods for reducing some of the apprehension you may feel about communication, whether you experience apprehension only occasionally or most of the time. Through your self-assessment you may have identified skills that need to be developed, but we will not provide information on developing skills in this chapter. We will help you with skill development in Chapters 4 through 9.

IMPROVING ATTITUDES

Achieving Self-acceptance

In Chapter 1 we defined self-acceptance as the ability to accept ourselves without any requirements or conditions. Self-accepting people do not judge themselves as human beings on the basis of their talents and inadequacies. Instead of evaluating themselves, they evaluate their behavior. We will begin trying to teach you to evaluate your behavior in this chapter and will continue that instruction in Chapter 4.

Self-acceptance has the particular definition that we have given you, but it is often confused with self-esteem or self-confidence. Self-esteem or self-confidence means that people value themselves because of what they have done well, and therefore, this feeling about self is dependent on what they do well in the future. If they continue to be successful, they will continue to feel good about themselves. If they fail, their self-esteem and self-confidence may deteriorate. A person achieves self-acceptance not by accomplishing or succeeding at anything, but by *choice!*

You can come to accept yourself if you choose to. You will be a self-accepting individual when you *choose* to allow yourself to be the way you are without unnecessary self-criticism. Self-acceptance does not occur spontaneously. If it did, all people would be self-accepting, and we would not need to write about it here. Self-acceptance can be increased by refusing to rate ourselves and practicing rating only our behaviors. If our behaviors are ineffective, we can criticize them and then change them. There is no sense in criticizing ourselves as human beings. To begin developing self-acceptance, it may help you to practice rating your behaviors, not yourself. Complete the following activity. If you have difficulty with it, be sure to consult with your teacher.

DIRECTIONS: Put an *X* next to each of the following statements that reflects a lack of self-acceptance (that is, each statement that rates the person, not the person's behavior).

_____ 1. I am unhappy with myself for being so shy.

_____ 2. I like the way I organized my speech.

_____ 3. I am pleased with myself for being such a good listener.

_____ 4. I don't like the way I answered many of the questions I was asked in the interview.

_____ 5. I am a poor speaker.

If you put an X next to statements 1, 3, and 5, you correctly identified all the statements indicating a lack of self-acceptance. All three of those statements provide judgments of the individual as a person. To make those statements reflect self-acceptance, they need to be changed so they are statements about behavior. Rewrite statements 1, 3, and 5 to correct them.

1. _____

_____

3. _____

_____

5. _____

_____

If you are uncertain if the statements you have rewritten rate behavior and not the individual, be sure to check them with your teacher. This is an important skill to develop because when you begin consistently to rate behaviors rather than yourself, you have achieved self-acceptance.

Achieving Acceptance of Others

By accepting ourselves without conditions and rating only our behaviors, we gain certain advantages. We may be more emotionally healthy, we are free to take risks and attempt new experiences, we expect people to accept us, and we accept other people more readily. This last advantage, the ability to accept others, is one that helps in controlling apprehension and will be the focus of our discussion in this section. One way in which we can develop our ability to accept others is to learn to accept ourselves, since people who are self-accepting tend to be more accepting of others.[1] If you do not accept yourself, you will undoubtedly think poorly of other people. And you may communicate that dislike for people when you interact. Some researchers have examined the relationship between self-acceptance and other-acceptance. Stock discovered that perceptions of others, feelings toward others, and acceptance of others appear to increase as understanding of self, feelings about self, and acceptance of self increase.[2]

Just as there are advantages to self-acceptance, there is an advantage to accepting others. The major advantage of acceptance of others is the lowering of apprehension associated with communication. One study found that people with low self-acceptance were more anxious than self-accepting people.[3] Since self-accepting people tend to accept others, we can assume that people who are low on acceptance of others also feel more anxious. One of the reasons we often experience apprehension about communication is that we are worried about how the other is judging us. Think of the last job interview you had. If you felt nervous about the interview, it was probably partly due to fear of being evaluated negatively. If you accept others and don't evaluate them as people but evaluate their behaviors instead, you will realize that it is your behaviors being evaluated, not yourself. And behaviors that we don't like can be changed; we can improve others' evaluations of our behaviors by changing those behaviors.

We can demonstrate acceptance of others in four basic ways. First, we can offer statements that express our sincere feelings or can question others about their feelings. For example, if you asked, "Are you feeling better today than you did yesterday?" the other person is likely to talk about his or her feelings. Your question indicates a genuine concern for the other individual and thus your acceptance of that individual.

A second way that we can indicate our acceptance of others is to make statements that show how important the relationship is to us and our desire to build a closer relationship. You may say, for instance, "Your friendship is so special to me. I hope we can remain friends even though I'll be away at college." Statements that indicate you are interested in the feelings and activities of the other also communicate that the relationship is important to you. By communicating that the relationship is important, you are letting the other know that you are not judging him or her as a person and that his or her successes and failures have nothing to do with the importance of the relationship.

A third way to express acceptance of others is to be responsive when communicating with them. A simple "Yes, I know" can express acceptance and warmth. Nodding and smiling are nonverbal means of demonstrating support and acceptance.

A final way in which we can express acceptance of others is by focusing our comments on their behavior. If, for example, you are unhappy with a friend's treatment of you, you can say, "I have been unhappy lately with the way you have been treating me. You have not returned my phone calls and have been late for our last two dates." Notice that these statements are about the other's behavior, not about the other as a person. The statement "You are a very inconsiderate person" does not focus on behavior and is likely to produce a defensive reaction.

In summary, we believe that you can improve your attitudes toward yourself and toward others by choosing self-acceptance and other-acceptance. You need to make a conscious decision to do this. In addition, you can practice self-acceptance and other-acceptance by focusing your evaluations on behavior. Behaviors can be changed and improved.

In the next section of this chapter we will examine the technique of reasonable thinking. This technique may not only help you develop more realistic beliefs about communication, but it may help you further to improve your attitude toward yourself and others.

Thinking Reasonably About Self, Others, and Communication

Thus far in this chapter we have considered how to achieve greater acceptance of self and others. Now we turn our attention to our attitudes about communication and how to learn to think more reasonably about it.

Shakespeare said, "There is nothing either good or bad but thinking makes it so.'"[4] He was telling us that our attitude toward something, good or bad, causes us to perceive that thing as good or bad. For example, faced with an upcoming speech, we might think, "This is a good opportunity to express my opinions on this topic. I'm looking forward to it." This attitude may propel us to study the topic carefully, plan the speech thoroughly, and deliver it with enthusiasm. Or we could think, "I hate giving speeches. I know I'm going to do a terrible job. Nobody is interested in this topic." By thinking this way about the speech, we may end up spending valuable preparation time complaining and planning ways to avoid doing the speech. The consequence of this may be a poor speech.

This is the idea that we mentioned earlier called *self-fulfilling prophecy*. We predict our own successes and failures and then act in ways that bring them about. In the example that we cited about giving a public speech, notice how you could bring about your success or failure by the way that you think about it. The person who thinks, "I'm excited about giving this speech. It is a good opportunity for me to express my views," brings about success because his or her attitude promotes careful preparation. The individual who says, "I hate giving speeches. No one will like it," predicts failure. The person's attitude prevents adequate preparation, which leads to an ineffective speech.

Self-fulfilling prophecies may become destructive spirals.[5] An example will clarify what we mean by that statement. If you have the attitude that no one will like you, and you are put in a situation in which you meet new people, you are likely to predict that these new people will not like you. When you meet those people, you will probably not act very friendly or try to engage them in conversations. Because you show a lack of interest in them, they are likely to show no interest in you. You will leave the situation saying to yourself, "See, no one likes me." What you may not say is, "Of course they don't like me. I made no effort to try to get to know them because of my poor attitude." When you fail to realize that you have brought the negative consequences upon yourself, you are more convinced than before that no one likes you. This is what we mean by a destructive spiral. Our attitude produces behavior that stimulates behavior in others that confirms our negative attitude, and on and on. The spiral is destructive because our attitude, and thus our behavior, becomes more and more negative.

Therefore, we may choose either of two attitudes—reasonable or unreasonable. Reasonable attitudes are realistic. If you do not know how to ski and you go skiing for the first time, it is reasonable for you to think that you might get hurt if you are not careful. If you did not prepare for a job interview, it is reasonable to think that you might not get the job. Unreasonable attitudes are unrealistic in that they have no basis in reality. If you have prepared carefully for an oral presentation, it is unreasonable to think that you will do a miserable job. It is unreasonable to think that no one will want to talk to you at a party unless you have some evidence that no one wants to talk to you.

A way has been developed to help us know whether our thinking is reasonable or unreasonable and to choose thoughts and attitudes that help us lead happy, productive lives. This method of reasonable thinking was developed by the psychologist Albert Ellis in 1951.[6] A sickly child with uncaring parents, Ellis often felt depressed and worthless. Then he began to realize that it was his attitude, not external events, that affected his life. His philosophy of reasonable thinking is now widely respected by medical and lay persons and is used in many disciplines throughout the world.

Reasonable thinking seeks to help a person to assess his or her own thoughts about life experiences realistically. The first and most basic principle of reasonable thinking is that thinking helps determine the emotions we have. People and events do not make us "feel good" or "feel bad"; we do it to ourselves.

A second major principle of reasonable thinking is that unreasonable thinking includes exaggeration (something is *terrible*), oversimplication (it's *all* her fault), overgeneralization (I *always* foul up), illogic (I'll *never* be able to do this), unvalidated assumptions (I *know* I'll mess up), and faulty and absolutist notions (I *must* give the speech perfectly). The term Ellis uses to describe these errors in thinking is *unrealistic beliefs.*

These unrealistic beliefs may fall into four basic categories: (1) statements of evaluation of human worth, either of oneself or of others; (2) need statements, which are arbitrary requirements for happiness or survival; (3) "awfulizing" statements, which exaggerate the negative consequences of a situation; and (4) words that reflect unrealistic demands on events and individuals.

Here are examples of these four categories of unreasonable beliefs:

1. Statements of evaluation of human worth, either of oneself or of others

UNREASONABLE:	Because I feel anxious, I am an inadequate person.
REASONABLE:	My apprehension does not mean that I am an inadequate person.
UNREASONABLE:	When I do poorly on a speech, I feel worthless.
REASONABLE:	When I do poorly on a speech, I realize I need to work more on my speaking skills.

2. Need statements—arbitrary requirements for happiness or survival

UNREASONABLE:	I need to overcome my fear of public speaking in order to be happy.
REASONABLE:	I can be happy whether or not I overcome my fear of speaking.
UNREASONABLE:	If I don't do well when I lead my group meeting, I'll be miserable.
REASONABLE:	Doing a good job at leading the group meeting is not necessary for me to be happy.

3. "Awfulizing" statements—exaggerating the negative consequences of a situation

UNREASONABLE:	People will think I'm the biggest bore when they talk to me.

REASONABLE:	It would be unfortunate if I bored anyone during conversation.
UNREASONABLE:	It is terrible to feel so apprehensive about a job interview.
REASONABLE:	It is inhibiting to feel apprehensive about a job interview.

4. Words that reflect unrealistic demands on events and individuals

UNREASONABLE:	I *should* be able to speak up more in a group.
REASONABLE:	I would like to speak up more in a group.
UNREASONABLE:	I *must* be able to talk easily with members of the opposite sex.
REASONABLE:	I would enjoy talking more easily with members of the opposite sex.

Perhaps the difference between reasonable and unreasonable beliefs is clear to you now. Do you remember the questionnaire that you completed in Chapter 2 to help you determine if you had any unreasonable beliefs about communication? If you identified any unreasonable beliefs at that time, list them here. You can find that questionnaire on pages 31–32.

1. _____

2. _____

3. _____

4. _____

5. _____

Next to each of the unreasonable beliefs you just listed, put the number of the category into which that belief falls. For example, if the first unreasonable belief that you wrote was, "I must maintain 100 percent eye contact in all speaking situations," you would put a 4 next to that statement. That is an unreasonable belief from the fourth category: words that reflect unrealistic demands on events and individuals. Do this for each of the unreasonable beliefs that you listed here. If you have any difficulty doing this, be sure to ask your teacher for help.

Often we do not realize that our thoughts are unreasonable. There are four guides we can give you to help you determine which thoughts are reasonable and which are unreasonable:

    1. *A reasonable belief is true.* If a belief reflects the truth, then it is reasonable. If, for example, you believe that you cannot throw a baseball 100

miles per hour, that is a reasonable belief if indeed you can't. Unreasonable beliefs are not grounded in reality and are untrue. The individual has no observable evidence for them. For instance, the belief, "I can never give a good speech" is not true in that the speaker cannot provide any evidence attesting to the truth of that belief.

2. *A reasonable belief is not absolutist.* It is not stated in terms of black and white but considers shades of gray. It is not stated in what general semanticists call "allness" terms. Absolutist statements imply that failure will always be the result, when that is just not true. "I will sometimes fail" is a reasonable belief because it is not absolute.

3. *A reasonable belief results in moderate emotion.* The emotions from reasonable beliefs may range from mild to strong reactions but do not severely upset the individual. The unreasonable belief "I will be devastated if I do not do well on the speech" implies very strong emotions or feelings.

4. *A reasonable belief helps attain goals.* Reasonable beliefs allow the person to pursue goals in a less fearful fashion and with a freedom to take risks that may help in the attainment of these goals. The reasonable belief "I will give the speech to the best of my ability" frees the individual to take the risks that will result in attainment of that goal. We will discuss goals in great detail in Chapter 4. As you read that chapter, you may see how important reasonable beliefs are in helping you achieve your goals as a communicator.

The activity that follows is designed to help you understand how to apply the four guides to test your beliefs. This activity should be done with a group. Your teacher may lead this activity in class. If not, it can be done with a few of your friends or roommates.

On pieces of paper, each member of the group or the entire class writes one reasonable belief and one unreasonable belief. Examples could be "I don't like to make mistakes in speaking" (reasonable), "All humans make mistakes in speaking" (reasonable), or "I have to get an A in speech class" (unreasonable). The beliefs are collected and put in a container of some sort. Each person then draws out one belief and tests whether it is reasonable or unreasonable by using the four guides. Here are the guides in the form of questions:

1. Is it true?
2. Is it absolutist?
3. Does it result in moderate emotion?
4. Does it help in goal attainment?

The ABC Model of Reasonable Thinking

At this point you may be getting very good at identifying reasonable and unreasonable beliefs and thoughts. That is an excellent start, but now you need to learn how to *change* those beliefs. Remember that our attitude may be a primary influence in the success or failure of our communication. The understanding and practice of reasonable thinking can help us control our attitudes to make certain that they are positive ones. We have emphasized that we *choose* our attitudes and feelings, and we want you to learn the ABC model of reasonable thinking to help you change negative attitudes into positive attitudes. This model was devised by the psychologist Albert Ellis,[7] who came to realize for himself that it was his attitudes about events that were making him miserable, not the events themselves.

A in the system stands for the *activating event,* or the occurrence that happens to trigger our feelings. *B* is the *belief* we then have about *A* and may be reasonable or unreasonable. *C* stands for the *consequences* or emotional response we have because of our belief about the event. Many people mistakenly think that *A,* the activating event, causes *C,* the consequence.

Let's look at an example:

ACTIVATING EVENT:	The customer asked for information. My mind went blank.
BELIEF:	I should have known what to say. I am so dumb.
CONSEQUENCE:	Self-condemnation; anger with self

Did the event (customer asking for information) cause the consequence (self-condemnation), or did the *belief* about the event cause the consequence? Let's try the example again:

ACTIVATING EVENT:	The customer asked for information. My mind went blank.
BELIEF:	I wish I had known what to say. It was unfortunate that I didn't remember the information.
CONSEQUENCE:	Understanding of self and determination to do better

You can see that the consequence was not caused by the event. It was caused by the belief the person had about the event. Look at the examples we just provided.

1. Which belief was reasonable? _____

2. Which belief was unreasonable and why is it unreasonable? _____

_____

Notice that the unreasonable belief was the one that led the person to feeling upset. That person's *choice* to accept that belief resulted in the negative consequences.

So far the ABC model has helped you realize the role of unreasonable beliefs in bringing about negative consequences. The next component of the model will help you handle unreasonable beliefs. That component is *D, disputing.* Disputing means that you challenge the belief with logic. The four guides that we gave you for examining unreasonable beliefs can help you with *disputing* that belief. If we return to our example of "I should have known what to say. I am so dumb," we can apply the four guides to dispute this unreasonable belief:

GUIDE 1:   Is the belief true?

ANSWER: Why *should* you have known the information asked for? Is it reasonable to think that you should always know the answers to questions you are asked? Where is the evidence that you are "dumb"? Is not knowing an answer to one question sufficient evidence to conclude this?

GUIDE 2:   Is the belief absolutist?

ANSWER: The belief suggests that you should always know what to say, so it does appear to be an allness statement.

GUIDE 3:   Does the belief result in moderate emotion?

ANSWER: No. In this case the belief results in self-condemnation and anger.

GUIDE 4:   Does the belief help you attain your goal?

ANSWER: The goal may have been to be a good salesperson. The resulting belief about the event did not encourage the person to try to do better next time.

By using the four guides to dispute the belief, we can see that it is unreasonable. Now we can change it to a reasonable belief and thus change the consequence to a more positive one.

Let's look at one more example:

ACTIVATING EVENT: I gave a speech in class and forgot part of it.

BELIEF: I am so stupid. I'll never be a good speaker.

CONSEQUENCE: Embarrassment, despair

Use the four guides to *dispute* the belief. This time, you fill in the answers.

GUIDE 1:   Is the belief true?

ANSWER: _____

GUIDE 2:   Is the belief absolutist?

ANSWER: _____

GUIDE 3:   Does it result in moderate emotion?

ANSWER: _____

GUIDE 4:   Does it help you achieve your goal?

ANSWER: _____

You have probably come to the conclusion that the belief in this example is unreasonable by disputing it with the four guides. Rework the example, changing the belief to a reasonable one and changing the consequences so that they fit the reasonable belief you have supplied.

ACTIVATING EVENT: I gave a speech in class and forgot part of it.

BELIEF: _____

CONSEQUENCE: _____

The last component of the ABC model is *E,* the *effect* of disputing the belief. If by disputing we realize that a belief is unreasonable, what shall we do? Our goal is to change the unreasonable belief to a reasonable one. By changing it, we change the consequences, with the *effect* that we understand and accept ourselves. Let's look at an example, adding the *effect* component of the ABC model.

ACTIVATING EVENT: The teacher called on me in class and I didn't have the answer.

BELIEF: I should have known the answer. People must think I am dumb.

CONSEQUENCE: Self-condemnation and embarrassment

DISPUTING: This belief is absolutist, implying that one should always know the answer. This belief does not result in moderate emotions. This belief does not help me attain my goal of participating effectively in class. Therefore, this is an unreasonable belief.

EFFECT: It wasn't so bad that I didn't know the answer. I often give correct answers, so the teacher and my classmates do not think I am stupid. I am not a dumb person. Next time I will try to be better prepared for class.

The ABC model will help you learn to practice reasonable thinking so that your attitudes do not interfere with your effectiveness as a communicator but instead help you grow as a communicator. Probably all of us from time to time fall into the trap of accepting unreasonable beliefs that make us feel bad about ourselves and prevent us from achieving our goals. By practicing the ABC model, we can change those unreasonable beliefs into reasonable beliefs, changing negative consequences into understanding of self and recognition of our limitations.

By increasing your self-acceptance and acceptance of others and by practicing reasonable thinking, your attitudes should no longer interfere with your effectiveness as a communicator. It will take time to reach this point, and you may find yourself slipping from time to time, but it is well worth the time and effort it takes.

CONTROLLING COMMUNICATION APPREHENSION

So far this chapter has concentrated on altering attitudes to improve communication effectiveness. We will now turn to controlling communication apprehension as a means of improving yourself as a communicator. Although we will provide you with techniques specifically designed to reduce fear of speaking, we need to point out that by improving your attitudes toward yourself, others, and communication in the ways that we have discussed, your apprehension about communication may be reduced. This is because one negative consequence of poor attitudes is fear. If, for example, you have the unreasonable belief that you are not a good speaker and can never be good, you will probably feel fear when confronted with speaking situations. So by working on improving your attitudes, you are already on the road to overcoming apprehension about speaking.

Before you continue reading, take a look at your personal communicator profile (Table 2.2) to refresh your memory about how you fared on the PRCA-24 and the subscales. Remember, a high score on the PRCA-24 indicates "traitlike" communication apprehension, which means that you generally experience apprehension in communication situations. If your overall score is moderate or low but you have a high score on one or more of the subscales (group, dyad, public speaking, or meetings), it means that you generally experience apprehension in that type of situation. The techniques for reducing apprehension that we will discuss are designed for people who experience this "traitlike" apprehension. Scholars are not as certain about how to help people who have only situational apprehension. Recall that situational apprehension refers to the experience of fear on occasion, but not necessarily in the same type of situation each time. For instance, most of the time when you give a speech you do not feel very apprehensive, but on a particular occasion you do. This is situational apprehension. We will discuss the situational features that may produce this type of apprehension and suggest ways that you can alleviate that occasional anxiety. Before we do that, we will discuss a method called *systematic desensitization* that is designed to help people who generally experience apprehension.

Scholars have suggested that communication apprehension may be a learned trait that is developed over a long period of time.[8] As a result, people vary in the degree to which they feel anxious about oral communication. Since the anxiety is learned, it can be unlearned. Complicated as it sounds, when a person has learned a habit, such as anxiety in a speaking situation, the more similar the present situation is to the anxiety-producing situation, the greater the intensity with which the individual will experience anxiety in the present situation. So if a person has learned to fear oral communication situations, the individual will feel this fear each time he or she thinks about or participates in the communication situation.

Psychologists have found that this fear can be overcome by a method called systematic desensitization. It has been used to help people overcome many types of fears, including communication apprehension.

The method is systematic in that it follows an organized plan. It involves desensitization in that the individual gradually becomes less sensitive (less fearful) to the situation. There are three stages in the systematic desensitization program. The first stage involves learning to relax properly. This is not as easy to do as it may sound. In the systematic desensitization method, you need to learn to relax all of your muscles as completely as possible. This can be done by purchasing a tape that has been created and produced by James C. McCroskey with instructions on how to relax[9] or by studying the muscle relaxation procedure that we provide,[10] which is based on that tape. If you look at the instructions for muscle relaxation on the following page, you can see that there are exercises to help you learn to relax each of the muscle groups. It takes time and practice to learn to relax in this way, but it is vital to the success of the systematic desensitization program. This is because the reason the program works is that tension and relaxation are incompatible responses—they cannot be experienced simultaneously. If you are completely relaxed, you cannot feel tension. If you do experience tension, you are not relaxed and have to try again to achieve the state of relaxation that you are seeking.

Instructions for Muscle Relaxation

Practice this procedure for about 30 minutes each day for three or four days. When you can use this procedure and feel completely relaxed, you are ready to begin pairing relaxation with the items on the hierarchy you create. This will be explained in greater detail in stages 2 and 3 of systematic desensitization.

For each of the muscle groups on the following list, hold the muscle for several seconds, concentrating on how the tension feels. Then relax the muscle and notice how the relaxation feels. Close your eyes as you follow this relaxation procedure.

1. *Hands.* Clench and relax left hand; repeat; relax; clench and relax right hand; repeat; relax.
2. *Forearms.* Bend left hand upward at the wrist, pointing fingers toward the ceiling; relax; repeat; bring right hand upward at the wrist, pointing fingers toward the ceiling; relax; repeat; relax.
3. *Biceps.* Flex biceps by bringing both hands up toward shoulders, flexing biceps muscles; relax, repeat; relax.
4. *Shoulders.* Shrug both shoulders trying to touch ears with shoulders; relax; repeat; relax.
5. *Forehead.* Wrinkle forehead; frown; relax; repeat; relax.
6. *Eyes.* Close eyes tightly; relax; repeat; relax.
7. *Tongue.* Press tongue into roof of mouth; relax; repeat; relax.
8. *Mouth.* Press lips together tightly; relax; repeat; relax.
9. *Neck.* Push head against the back of the chair; relax; repeat; relax; bend head forward and touch it to chest; relax; repeat; relax.
10. *Back.* Arch back off chair, sticking out chest and stomach; relax; repeat; relax.
11. *Chest.* Take a deep breath and hold it; exhale and relax; repeat; exhale and relax.
12. *Stomach.* Suck in stomach, trying to make it touch your back; relax;

repeat; relax; tense stomach muscles, making them very hard; relax; repeat; relax.

13. *Buttocks.* Push buttocks into the chair; relax; repeat; relax.
14. *Thighs.* Stretch out both legs, lifting feet off floor; relax; repeat; relax.
15. *Legs.* Point toes upward toward face, stretching muscles in calves; relax; repeat; point toes downward; relax; repeat; relax.

Stage 2 involves the development of a list of situations, called a hierarchy, that make you feel anxious. The list starts with the situation that arouses the least anxiety and progresses through situations that arouse increasing levels of anxiety. Let's look at a sample hierarchy for communication apprehension about public speaking.

Sample hierarchy for systematic desensitization

1. Your teacher announces that everyone in the class will be giving a speech during the semester.
2. You are assigned to give a speech in two weeks.
3. You are in the library finding sources for your speech.
4. You are in your room making an outline of your speech.
5. You are preparing the final note cards you will use for your speech.
6. Two days before the speech, you are practicing it alone in your room.
7. You are rehearsing your speech for your roommate the night before the speech.
8. You are on your way to speech class on the day of your speech.
9. You are looking over your note cards in class before the class begins.
10. You are called on to give your speech.
11. You are standing in front of the class about to begin your speech.
12. You have forgotten to display the visual aid you planned for your introduction.
13. You have finished your speech and are walking back to your seat.

Notice that the situations listed on the hierarchy start from the least anxiety-provoking to the most anxiety-provoking. Notice also that this list could differ from individual to individual. What one person finds as the most frightening situation, another person may not. Even though you may not experience a great deal of apprehension about public speaking, you undoubtedly feel some nervousness when you give speeches. What changes, if any, would you make in the hierarchy? On the lines below, put the numbers that correspond to the items in the hierarchy so that they go from least anxiety-producing to most anxiety-producing from your point of view.

1. _____   4. _____

2. _____   5. _____

3. _____   6. _____

7. _____   11. _____

8. _____   12. _____

9. _____   13. _____

10. _____

You would use the revised hierarchy for your own program of systematic desensitization. You might want to compare your ranking of the situations to rankings made by classmates and discuss why you ordered the items as you did, asking them why they listed the items in the orders that they did.

Hierarchies like this one for public speaking can be constructed for any type of communication situation. If you received a high score on any of the subscales of the PRCA-24, you should construct a hierarchy for each of those types of situations. You will need these to begin a program of systematic desensitization to reduce your apprehension about those types of situations. If you have problems doing this, seek the help of your teacher.

The final stage of the program of systematic desensitization involves putting together the first two stages. You begin by practicing the relaxation method until you are able to achieve a state of complete relaxation. Be sure to sit in a very comfortable chair in a room without distractions. Then you imagine, as vividly as you can, the first item on your hierarchy. You will probably feel some tension as you imagine the situation. Stop thinking about the situation and concentrate on returning to a relaxed state. Go back to the first item on the hierarchy and try to put yourself in that situation once again. If you feel tension, stop thinking about it and try to relax. When you are able to think about the first situation on the list without feeling tension, go to the second item on the hierarchy and try to imagine yourself in that situation. If you feel tension, try to relax again. When you are relaxed, imagine the second item on the list again until you are able to imagine it without feeling tension. Repeat this procedure until you can imagine all of the items on the hierarchy without experiencing tension. This procedure teaches you to experience the pleasant feeling of relaxation when confronted with the situations that originally provoked anxiety. In other words, you learn a new habit—you learn to relax in communication situations instead of feeling apprehension in them. You should follow this procedure for about five to seven sessions. Sessions should last no longer than one hour.

If you master this procedure, you may be successful in reducing your communication apprehension. This procedure is recommended for those of you who experience more traitlike apprehension, although it may be effective if you experience only situational anxiety. In the final section of this chapter, we will take a look at features of communication situations that may provoke occasional apprehension. By understanding these situational features and following the suggestions that we give, you may be able to reduce the frequency with which you experience situational apprehension.

Before we examine situational features that may contribute to communication apprehension, we would like to present a shortened version of the relaxation technique we just described. If you do not have time to follow the procedure we have described, you may find this shortened version helpful.

Whenever you are going to be faced with a communication situation that makes you feel apprehensive, sometime prior to that situation you should follow this procedure. You may do this immediately before the situation or whenever you have time on that particular day.

Sit in a comfortable chair and relax. Imagine yourself in a place that makes you feel relaxed, such as at the beach or alone in your room. Try to empty your mind of thoughts that make you feel tense. Breathe deeply and slowly. When you feel completely relaxed, imagine yourself in the situation you are about to face. If you become tense, try to get back that relaxed feeling you had by thinking about the place that made you feel comfortable. When you return to a state of relaxation, try again to imagine yourself in the situation you are about to face. This time, you may be able to remain relaxed, but if you cannot, put that image out of your mind and go back to trying to relax. Keep repeating this procedure as often as you need to until you can feel relaxed as you imagine yourself in the situation you fear.

CONTROLLING SITUATIONAL APPREHENSION

If you did not receive high scores on the PRCA-24 or its subscales, apprehension about communication may not be a problem for you. However, there may be times that you experience fear in specific communication situations. Although we cannot guarantee that you will never experience situational apprehension again, we think that if you understand situational features that seem to produce apprehension, you will be better prepared to deal with it. Sometimes just knowing why we are feeling anxious can help reduce that anxiety. And by knowing the features of situations that can produce apprehension, you can take the necessary steps to handle those features in a way that reduces your apprehension.

Daly and Buss have systematically examined situational features that produce anxiety reactions.[11] Although they have been concerned mostly with features of public speaking situations that cause fear, Buss has shown how these same features can produce fear in other types of communication situations.[12] We will discuss each of these situational features and provide suggestions for dealing with them.

Novelty   Novelty refers to the newness of a communication situation. As Daly and Buss suggest, we can look at three types of novelty: novelty of environment, novelty of role, and novelty of audience.

Novelty of environment refers to the setting in which the interaction takes place. The first time you visit a friend's house you may be a bit uncomfortable, partly because it is a new place. Students typically seem uncomfortable in a new classroom, as do their teachers. Unfamiliar places tend to increase communication apprehension. That is why you may feel much more at ease if you throw a party at your place, rather than attending a party held at a place that is novel to you. The best suggestion we can give you is, if at all possible, try to check out the environment prior to the communication event.[13] If, for example, you are going to be giving a public speech, try to get into the room prior to the speech so that you can familiarize yourself with it. If you will be interviewed for a job, go to the place where you'll be interviewed. Even if you cannot get into the room prior to the interview, you can at least become familiar with the building and its surroundings. The more you acquaint yourself with the setting, the less novel it will be, and the more at ease you should feel.

The second type of novelty Daly and Buss describe is novelty of role. You may be very comfortable in the role of daughter or son, but if all of a sudden you had to take on the role of parent, you might be very ill at ease initially. You are likely to feel apprehension in a new role. The first time you lead a meeting of your classroom group, the first time you give a speech, or the first time you act as a tour guide for your summer job, you are likely to feel uncomfortable in your new role.

There is not a great deal that you can do to reduce the apprehension produced by a novel role. However, this should tell you how important it is to expose yourself to a wide variety of communication situations. As you gain greater social experience, fewer and fewer roles will be novel. And when you are faced with a new role, you will be better able to adapt to it because of your experience in trying out new roles.

The final type of novelty is novelty of audience. By audience we mean the person or persons with whom you are communicating. Unfamiliar people tend to increase our apprehension about communicating. You have probably experienced this type of anxiety. When you went to college, probably everyone was new to you. The teachers were unfamiliar, the students, your roommate, and your adviser. Each time you attend a social event at which there are many people you do not know, you may experience some discomfort. And the first speech you give in your speech class may make you the most anxious, partly because the audience is new.

Again, there is not a great deal you can do to reduce the apprehension produced by a novel audience, unless it is possible to find out what that audience is like prior to the communication event. For instance, if you will be attending a party where you are not likely to know many people, ask the host who will be at the party and what they are like. The more you can find out about the people who will be there, the more comfortable you should feel. This is because the anxiety produced by a novel audience stems from uncertainty about how to act.[14] You will feel more confident about how to act if you can become familiar with the audience prior to the event.

Audience Characteristics   Daly and Buss describe various characteristics of the audience that can increase apprehension. These include size, audience status, audience response, and homogeneity of the audience.[15]

In general, the larger the audience, the greater the apprehension. Although Daly and Buss are talking about an audience for a public speech, the same probably holds true for other types of situations. For example, you may find yourself feeling more anxious in a larger group discussion (eight to ten people) than in a small group (four or five people). Perhaps you are hesitant to ask questions in a large lecture class but feel little discomfort about volunteering in a small class. Large parties may make you ill at ease, whereas small parties do not. Since you probably cannot reduce the size of the audience, you have to adjust to it. Try to think of the individuals in the audience rather than focusing on them as a large mass of people. Think of them as Kathy, Joe, Henry, Sally, Sue, Gert, Fred, and Tiny, not as a group. If you do not know them, think of them as the woman in the first seat with the pretty red hair, the woman in the second seat with the unusual hat, the man in the third seat with the jet black hair, and so on.

If you perceive that there is a status difference between you and the other person or persons with whom you are communicating, this is likely to increase your apprehension. That is why students sometimes report that they are uncomfortable talking to teachers, advisers, deans, or other college personnel. Perhaps physicians, lawyers, counselors, and employers make you feel ill at ease. It is probably the status difference that you perceive between you and the other that makes you so apprehensive. The higher the status of the audience, the greater the anxiety you will experience.

You cannot change the status of the others, but you can change the way you perceive that status difference. Try regarding the other as a person who is similar to you in many ways. True, the individual differs from you too, but try to minimize the differences and maximize the similarities. When students run into their teachers outside of the classroom setting, they often begin to see those teachers as people and feel more comfortable talking to them. By regarding the high-status person as similar to you in many ways, you may reduce the fear you feel when speaking to that person.

The third audience characteristic that can produce situational apprehension is how that audience responds to you. If you are presenting a public speech and people look bored or hostile, you are likely to feel apprehension. If they are smiling and nodding, you will undoubtedly feel much more at ease. If the interviewer glares at you or stares blankly, your anxiety may increase. If you are talking with a stranger in a social situation and that person asks you many questions about yourself and responds enthusiastically to what you have to say, you are likely to feel very comfortable.

Although you cannot control other people, you can behave in ways that tend to elicit positive responses. By improving your communication skills, you can increase your effectiveness and thereby increase the positive responses of others. For example, in Chapters 8 and 9 we will teach you a number of techniques to gain and maintain attention in a public speech. By using these techniques well, you can probably elicit very positive responses from your audience most of the time. Thus the best way to reduce the apprehension produced by negative audience reactions is to improve yourself as a communicator.

The final audience characteristic is the homogeneity of the audience. This refers to how similar or different you perceive audience members to be in comparison to one another. If you perceive the audience members to be vastly different from one another, you are likely to experience apprehension. A diverse audience increases anxiety because it makes it difficult for you to figure out how to act in ways that will be acceptable to all the types of people in the audience. Thus if you are in a class in which the students are quite diverse, you might experience apprehension about speaking out in that class. You may have experienced this at a social situation in which there were many different types of people present.

Again, like most audience characteristics, you cannot change who is in the audience and what those people are like. In this situation you should assume that you probably cannot please everyone and just do your best. The other thing that you can do is to look for similarities among audience members. They may be different in some ways, but they are certainly similar in others. By focusing on the similarities, you can plan communication messages that appeal to what they have in common.

Inappropriateness Inappropriate actions on the part of the speaker can increase apprehension.[16] You may not feel very anxious in a communication situation until you make a mistake or act in a clumsy manner. For example, if you drop your notes when presenting a speech, you may feel a sudden rise in anxiety. If you spill your drink in a social situation or trip as you are walking across the room, you may experience apprehension. If you say the wrong word in an obvious way during a job interview, you may suddenly feel uncomfortable. Any of these kinds of mistakes can produce situational apprehension.

If you make this kind of mistake in a communication situation, you can simply ignore it. Chances are no one will say anything about it, and people will realize that we all make mistakes. Another option you have is to make a joke about it. When people stumble over their words, they sometimes are heard to make jokes such as "Rented lips" or "First day with the new mouth." Jokes are an effective way to diffuse the social tension that results when someone makes a mistake that others see.

Novelty, audience characteristics, and inappropriate speaker actions are three situational features that can produce communication apprehension. Daly and Buss discuss others, but those others concern public speaking situations. The three that we have focused on can be handled in the ways that we have suggested. So the next time you feel yourself becoming anxious in a communication situation in which you do not normally experience apprehension, try to identify the situational features that are causing your anxiety. This alone may make you feel more comfortable. In addition, try the techniques we have suggested to handle these situational features.

SUMMARY

This chapter has focused on techniques for improving attitudes and reducing communication apprehension. These techniques can be learned fairly easily but require practice.

There are three areas in which attitudes can be improved. First, we need to improve our attitude toward ourselves, by striving for self-acceptance, the ability to accept ourselves without any requirements or conditions. The most effective way to develop self-acceptance is to practice rating our behaviors, not ourselves as human beings.

Second, we should strive for other-acceptance. People who are self-accepting often accept others as well. But to try to improve our attitude toward others, we need to concentrate on evaluating their behavior, just as we evaluate our own behavior.

Finally, we need to improve our attitude about communication by developing reasonable attitudes. Reasonable attitudes are realistic. Unreasonable attitudes involve exaggeration, oversimplification, overgeneralization, illogic, unvalidated assumptions, and absolutist notions. We can test our beliefs to determine if they are reasonable by applying four guidelines. First, reasonable beliefs are true. Second, reasonable beliefs are not absolutist. Third, they result in moderate, rather than extreme, emotion. Fourth, reasonable beliefs help in goal attainment. Once we have identified our unreasonable beliefs, we need to apply the ABC model to turn them into reasonable beliefs. This technique involves identifying and disputing our unreasonable beliefs so that we can have a more positive attitude toward communication.

In addition to improving our attitudes, many of us need to reduce our apprehension about communication. This can be done by learning and practicing systematic desensitization. There are three stages of systematic desensitization. First, we need to learn to relax as completely as possible by practicing relaxation of each of the muscle groups. Stage 2 involves the development of a list of situations that make us feel anxious. This is called a hierarchy. The final stage involves pairing relaxation with the items on the hierarchy. To do this we need to relax by following the muscle relaxation procedure. Then we go to the hierarchy, focusing on the least threatening item on it. We need to try to imagine that situation. If we feel anxious, we try to relax again and then imagine the situation a second time. We repeat this procedure until we can feel relaxed as we imagine all of the items on the hierarchy.

Many people experience apprehension occasionally, which is called situational apprehension. There are three major situational features that can produce occasional apprehension. First, the novelty of a situation can produce fear, including novelty of the environment, of the speaker's role, and of the audience. Second, audience characteristics may create anxiety in a speaker. These characteristics include the size of the audience, the status of the audience, how the audience responds, and homogeneity of the audience. The final situational feature that often produces apprehension is inappropriateness on the part of the speaker. When we experience situational apprehension, we need to examine the features of the situation that might be making us feel nervous so that we can adapt to those features.

chapter 4

Setting Personal Communication Goals

CHAPTER OBJECTIVES

1. To understand what goal setting is and its importance in improving as a communicator.
2. To learn the steps of the goal-setting process.
3. To complete the goal-setting process for a first communication goal.

INTRODUCTION

Now that you have assessed yourself as a communicator and have begun learning techniques to improve your attitudes and reduce apprehension, you are ready to begin mastering the skills that are necessary for all types of communication situations. In this chapter we will concern ourselves with goal setting. Chapter 5 will explain situation and listener assessment.

We will begin by explaining what goal setting is and how it is important to you as a communicator. We will then teach you the step-by-step process of goal setting. By the time you complete this chapter, you will have completed your first goal preparation and will have an important tool for improving yourself in any type of communication situation.

WHAT IS GOAL SETTING?

In order to manage the communication process, we need to manage ourselves. We cannot control the behavior of other people, but we can control our own behavior. Goal setting is a technique that helps you manage your own behavior to maximize your effectiveness as a communicator. Many communication situations we must face are unfamiliar. Those that are familiar involve new elements to which we must adapt. The method of goal setting helps us prepare for situations so that we can reduce the possibility of making mistakes. The authors of this book have taught the goal-setting technique to a large number of students, and their response to it has been very positive. They claim that it helps them feel prepared to face communication situations and thus increases their confidence.

As we introduce you to goal setting, it is vital that you realize that *you set goals for your behavior,* not for your listener's behavior. A *goal* is a specific statement of what you are trying to accomplish by talking.[1] It is always stated in terms of the behaviors you will perform, not in terms of what you want the other person to do. For example, your goal should be stated as "I will prepare for and present a public speech." Your goal should *not* be stated "The audience will love my speech." You cannot control the audience's behavior, but you can manage your own.

Goal setting is a step-by-step procedure designed to achieve the following:

1. Help you formulate your precise goal statement
2. Help you specify behavioral outcomes that you would have to see in order to conclude that you had successfully achieved your goal
3. Help you list steps that you would need to do to prepare for and carry out your goal

We will explain each of these three aspects of goal setting later in this chapter, but let's look at a brief example now.

Suppose you took a course last semester in which you thought your final grade would be a B but you received a C. You make the decision that you will talk to your teacher about your grade. Through the process of goal setting, you would do the following:

1. *Formulate a specific statement of your communication goal.* In this case your goal statement might be "I will talk to my teacher to find out why I received a grade of C and to try to persuade him to change the grade to a B if I deserve the higher grade."

2. *Specify behavioral outcomes that would help you determine if your goal was achieved.* In essence, what you are doing in this step is listing behaviors that you would have to perform in order to consider yourself successful at accomplishing your goal. In this example your list might consist of the following behavioral outcomes:

I will explain to the teacher why I thought I would receive a B.

I will ask the teacher why I received a C in the course.

I will not insult the teacher by calling him names if he refuses to change the grade.

I will maintain eye contact about 70 percent of the time.

I will not interrupt him when he is talking.

I will ask if he will change the grade.

I will thank him for his time.

3. *List steps that you need to do to prepare for and carry out your goal.* In this example your list might look like the following:

I will call my teacher and make an appointment.

I will get out all the papers and tests that I have from the course.

I will go over the course syllabus to make sure that I completed all assignments.

I will calculate my final grade according to the· grading policy specified on the syllabus. If it comes out to a B, I will continue with my goal. If it comes out to a C, I will call and cancel my appointment.

I will bring my calculations with me to the appointment.

I will arrive on time and introduce myself.

I will state the reason for my visit and explain my calculations.

I will not interrupt while the teacher responds.

I will ask if my grade will be changed.

I will thank the teacher for his time.

Each of these steps of goal setting will be explained in much more detail, but it should be clear at this point that goal setting is a method for making a careful plan to help you achieve your communication goals. It is like planning your route for a trip so that you can arrive at your destination in an efficient manner.

THE IMPORTANCE OF GOAL SETTING

Goal setting is a general skill needed to become an effective communicator. There are three major ways in which goal setting is important to you: (1) It helps you formulate a specific statement of your goal, (2) it helps you recognize when you have been successful in achieving your goal, and (3) it helps you make a specific plan for carrying out your goal.

Formulation of a Specific Goal Statement

It is important to know what our goals are in a communication situation. Remember that we said that goal statements are made in terms of our behavior. A clear goal statement gives direction to our behavior. If we do not know what we are trying to achieve by talking, we are likely to be very dissatisfied with the act of communication. Have you ever been involved in an intimate relationship that started deteriorating after it had been going so well? Perhaps you decided to talk to the other person because you wanted to "make things like they used to be." Chances are that your conversation ended up in an argument or that you left it feeling very frustrated. One reason for such a bad ending is that you were not clear about what you wanted in the first place. You wanted things to be better or to be like they used to be, but that is not a very clear goal. Your vagueness was probably communicated to your partner, who probably even asked you, "So what do you want me to do?" But because you didn't know what you wanted, you could not work out a satisfactory arrangement with your partner. In this example it was the lack of a specific goal that caused the problem with the communication. You have probably experienced other situations in which the speaker did not have a clear goal, such as when a public speaker did not seem to make a clear point. This is another case where the major problem was a lack of a precise goal statement. Goal setting can help us avoid these frustrating situations.

Let's look at some examples of good and bad goal statements so that you can see the difference between a specific goal statement and one that is vague.

VAGUE: I will make a good impression on the interviewer.

GOOD: I will mention at least three of the reasons why I feel I am qualified for the job during the interview.

The first example is vague because it does not provide direction for our behavior. Of course you want to make a good impression, but how will you do that? You can do it only by managing your own behavior. The second goal statement specifies exactly what you want to achieve in the interview and directs your behavior.

VAGUE: I will be an interesting conversationalist at the party.

GOOD: I will introduce at least two topics in each conversation I engage in at the party.

Notice again that the first goal statement does not provide any clues as to how you should behave, whereas the second one does. Try to correct the following vague goal statement to make it a good one.

VAGUE: I will be a valuable member of my group.

GOOD: _____

_____

To determine if the goal statement is written correctly, make sure that it is stated in terms of behaviors you could actually see someone performing.[2] For example, you could see someone introduce two ideas to the group. You could not, however, see someone be a valuable member of the group. To be a valuable member involves behaviors that assist the group in achieving its task. Thus your goal statement should focus on specific behaviors that you would perform. If you are not sure if the goal statement you have written is correct, be sure to check with your teacher.

Recognition of Success

Goal setting is also important because it can help us recognize when we have been successful in achieving our goals. It does this by forcing us to be specific about what success would look like. Many times we are not sure if our communication has been successful, partially successful, or unsuccessful. For other things that we do we can often recognize success instantly. If you play basketball and your goal is to make a basket, you know immediately whether or not you have achieved your goal. If you are trying to get a computer program to run and it does, you know you have been successful. But when we communicate, success and failure are not so clear-cut or so visible. How many times have you given a speech in class and after it was over thought to yourself, "That was terrible"? And of those times, after how many did someone in the class say, "That was a great speech"? The reason this occurs is that we don't know what success looks like, and if we lack confidence in ourselves, we tend to assume failure. Goal setting can help you build your confidence as a communicator because it can help you see when you have been successful and to what extent you have succeeded. You'll probably discover that you have more successes than failures and that you will almost always be at least partially successful. Goal setting does this by forcing you to list specific behaviors that act as standards against which you can measure your success. You can look back at the list of standards to see which ones you have met and which ones you have not. This gives you a concrete tool for assessing the success and failure of your goals.

Formulation of a Specific Plan

The third way in which goal setting is so important is that it helps us make a specific plan for carrying out our goals. Part of the goal-setting process involves creating a list of all of the behaviors that you will have to perform to prepare for your goal and carry it out. In our example of the student going to see the teacher about a grade, you can see the list of steps needed to prepare for the goal. Without creating a list, a student might forget to call for an appointment or might fail to calculate the grade to find out if he or she was correct in feeling that the final grade was too low. You can see how listing these steps can help the student communicate more effectively when speaking with her teacher.

THE STEPS OF GOAL SETTING

In this section we will take you step by step through the process of goal setting. What we want you to do as you read along is to complete the activities so that you can begin setting your own personal communication goals. By the end of this chapter, you'll have made some specific plans for carrying out goals that are important to you.

Step 1: Defining Goal Areas

Before you can begin to define precise goal statements, you need to decide in which areas you need to improve and in what order you want to tackle those areas. This should be fairly easy for you at this point because in Chapter 2 you participated in a number of activities designed to help you assess your strengths and weaknesses as a communicator. Go back to your work in Chapter 2 and look at the types of communication situations that represent areas in which you need improvement. Perhaps you discovered that you have trouble initiating conversation with strangers, that you hesitate to speak out in class, and that you fear giving public speeches. These would be the areas in which you would want to begin setting goals. By going back to Chapter 2, you can discover the communication areas in which you need improvement. Take a minute to list these areas.

Area in need of improvement	Priorities based on the three guidelines	Totals

Now that you have your goal-setting areas in front of you, your next task is to prioritize them. There are three guidelines that you can use to help you put these areas in the order in which you'll tackle them. First, consider which of the areas is most important to you right now. For example, suppose you have identified the following goal areas: public speaking, speaking in task groups, and speaking to authority figures like teachers and advisers. As you look over these three areas, think about where it is most important for you to improve. Perhaps you have just become an officer in a club on campus and you know that you'll be serving on a committee and participating in meetings of the executive council. This might be the area that you put first on your list, since it seems important for you to begin improving in this area as soon as possible. Think about which area should be second on your list. Maybe you will not be doing any public speaking in the near future, so you can put that third on the list and speaking to authority figures second. Do this for the goal-setting areas you have listed; put them in order based on their importance to you. Do this by numbering them from

1 to 5 on the first set of lines under the heading, "Priorities Based on the Three Guidelines."

The second guideline you can use to help you prioritize your list is to consider in which communication areas you will have opportunities in the near future to participate. Suppose you have identified social conversation, group discussion, and public speaking as the three areas in which you feel you need improvement, and this is the order of importance you have established. Will there be opportunities within the next few weeks for you to participate in social conversations? Chances are that the answer is yes, so you can leave that area in the number 1 spot. Will there be opportunities for you to meet in small task groups? If the answer is no, you might want to move that area to third place on your list. Since you are probably going to have opportunities in the course you are presently taking to give speeches, you might want to move public speaking to the second place on the list. Go through each of the areas you have listed, and if there are any for which there will be few if any opportunities to participate in, put them lower on the list of priorities. Again, rank order the five areas, using the second set of lines in the priorities section of the chart.

The third guideline you should use in putting your list in order is to consider which areas you consider more difficult and which less difficult. The key to improving yourself as a communicator is to begin having successful communication encounters so that your confidence can begin to grow. It is best, therefore, if you begin with goal areas that seem easier and gradually move to the more challenging areas. If, for example, your list of goal areas as you have just reorganized them consists of public speaking, social conversation, and speaking to authority figures, you should now consider which area is most challenging and move it down on the list. Perhaps public speaking represents a greater challenge to you than social conversation. You may want to switch those two areas on your list. Using the third set of lines, rank order the five areas according to this guideline.

Now that you have the three guidelines in mind, take an average rank for each area and write that number under the heading, "Totals." To compute an average rank for each area, add the three numbers you listed for that area and divide by three. The area with the lowest average rank is the one you'll work on first. If any ties resulted, you can make the decision about which area will be given priority.

Step 2: Formulating Specific Goal Statements

In this next step of goal setting you will work with the goal area that is first on your final list. And for each of the remaining steps of goal setting, continue working with that first area. After you have completed the steps of goal setting for your first area, repeat them for each of the remaining goal areas you have identified.

Step 2 of goal setting involves formulating a specific goal statement for a specific communication situation. This is the step that moves you from the broad area to the precise goal that you will carry out. For instance, suppose that on your final list, social conversation is the area that you want to work on first. You now need to decide on a specific type of situation in which you would like to begin practicing social conversation. To do this you can go back to the three guidelines we gave you for ordering your goal areas: (1) Which type of communication situation is most important to you? Perhaps you find yourself alone and uncomfortable at parties, and you want to begin meeting new people and having more fun at parties. Parties, then, might be the type of situation that is most important to you. (2) Which type of situation are you likely to encounter in the next few weeks? If you rarely go to parties and there are none coming up, you might want to pick a new type of situation in which you could practice social conversation, such as in the dining hall or after class with a fellow student. (3) Which type of situation is the easiest for you? If you think that parties represent a situation that is relatively easy for you, you might want to pick a party for your first goal.

You are now ready to pick the type of situation in which you will carry out your first goal. Make a list of all of the possible types of situations you could be in to practice that goal. If you need help, refer to the examples provided.

Types of situations in which I could practice

1. _____

2. _____

3. _____

4. _____

5. _____

6. _____

Examples for social conversation

1. Fraternity or sorority parties
2. After class
3. In the dormitories
4. In the dining hall
5. In the apartment complex
6. Riding the bus to campus

Examples for group discussion

1. With my group of classmates working on a project
2. At the meetings of the publicity committee
3. In my Bible study group
4. With a group of people eating dinner in the dining hall

5. In a dorm meeting
6. At a meeting of my study group

Examples for speaking to authority figures

1. With my teacher after class to ask a question
2. With my adviser
3. With an employee in the career placement center
4. With my physician or counselor
5. With my roommate's father or mother
6. With my landlord

We have provided you with these examples to stimulate your thinking, but our lists are not exhaustive. You may even think of situations you could add to your list later on. That is fine. This initial list is to get you started. It can always be revised and updated.

Now that you have a list of possible communication situations within your particular goal area, you are ready to select one so that you can continue with goal setting. Return to the three guidelines. Of the situations you have listed, which one is most important to you, will you have the opportunity to encounter soon, and is relatively easy for you? Pick a situation and list it here:

Type of situation I have selected: _____

With a specific situation in mind, you are ready to formulate your specific goal statement. This is a statement of what you hope to accomplish in the situation you selected. Before you write your goal statement, keep in mind these two general principles:

1. *Your goal should be realistic.* You need to select a goal that is possible. "I want to carry on a five-minute conversation with a stranger on the bus" and "I will ask my teacher two questions about the project after class" are both examples of realistic goals. The more realistic your goal, the greater your chances for success. Remember that success builds confidence. And confidence leads to taking advantage of more communication opportunities, which leads to greater skill.

Unrealistic goals may be worth dreaming about, but they are not what you should seek, especially now when you are trying to improve your communication. "I want to be popular" and "We will fall in love by the end of our conversation" are examples of unrealistic goals. If those things happen, that is wonderful, but you don't want to consider them your goals.

2. *Your goal should be stated in behavioral terms.* This means that your goal statement should include the specific behaviors that you want to perform rather than how you want to feel or how you want the other person to act. Here are some examples of goal statements that are written in behavioral terms:

I will initiate a conversation with a classmate at the end of class.

I will present a five-minute extemporaneous speech in my speech class.

I will ask my adviser what courses I should take in the fall.

I will ask two questions in my history class.

Notice that none of these statements are statements about feelings or statements about how you would like the other person to act. We advise staying away from those kinds of goal statements because you cannot control another's behavior; you can only control your own. And it is easier to control your behavior than it is to control your feelings, so your chances for successfully completing your goal are reduced if you state your goal in terms of feelings or the behavior of the other person.

Look at the following goal statements and decide what is wrong with each one:

1. I will feel confident when I present my speech in class.
2. My teacher will say, "That was a good question," when I ask a question in class.
3. We will enjoy our five-minute conversation on the bus.
4. My group members will think I am intelligent when I offer ideas.
5. Pat will ask me out on a date by the end of our conversation.

If you cannot determine what is wrong with these goal statements, your teacher can help you. For further practice, try rewriting each of these goal statements so that they are stated in behavioral terms. This may be difficult at first because it is not something that you are used to doing. After a while, however, it will become a habit, and you'll find it very easy to do.

At this point you are ready to write your specific goal statement. You have already identified the goal area and the type of situation in which you'll carry out your first goal. Take a minute now to write your final goal statement, using the correct ones we have provided as models.

My final goal statement: _____

_____

Keep in mind that this is only your first goal. You can go back through this process any number of times to write goal statements for yourself. In fact, your improvement as a communicator will increase as you complete more and more goals.

Step 3: Writing Criteria for Success

Earlier we said that goal setting can help us by forcing us to list standards by which we can judge success and failure. We need to know when we have successfully achieved our communication goals so that we don't assume we have failed when we have not. If you lack confidence in yourself as a communicator, you probably have a tendency to assume that you have failed when you actually don't know how well you did. To know how well you did, you will need to make a list of criteria or standards by which you can judge yourself.

Just as you wrote your specific goal statement in behavioral terms, you need to do the same for your criteria for success. Remember, you cannot control anyone else's behavior, and it is easier to control your behavior than your feelings, so by establishing behavioral standards, you have the most objective measure you can find for evaluating your success. Let's look at an example before you try your hand at writing some criteria.

Suppose you wrote for your goal statement "I will carry on a five-minute conversation with a stranger at the party on Saturday." Think about some of the *behaviors* you would have to do in order to consider yourself to have had a successful conversation with a stranger. Here are some possibilities:

1. *I will maintain the conversation for at least five minutes.* This one is necessary because you specified it in your goal statement. If your conversation only lasts three minutes, you will be partially successful. If you don't engage in a conversation with a stranger, you will have been totally unsuccessful, unless, of course, you knew everyone at the party and nobody qualified as a stranger. We'll talk about this idea later.
2. *I will make sure I introduce myself at some point in the conversation.* It is generally a good idea to introduce yourself to a person you begin a conversation with. It is not necessary to begin that way, but before you end the conversation, it is a good idea.
3. *I will maintain at least 50 percent eye contact.* It is a norm in our society (although not in all societies) to look at a person while the two of you talk. It is not appropriate to stare (maintain 100 percent eye contact), but you are expected to engage in eye contact at least 50 percent of the time.
4. *I will ask at least five questions and make at least five comments.* A conversation proceeds through the asking and answering of questions and the offering of comments. Therefore, to have a successful conversation, you need to do your share of asking questions and making comments. The number five is arbitrary, but you need to pick a number so that you have something by which to gauge yourself. Don't worry about trying to count your comments and questions during the conversation. After the conversation is over, think about your behavior and try to assess how many comments and questions you initiated. The specific number is not important. You are simply trying to decide whether or not your contribution was sufficient.
5. *I will do approximately 50 percent of the talking.* If you barely say anything during a conversation, it will not be much of a conversation. A good rule of thumb is that you should talk about 50 percent of the time and listen about 50 percent of the time when speaking to one other person. When there are three people, you should talk about one third of the time, and so forth.
6. *I will end the conversation by saying, "Nice talking with you."* In our

culture there are standard ways of opening and ending conversations. You are always safe if you use these standard ways. For a conversation with a stranger at a party in which people mingle and move on to talk to others, it is perfectly appropriate to use a common ending. But you need some sort of ending; it is generally not appropriate just to walk away.

Keep in mind that these are examples of criteria you might use to evaluate your conversation with a stranger at a party. It is up to you to write your own criteria on the basis of the particular situation you find yourself in and your own strengths and weaknesses as a communicator. For example, if you discovered through your self-assessment in Chapter 2 that you have a great deal of difficulty with eye contact, you might want to list the criterion "I will maintain about 30 percent eye contact." Perhaps this would represent an improvement over what you usually do. If you set your standard too high, you are bound to fail. So just as you set your own goals so that they increase in difficulty, you set your own criteria so that each time they represent an improvement.

With the list of criteria we just generated, we would have a set of standards by which we could judge our conversation with a stranger at a party. If we did each of the things on the list, we would be successful. If we did some of them but not others, we would be partially successful, and so on. But we would have something concrete to help us assess how well we had achieved our goal. Without the list, we probably would assume that we had not done very well or that we had done a great job, without using any clear-cut standards to make our assessment. Notice what else this list of criteria does for you. You can go back to it and see where your weak areas are. Suppose you had your conversation with a stranger and did everything on the list except introduce yourself. You now know what you need to do next time in a similar situation in order to improve over the last time. Knowing what you need to do to improve is at least half the battle.

Before we continue this discussion of criteria, it is time for you to try your hand at writing some for your first goal. Go back to the final goal statement that you formulated. On the lines below, list some possible criteria for success; that is, list behaviors you would have to perform in order to consider yourself successful in achieving your goal. (If you need more space, use a separate sheet of paper.)

1. _____

2. _____

3. _____

4. _____

5. _____

6. _____

Look at your list. Are all of your standards written in terms of *your behavior?* You cannot control the other person's behavior, so be sure that none of your criteria are written in terms of what the other should do. If you had written, "My partner will ask me my name," you would want to change it to, "I will tell my partner my name." Are any of your criteria written in terms of feelings? Did you write, "I will feel confident when I end the conversation"? If you did, you want to change it to, "I will end the conversation by saying . . ." because you cannot easily control your feelings. Besides that, you can have a successful conversation even if you don't feel confident. By listing feelings as criteria, you doom yourself to failure.

Just to make sure that you understand this notion of writing criteria for success, pick two of the following goal statements and list criteria for them. Do this on a separate sheet of paper. You may want to go over them with your teacher.

1. I will ask two questions in my math class.
2. I will talk to my adviser about my schedule for next spring.
3. I will present a five-minute oral presentation in my business class.
4. I will offer my ideas at least twice at the next meeting of my study group.

Step 4: Listing Steps for Preparation and Implementation

At this point you have specified your goal statement and have listed criteria to help you assess your success as you carry out your goal. You now know where you want to end up and what you want your behavior to look like as you implement your goal, but you have not yet planned how you will arrive at your destination. You have also not specified what steps you'll take in order to produce the behavior that you want to produce. Step 4 is designed to help you make your specific plans for the preparation and implementation of your goal. The more carefully you complete this section, the greater your chances of success. Think how carefully you prepare for other events. You study for tests, you practice for athletic competitions or rehearse for a play, you carefully plan the meal you'll cook. But so often we neglect to prepare for our communication encounters. We leave them to chance and then wonder why we are not more effective. Although careful preparation is no guarantee, it will increase the likelihood that we will be effective.

Essentially, what you do in this step of goal setting is to focus first on preparation for your goal and then on implementation. Let's look at preparation first. What you need to do is to list, in the order that you will do them, all of the steps that are necessary to help you prepare for your goal. Let's look at an example.

Suppose your goal is to present an oral report to the class. There are many steps involved in the preparation of an oral presentation. We will teach you about these in Chapters 8 and 9, but for now, here are some of the steps:

1. I will select a topic for my report.
2. I will narrow down my topic so that it can be covered in the allotted time.

3. I will make an outline of the major and secondary points I plan to make.
4. I will find at least two current sources on my topic to get the latest information.
5. I will prepare note cards to be used when I give the report.
6. I will prepare my visual aid.
7. I will rehearse my presentation at least twice with my roommate.
8. I will make any final changes in my report.

It is fairly easy to see that there is a great deal of preparation involved for an oral report, but there is plenty of preparation you can do for other kinds of communication goals. Here's another example.

Suppose you have been invited to a dinner party at your friend's parents' house. Most of the people there will be older than you, and you do not know any of them except for your friend and her parents. You decide on a goal: "I will carry on five-minute conversations with at least two strangers at the party." How might you prepare for such a situation? Here are some steps:

1. I will ask my friend to tell me who will be at the party, what they do for a living, where they live, and how they know her parents.
2. I will ask my friend to tell me about the major interests of the people at the party so that I'll have some topics to talk about.
3. I will think of answers to questions they are likely to ask me, such as what I am majoring in in college and what I plan to do when I graduate.
4. I will think of two good ways to initiate conversations, such as "Wasn't dinner wonderful?" or "How long have you known the Hastings?"

For any communication situation except for those that occur on the spot, you can do some preparation. You can prepare for your participation in a class, a meeting with your teacher, a conversation with a stranger, or an interview. You are now ready to list the steps you should follow in preparing for the goal you are planning. Take some time now to do this. Keep in mind that if you think of something else you can do, you can add it in later. (If you need more space, use a separate sheet of paper.) Check with your teacher if you have any questions.

Steps I'll perform in preparing for my goal

1. _____

2. _____

3. _____

4. _____

5. _____

In this fourth step of goal setting, we have concentrated so far on the steps in preparing for your goal. The second part of this step is to list the activities you'll perform in the actual implementation of your goal. We can carefully prepare in advance but be lost when we try to carry out our goal if we don't think about what we'll actually do when we get there. It would be like preparing a poster for a presentation and not thinking about when you will use it during the speech or where you would put it to display it to the audience. You might have a great poster, but you could end up doing a miserable job of using it.

In completing this part of goal setting, you want to try to place yourself in the situation and think about what you'll need to do. If we go back to our example of an oral report in class, we might end up with a list like the following:

1. I will volunteer to go first when the teacher asks.
2. I will walk to the front of the class, making sure to bring my notes and my visual aid. I will already have the tape on the back of my aid.
3. I will place my visual aid face down on the desk and my note cards on the lectern.
4. I will look at my audience and begin my introduction, glancing at my cards but not reading them.
5. When I reach my second major point, I will place the visual aid on the blackboard so that my audience can see it. I will explain what is on the aid, then remove it.
6. At the conclusion of my report, I will ask the audience if they have any questions. If they do, I'll try to answer them. If not, I'll sit down.

Notice that what you are trying to do is to make the most specific plan you can. Things may happen that you couldn't anticipate, but if you have a good solid plan, you won't be at a loss. You'll simply have to make adjustments. Suppose another student volunteers to present his report first. You can just tell the teacher right then that you would like to be second and then carry on with the rest of your plan.

It is time to complete this step for your own first goal. On a sheet of paper, list the steps you'll do in the implementation of your goal. It is a good idea to check this list with your teacher, as well as the other work you have done so far.

You now have just about completed your first goal-setting activity. You have a clear goal, a list of standards by which to judge yourself, and a list of steps you'll perform in the preparation and implementation of your goal. Put all of these together on one or two sheets of paper and make any changes in them that you feel are necessary. You are now ready to move to the final stage of goal setting.

Step 5: Planning for Contingencies

It would be nice if communication were so predictable that we could be sure our plan would be carried out smoothly. Actually, if communication were that predictable, it would probably be very boring. But communication is not totally predictable because we cannot be sure how the other person will act or what circumstances will arise that will require us to alter our plan. In this final step of goal setting, we plan for various circumstances. If you set a goal to talk to your adviser and your adviser misses the appointment, have you failed? Of course not, but you may be inclined to blame yourself if your confidence is low. If you plan on carrying on a ten-minute conversation and a third person interrupts the conversation, is it your fault? Did you fail because your conversation lasted only five minutes? Again, no.

In this final step of goal setting, you will complete two parts. First, you need to plan for the best, worst, and most likely outcome that could occur when you carry out your goal.[3] You also need to plan what you'll do in each of the three situations. For our goal of giving an oral report in class, what might be the best possible outcome? Perhaps the teacher would say that it was a model presentation or several classmates would say that the speaker did a great job. Perhaps the student would receive an A on the presentation. It is up to you to decide what you would consider to be the best possible outcome and how you would handle it.

What might be the worst possible outcome for our goal of presenting a report in class? The student might forget to bring the note cards to class or might drop them during the presentation. Or perhaps the teacher would ask the speaker to sit down because he or she seemed poorly prepared. Again, think about the worst thing that could happen and how you would handle it. For both the best and worst scenarios, be sure to try to stay realistic. Of course, the worst possible thing might be that the roof would cave in, killing everyone in the class, but that is so highly unlikely that there is no sense in preparing for it.

Now that you have considered the best and worst possible outcomes, what is the most likely thing that will occur when you attempt your goal? For our public speaker, the most likely outcome is that he or she will present the report as planned, perhaps stumbling over a few words, but generally giving the prepared presentation.

You might be wondering why it is important to plan for the best, the worst, and the most likely outcomes. There are two major reasons. First, by preparing for all three cases, you can anticipate how you would handle each one. Then whichever one occurred, you would be prepared with a plan of action. So, for example, if the teacher did ask our speaker to sit down, the speaker would be prepared to handle that possibility. He or she might reply, "I am prepared, but I'm a little nervous, and that makes me seem unprepared." By the way, a teacher would not typically ask a student to sit down because he or she appeared unprepared. Our goal setter would only list this for the worst possible thing that could happen if the teacher had a reputation of doing that or if the student had seen the teacher do that. You'll learn more about how to anticipate the best, most likely, and worst possible outcomes when you read Chapter 5. This chapter teaches you how to assess the situation and your audience so that you have a better understanding of both and can adapt your behavior accordingly. In any event, planning for a best, worst, and most likely outcome prepares you with a response for each.

The second reason it is useful to prepare for the best, worst, and most likely outcomes is so that you can see that usually the worst realistic thing you can think of is not really so terrible and the best is not so great after all. If your goal was to approach a stranger at a party and he or she said, "Bug off. I'm not in the mood to talk" (your worst-case scenario), what is so terrible about that? Sure, you don't feel very good about it, but it is obviously the other person who has the problem, not you. And if you had prepared for how you would deal with this, you could come off appearing like a terrific person. If you didn't prepare, you would proba- bly just storm away or throw an insult at the person, like anyone would do in that situation. In any event, by planning a best, worst, and most likely outcome, you can see that what will probably happen *is* the most likely outcome you planned. You can also see that most of the time, the worst is not so bad after all.

Take out the sheet of paper with your final lists for your first goal, and write out the best possible outcome and how you would handle it. Do the same for the worst and the most likely outcomes. Remember to be as realistic as you can. You may want to go back over this and make some changes after you have read Chapter 5.

The second aspect of this final goal-setting step is to consider the possibility of something going wrong when you carry out your goal. Try to answer the question "If something goes wrong, when would it be my fault, the other's fault, or the fault of circumstances?" Keep in mind that when you carry out a goal, failure is a possibility. But just because you experience failure does not necessarily mean that it was your fault. It certainly could be, but then you can look at your list of criteria for success to determine in what specific ways you failed. Sometimes you may fail because it is the fault of the other person or the fault of circum- stances. You need to recognize this so that you don't blame yourself for failures that you could not control. This is important if you want to continue building your confidence as a communicator.

So suppose when you try to talk to a stranger at a party, he or she tells you to get lost. Your goal may have been a failure, but it was *not* your fault. Or suppose you have to give a speech and the speakers ahead of you took too much time and the teacher had to cut you off partway through your speech. Was the failure your fault? Obviously not. It is important to learn to recognize when you have failed because of something you have done and when the goal has been a failure because of other people or circumstances. Why blame yourself when there is nothing you could have done?

Take a look at the paper on which you have done your goal setting, and answer the question "If something goes wrong, when would it be my fault, the other's fault, or the fault of circumstances?" When you have completed that, pat yourself on the back because you have just completed all five of the steps of goal setting. Don't run out and attempt your goal quite yet, though. Keep reading, and consult your teacher to find out when you should try your goal. Remember, our goal is to help you collect successes so that your confidence will grow. You don't want to attempt a goal until your teacher says you are ready.

SUMMARY

Goal setting is a very important technique for improving as a communicator because it helps us prepare for communication situations. By careful planning we are more likely to experience success in communication situations.

There are five major steps in goal setting: defining goal areas, formulating specific goal statements, specifying criteria for success, listing steps for the preparation and implementation of goals, and planning for contingencies. Each of these steps must be carried out each time you plan a communication goal. You'll discover that the process gets easier each time you complete it. Remember that goal setting is a process designed to help you formulate clear goals, specify standards you can use to judge your effectiveness, and specify what you need to do to prepare for and carry out your goal.

chapter 5

Assessing the Communication Situation and Listeners

CHAPTER OBJECTIVES

1. To understand the importance of situation and listener assessment in the communication process.
2. To understand the four major features of a situation that are examined in a situation assessment.
3. To understand the three major aspects of the listeners that are examined in a listener assessment.
4. To complete an initial situation and listener assessment for the first personal communication goal.

INTRODUCTION

In Chapter 4, we introduced you to a very important skill called goal setting. This is a skill that you need for any type of communication situation. As you saw from the examples in that chapter, goal setting is used in dyadic (one-to-one), small group, and public speaking situations. Thus it constitutes a general communication skill that we need to develop to be effective communicators.

A second general communication skill that we need to develop is situation and listener assessment. Like goal setting, this is a skill that is needed in all types of communication encounters. In fact, situation and listener assessment is an integral part of goal setting because by understanding a communication situation and the listeners, you will be better able to write criteria for success and the step-by-step plan for achieving your goal. At the end of this chapter we will ask you to make any changes in the goal analysis that you completed in Chapter 4 based on what you learn in this chapter. You should be able to make a number of changes because situation and listener assessment provides you with a greater understanding of a specific communication situation.

WHAT IS SITUATION AND LISTENER ASSESSMENT?

Situation Assessment

By *situation* we mean a particular time and place in which we feel that we have something that can be accomplished by speaking. (This definition is based on the definition of *rhetorical situation* provided by Bitzer.)[1] In essence, we are always in situations, but in order for it to be a *communication situation,* we must feel that there is something that can be achieved by talking. That something is our *goal.* We are motivated to talk because we have a goal that we feel can be achieved by speaking with another.

When we feel that we have a goal that can be accomplished through speaking, the time and place in which we attempt to communicate to achieve our goal is a communication situation. Features of that situation influence our behavior and essentially dictate behaviors that are in the realm of appropriateness. Suppose you hosted a party at your home that was to begin at 9:00 P.M. As you were getting ready at 8:00, one of the guests arrived. What would your reaction be? You might be a bit perturbed or embarrassed, but you would at least be a bit uncomfortable because people do not *typically* arrive that early. Suppose that as you continued to get ready, your early arriver went into the kitchen and started helping himself or herself to food. By this time your patience would be wearing very thin. You would be relieved when other guests started arriving.

Why would you feel upset or uncomfortable by your guest's behaviors? Because people do not typically do those things. In other words, there are *norms* or expectations for behavior that operate in all situations. When people violate norms, the rest of us feel very uncomfortable and sometimes angry.

Suppose your early arriver began talking about very morbid topics at your party, such as a recent funeral he or she attended. And suppose this guest continually interrupted conversations and then monopolized them. No doubt you would not invite this person back to your home. Notice that norms for both general behavior and communicative behavior are operating in the situation. People do not usually talk about morbid topics at a party, nor do they interrupt others and monopolize conversations. Your guest violated norms for conversational behavior.

To make sure you understand the notion of conversational norms, take a minute to list some other norms (expectations for behavior) for communicating with strangers at parties:

1. _____

2. _____

3. _____

4. _____

5. _____

If you have trouble listing norms for communication at parties, return to this activity after you have read the sections on situation assessment and see if you can fill the norms in then. If you still have trouble, be sure to speak with your teacher, who can clarify this concept.

Thus by situation assessment we mean that we observe and analyze the situation to determine the norms for communication so that our behavior is appropriate for that situation. We should also observe the general norms for behavior, such as what to wear, what time to arrive, and so forth, but in this book we are concerned mostly with norms for communication. Perhaps our guest in the earlier example intentionally violated general and communication norms. But a more likely explanation is that this individual was deficient in the skill of situation assessment and simply did not know that his or her behavior was inappropriate. There may be times when you decide to violate norms for a particular purpose, but our goal is not to convince you never to violate norms. Our goal is to teach you the techniques of situation assessment so that your norm violations occur by choice rather than out of ignorance.

Where do these norms come from? Certainly they have developed over time as humans have come together to interact. Norms are culturally based; they differ from culture to culture. They even differ across regional groups within the United States, across ethnic groups, age groups, and so on. So the key to being skillful at situation assessment is to know the techniques rather than to try to memorize norms for different types of situations. Later in this chapter we'll examine the features of situations that will provide clues as to what communication norms are in operation.

Listener Assessment

Just as some communication behavior is more appropriate than other behavior for a particular situation, some communication behavior is more appropriate for a particular listener or group of listeners. We are using the term *listener* to refer to any other participant in the communication situation, whether it be a social conversation, group discussion, or public speech. We have learned over the years to modify our choice of words depending on to whom we are talking. So your language choices are different when you talk to your best friend than when you talk to your teacher. And they are different again when you talk to your parents.

You have also noticed that your topic choices vary, depending on who your listener is. How much you talk and whether or not you initiate the talk also depends on who your listener is. The term *listener assessment* means that we study and observe our listeners so that our communication behavior is appropriate for the listeners. Later in this chapter we will examine the particular aspects of the listener that we need to observe and analyze.

Notice the similarity between situation assessment and listener assessment. In each case we are trying to gain the fullest understanding possible so that we can *choose behaviors* that are appropriate for both the listener and the situation. Although much of our communication behavior seems to be almost automatic, keep in mind that we choose our behaviors. This is not to say that we are not influenced by the behavior of others but that we can and do make many choices in our communication. We can choose to talk about a particular topic; we can choose the language we'll use; we can frequently choose to whom we'll talk. There are many aspects of communication that provide opportunities for choice. By becoming skilled at situation and listener assessment, you can make your choices more effective ones.

THE IMPORTANCE OF SITUATION AND LISTENER ASSESSMENT

You might be wondering how this will help you improve as a communicator. First, as we have just said, you will be better able to select communication behaviors that are appropriate for the situation and the listener. A second value of situation and listener assessment is that it will enhance the possibility of your accomplishing communication goals. In this chapter we will emphasize that you will probably not be successful at achieving your goals if you do not take the listener into account. Your success depends on cooperation with another individual or group of individuals because all communication goals by definition require interaction with another person. Thus by developing assessment skills, you can increase the possibility of having successful interactions.

Another important benefit of situation and listener assessment is that it can help you feel more confident in communication situations. Perhaps one of the reasons that you sometimes lack confidence is that you are not sure of what to say or do. For many people who fear public speaking that is the case. They think the audience will be bored by their topic, and they don't know how to start their speeches. By observing and analyzing listeners and situations, you will gain greater confidence because you will feel more certain about what is appropriate behavior.

Finally, listener and situation assessment skills can help improve your attitude toward communication. Instead of having the unreasonable belief that "I never say the right thing at parties," you can have the reasonable belief that "I will know what to say if I carefully analyze the listener and the situation." You will gain a greater sense of control over yourself in communication situations, and this will help you develop rational beliefs about communication. It is when we feel out of control that we have a tendency to think irrationally.

HOW TO ASSESS A COMMUNICATION SITUATION

In this section we'll present you with information on how to assess a situation. We'll do this by discussing the features of situations that you need to observe and think about in order to understand the norms for communication that are in operation. Throughout this section we'll ask you to complete activities designed to increase your skill at situation assessment and to prepare you for your first communication goal.

Review of Your Personal Communication Goal

So that you continually keep your first communication goal in mind, go back to page 80 and find your final goal statement. Write that goal here:

My goal: _____

_____

Tentatively decide on where you might be to achieve that goal and write that here:

_____

Why did you select that particular place? _____

_____

Who would be there? _____

Why would they be there? _____

_____

These answers are for your own use to help you prepare for your first communication goal. It is not necessary to consult with your teacher at this point unless you have any questions. You may change some of these answers later, but by having a tentative idea of where the situation would take place and who would be there, you can begin to complete a situation assessment for your first personal communication goal.

Features of a Communication Situation

Situation assessment involves observing the features of situations that provide clues about the communication norms in effect. You probably already assess situations to some degree, but you may not have a systematic procedure for doing this. Our procedure involves thinking about and observing each of the situational features described in this section. Not every one will necessarily apply in each situation, but we need to think about each one of these. In Chapters 6 through

9 we'll discuss situation assessment for dyadic, group, and public speaking situations so that you can see how the technique applies to three major types of communication situations. In this section we'll explain general features that you can think about in any type of situation. There are four situational features that you need to consider.

The Nature or Purpose of the Situation   Communication situations differ in nature or purpose, that is, in why the people are gathered. There are different reasons why people gather together, and your first assessment task is to determine the nature or purpose of the situation. Two people may interact because one will interview the other for a job. Thus the nature or purpose of the situation is the employment interview. A large group of people may come together because one of them is going to preach. The nature of the situation, then, is the sermon. As you are already aware, there are many different possible purposes for communication situations.

In assessing the nature or purpose of the situation, you are not trying to determine each individual's reason for being in the situation, because the individual reasons are many and varied. Even though the nature of the situation, for instance, is the job interview, the applicant may be there simply because of some outside pressure to be there, not because of a sincere interest in the job. When you consider this feature of the situation, you are trying to assess the overall purpose of the gathering.

We need to be as precise as possible in specifying the nature of the situation because several situations could have the same overall purpose but be very different in nature. For instance, the overall purpose of a formal dinner party, a beer bash, and a Halloween party may be for people to have fun, but these are quite different from one another and have very different norms. So when you assess this feature of a situation, be as specific as possible.

Now, let's come back to the reason why we need to consider this situational feature, to begin understanding the communication norms that are in operation. Notice that just by knowing the nature of the situation, we already have some clues as to the communication norms because of our experience in similar situations. So, for example, if we consider the case of a beer bash, we can determine some of the norms. One norm is that people do not generally carry on long conversations with one person; instead, they tend to engage in many short conversations. Another norm is that people typically end conversations in this type of situation by excusing themselves to refill their drinks or get some refreshments. Can you list some other communication norms?

1. _____

2. _____

3. _____

You may want to discuss these with your classmates and teacher. You'll probably find that someone else has observed a norm that you didn't think of. You may discover that people disagree about the norms, too, but remember that there are other features of the situation to consider that also influence norms. Each one of you is probably remembering your own experience with a beer bash, and some of the norms you are listing may be due to other features of the situation.

Our ability to list norms for a particular type of situation depends on how much experience we have in that situation or how much vicarious exposure we have had to it through reading, watching movies or television, or listening to others talk. If we are totally unfamiliar with a type of situation, we may not be able to list any communication norms. For instance, if you have never experienced directly or vicariously an oral comprehensive examination, such as the kind a doctoral student takes, you probably could not list any communication norms. This should tell you that as you begin to acquire greater experience in varied situations, you will become better at assessing the norms that influence behavior in those situations. The best advice we can give you is to gain as much experience with new situations as possible.

So what should you do if you find yourself in a totally new situation? If you know the situation is coming up, you should try to get information from others about the situation and the communication norms. If you have no opportunity to prepare, try to hang back a bit and observe what others do. It is better not to say much than to say the wrong things at the wrong time and to the wrong people.

Now that you are acquainted with the first situational feature, the nature or purpose of the situation, go back to your first communication goal. List the nature of the situation, being as specific as possible:

Nature of the situation: _____

With that in mind, list the communication norms that typically operate in that type of situation. List as many as you can think of, using a separate sheet of paper if necessary. Again, these answers are for your own use as you prepare for your communication goal.

1. _____

2. _____

3. _____

4. _____

5. _____

6. _____

The Physical Setting A second situational feature that provides clues to the communication norms is the actual physical setting of the situation. People gather in all kinds of locations. They have parties in banquet halls, restaurants, their homes, dorms, parks, and so forth. They have group meetings in all kinds of places too. Thus when we assess a communication situation, the second feature we should consider is where the situation is occurring and how the physical setting influences communication behavior. Let's look at a few examples. If you are at a party where the music is very loud, how is communication influenced? As you know, people tend not to talk much. When they do, they have to shout, and so they tend to talk only if necessary, and they certainly do not talk about serious subjects. They tend to ask one another questions that require very brief responses or nonverbal responses, such as a nod or a smile. This is an example in which communication behavior is heavily influenced by the physical setting.

Consider another example. You are working with a group of classmates on a project. You have decided to meet in one group member's apartment. The apartment doesn't have a room where you can all sit comfortably in a circle, like you usually do when your group meets. Instead, you are arranged so awkwardly that it is difficult for group members to talk to the whole group. You discover that members tend to talk only to members sitting next to them and that the entire meeting is chaotic. Notice again how the actual physical location has had a strong influence on communication behavior.

In the examples cited so far, the physical setting limited the communication behaviors that were possible. This is often the case. So when you assess the physical setting, you need to look for the aspects of the situation that may hinder communication. In addition, you need to try to identify the communication norms that operate in that type of physical setting. Let's look at aspects of the location that you should observe because of their potential to influence communication.

1. *Size of the room.* How large or small the location is can have an effect on communication. Consider the difference between a very large class in a huge lecture hall versus a small class in a seminar room. In which setting is it the norm to limit your participation to brief comments and questions? Usually in the large lecture hall. Part of the explanation for this is that the room is so large that it is difficult for the teacher to hear the students' comments and questions, and it is difficult for the students to hear one another's questions. Rather than to have to shout or repeat themselves, students tend not to speak out much.

If we took a very small class and put the students in a large room, you would also notice an impact on communication behavior. The students would probably spread out in the room, perhaps sitting toward the back. This sometimes happens at public speeches when the audience is small but the room in which the speech is held is very large. You may have been in situations like this. Chances are that if you were, you noticed that people did not talk much either to each other or to the teacher or speaker. In this type of setting, people tend to feel isolated, and so they are not drawn into discussion.

2. *Distractions.* A second aspect of the physical setting that we need to consider is distractions. These can take a number of forms, but they all have the potential to hinder communication. Noises can cause people's attention to wander or make it difficult for them to hear one another, as in the case of the party with the loud music. When the temperature is too hot or too cold, people tend to talk less or to talk about how uncomfortable they are. The same is true if the furniture is uncomfortable or if there is nowhere to sit. Again, the possibilities are endless. You need to take a look at potential and existing distractions when you examine the physical setting. Whenever possible, of course, you should try to remove distractions. We'll discuss specific examples in Chapters 6 through 9, when we examine dyadic, group, and public communication.

3. *Organization of the Setting.* People who own singles clubs and bars try to arrange the physical setting to maximize interaction. They are aware that improper organization of the setting can result in poor business. If people cannot meet others easily, they will go somewhere else. You might be surprised to hear that the way a place is organized can make it difficult for people to communicate unless you have experienced such a place. The third aspect of the physical setting that you need to consider is how it is organized. Is it organized in a way to enhance or hinder talk?

Remember the example of the classmates meeting in one group member's apartment? It was the inappropriate organization of the setting that made it impossible for the group members to communicate. If you have ever thrown a party in a place in which the rooms were so small that the guests had to split up into several rooms, you have experienced the effect of setting organization on communication. What happens in this party situation is that groups of guests who already know each other split off into separate rooms. If your goal was to get all of your groups of friends to know each other better, you would be disappointed. You could have had much more success had you given the party in one large room. Of course, you wouldn't want the room to be too large because then what would happen? People would still break off into clusters around the outskirts of the room.

Thus when you observe a physical setting to determine how it may hinder or influence communication, be sure to consider the three aspects of size, distractions, and organization. For your first communication goal, you have already determined the setting. If you feel you want to change the setting, do so now. Next, write down the possible ways that these three aspects of the setting may influence communication:

1.   Size of the room: _____

_____

2.   Potential distractions: _____

_____

3.   Organization of the setting: _____

_____

If you had trouble completing this activity, it is probably because you do not have enough information about the setting. There are many times when we do not know what the specific setting looks like until we get there. Advance preparation is always preferred, but it is not always possible. You may have to think about these aspects of the physical setting when you arrive. That is fine. It simply means that you will have to do some adjusting on the spot.

There are some physical locations that seem to impose norms for communication behavior rather than simply hinder or influence communication. For example, a church or synagogue seems to impose communication norms. In this type of physical setting, even if no formal service is taking place, people typically talk quietly and seriously, if at all. It would be rare to find people shouting or laughing loudly or mingling with other visitors. Libraries are similar. The norm is to talk quietly or not at all because you might disturb others who are trying to concentrate. When you assess the physical setting, consider whether the type of setting imposes norms for communication. For your first personal goal, think about the setting and whether or not it imposes any norms. If so, list them here:

1. _____

2. _____

3. _____

Presence of Others   A third aspect of a communication situation that we need to consider when conducting a situational assessment is whether or not there are other people present and whether or not they are directly involved in the interaction. What we are observing in this case is what might be called the presence of a nonimmediate audience. What we say and how we say it can be strongly influenced by others in the situation who are not directly involved in the interaction. Our communication is influenced by this in two ways.

First, when there are others present who may be able to hear the interaction, one or both participants in the conversation may "play to the audience." That is, what they say and how they say it may be more for the benefit of the other people present than for the interaction partner. You may have been in situations like this. Suppose you are at a party with a close friend of yours, and there are many other people who can probably hear your conversation if you talk slightly louder than necessary for your friend to hear. Have you ever found yourself trying to impress those others while talking with your friend? Perhaps you tell your friend of some accomplishment or adventure because you want those other people to think highly of you. Even if you have never done this, you undoubtedly have found yourself in the position of the friend. You probably have spoken with people, aware that they were talking more to the "audience" than to you. Keep in mind that this tendency to try to impress a nonimmediate audience is not a *norm* generated by this situational feature. But it is a way in which communication may be influenced when others are present.

Communication may be influenced in this way in other types of interaction, not just in a conversation between two people. A group of students discussing a topic in a classroom may alter their communication when they know the teacher is within earshot. Or a teacher who is aware that his or her colleagues are outside the classroom door may alter a lecture to try to impress the colleagues. This behavior can occur in any type of situation in which others who can hear are present.

A second way in which communication can be influenced by the presence of a nonimmediate audience is that the people interacting may refrain from saying what they would actually like to say because of their awareness that others can hear. In this case, instead of trying to impress the other people present, the individuals involved in the interaction are keeping information from those present. And in the process, they keep information from their interaction partner. Perhaps you have been in a situation in which someone very close to you tried to get you to talk about a highly personal or relationship matter when there were other people present who could possibly overhear. You may have found yourself upsetting your friend because of your reluctance to discuss the matter in front of other people. If you have been in this situation, your friend violated a communication norm. The norm is that private talk should be carried on in private. The presence of a nonimmediate audience sets up this norm because as long as others are present who can probably hear, you are not in a private situation. Think of the number of times you have been in a restaurant, where you get the feeling that you are in a private situation, but you have overheard other people's conversations.

Thus when assessing a potential communication situation, you need to consider whether or not there are other people present who can probably hear what is being said. You may discover yourself or someone else in the interaction trying to impress those others. And you should certainly observe the norm of private talk in private places. It is embarrassing to you, to your partner, and to others if highly personal topics are discussed when others can overhear.

Now return to the communication goal for which you are preparing. If you have already picked the setting for your goal, think about whether or not others are likely to be present. If so, consider how their presence may influence your communication and that of your listener:

Others likely to be present in the situation where I plan to carry out my first goal:

_____

Their presence may affect my communication and that of my listener(s) in the

following ways: _____

_____

_____

If you believe that the presence of others will affect the outcome of your goal attempt in any negative way, you should reconsider the setting that you selected. For example, if your goal is to discuss your relationship with an intimate other, the setting should be a private one. If you had originally chosen a public place in which others might be present, you probably should alter your plan at this point. If you decide to select a new location at this point, go back through the steps of situation analysis that you have completed thus far and redo them.

Time   A fourth situational feature that we need to take into account when communicating is time. We can look at time in two ways. First, we need to consider what time of the day it is and what day it is. Second, we should think about how much time is available and appropriate for the interaction.

In considering what time of day it is, you have to keep in mind that there are particular times of the day that are more conducive to successful interaction than other times. So, for instance, many people need time to wake up in the morning, and an attempt at a serious conversation with those people before 9:00 A.M. may be frustrating. Consider the plight of the poor teacher who tries to get a class involved in a discussion at 8:00 A.M. If you have ever taken an early class against your will, you have probably observed how reluctant people are to participate early in the morning.

Since not everyone finds it difficult to get involved in communication in the early hours of the day, you will want to try to determine who is willing to talk at that time and who is not. Generally, you cannot determine this with strangers, so our advice is to plan your communication goals for later in the day. With friends and family members, however, you generally know who is a morning person and who is not. We'll discuss this idea in more depth in the section of this chapter on assessing the listeners.

Just as early in the morning is not the best time to try to talk to people, neither is late at night or right before lunch or dinner. When people are hungry and tired, they are typically less cooperative than they are when their stomachs are not rumbling or they are not ready to go to sleep. So as you plan communication goals or try to assess why you were unsuccessful in a situation, consider the feature of time of day.

Time of the week is also part of this first consideration. Would you rather have a Friday afternoon class or a Wednesday class? Keep in mind that by the end of a week, many people are tired from working and are looking forward to a couple of days off. This is not true for everyone, since many people do not work a Monday-through-Friday week. Your listener assessment techniques will help you here. But the general assumption you can make is that Friday is a bad time to try to make an appointment with a teacher or to give a speech. If you have to give a speech in one of your classes, you might want to pick a speaking day other than Friday, if you have a choice. If, on the other hand, your communication goal is to carry on light conversation with a stranger, Friday may be a good choice.

The second consideration of time is how much time is available for the interaction. You need to make sure that there is enough time for what you want to do but that you don't exceed your time limit if one has been imposed. Let's look at an example. For serious topics, you generally need more time. If you have had a disagreement with a friend, it is not wise to try to talk about it when one of you has to rush off to a class. There is insufficient time to discuss the issue, and one or both of you will feel very frustrated by the encounter. Whenever possible, then, consider how much time you will need and plan your communication so that there will be sufficient time. Have you ever gone up to a teacher after class to try to talk about an assignment? Perhaps you were dissatisfied with the teacher's brief response. This is a situation in which you did not try to guarantee yourself sufficient time for the interaction. How can you do this? The best solution is to make an appointment, letting the teacher know how much time you think you'll need.

The other side of this coin is to make sure that you do not exceed any time limits that have been imposed. For most appointments you make there will be a time limit. If you have to present a speech or a report, there will be a time limit. In doing situational assessment, examine any limitations on time so that you can prepare accordingly.

Thus the situational feature of time imposes several norms. First, your attempts at communication should not occur early in the morning, immediately before lunch or dinner, or late at night, unless your listener assessment indicates otherwise. Second, your attempts at communication should take place early in the week if they concern business and later in the week if they concern pleasure. Again, this is a general rule of thumb that may be contradicted by your listener assessment. Finally, you should make sure that there is sufficient time for the interaction you have planned but that you do not exceed any time limits.

For the first communication goal that you are planning, examine the feature of time and answer the following questions:

1. Considering your goal, what are some of the best possible times for you to

attempt to carry out your goal? _____

_____

2. On what day or days of the week should you attempt your goal? _____

_____

3. How much time do you need to carry out your goal? _____

_____

4. How can you guarantee that there will be enough time available? _____

_____

5. Are there any limits on the time available? If so, how will you deal with

those limits? _____

_____

You have now completed a situational assessment. You have examined the four major features of a situation that influence communication. You have looked at the nature or purpose of the situation, the physical location, the presence of other people, and the feature of time. At this point, we need to make some general comments about situation assessment.

First, whenever possible, you should try to assess communication situations as you plan for them. Advance assessment gives you more time to make careful plans. But even though we advocate careful planning and prior assessment, you have to be prepared to alter your plan because situations can change unexpectedly. In addition, you may have made some incorrect assumptions about a situation. For instance, you may have assumed that there would be other people present. When you arrived, you found that you were wrong. Or you may show up for a half-hour appointment, only to be told by the other that the appointment will last only 15 minutes. So you must always be prepared to alter your plans.

Second, there will be times when you can do very little situation assessment before you enter the situation. In these cases you must do most of your observing, thinking, and planning on the spot. There is nothing wrong with this. As you become more adept at situation assessment, you will find it easier and easier to do on-the-spot assessments.

Finally, in addition to conducting a situation assessment, you will also be conducting a listener assessment. We will describe that procedure in the next section of this chapter. You will discover that there will be times when you have to weigh listener and situational features and make decisions in favor of one over the other. For example, you may not like to show affection in public, but if someone you are very close to is leaving for Europe for a year and you are saying good-bye at the airport, you will need to decide whether the other's need for affection from you outweighs the situational feature of the presence of a nonimmediate audience. We will discuss this concept when we have completed the section on listener assessment.

HOW TO ASSESS YOUR LISTENERS

In this section we will examine the aspects of listeners that we need to take into account as we plan and carry out our communication goals. This is very similar to situation assessment. What we are trying to do is to plan communication that is appropriate for the listeners so that we will increase our chances for success. In order to determine what is appropriate, we have got to think about several aspects of our listeners, just as we did in assessing situations. But in many respects we think listener assessment is even more important because we are convinced that we will not be successful at achieving our goals if our communication encounters with others do not result in satisfaction for them. The "do it because I said so" strategy may work when it comes from someone in authority, like a parent, boss, or teacher, but it does not typically work in other types of relationships.

In this section we will examine three major aspects of our listeners. Be sure to complete the activities because they will help you conduct the listener assessment for your first communication goal.

The Nature of Our Relationship with Listeners

The first aspect we need to consider is the type of relationship we have with the listener or listeners. We can begin by examining whether the relationship is unequal, such as a superior-subordinate relationship, or equal, such as a friendship. Let's examine what we mean by this distinction. There are many types of relationships that could be categorized as unequal in the sense that one person is in a position of authority over the other. Teacher-student, employer-employee, doctor-patient, and parent-child relationships are some examples. The authority one holds over the other is stronger in some cases than in others. So we don't want you to treat this distinction of equal versus unequal as black or white. There are degrees of the authority one person can have over another.

An equal relationship is one in which there is no apparent superior-subordinate relationship. Many of our friendships fall into this category, although there are times when someone who is in authority is also our friend. These are often the most difficult relationships because we have to find a way to deal with a two-sided relationship. We have to deal with the person as an authority and as a friend.

Why do you need to consider whether a relationship is equal or unequal? Because communication needs to be appropriate for the type of relationship. We cannot list all the possible ways in which communication is influenced by the nature of the relationship among the participants, but we can give you some general principles or norms.

First, when a relationship is unequal, the person in the subordinate position typically allows the other person to take the lead in communication. For example, as students, you do not walk into class and tell the teacher what you want to hear about that day. You give the lead to the teacher. If you are on a committee, you let the chairperson begin the meeting. You don't walk in with your own agenda. If you participate in a job interview, you allow the interviewer to begin the interview. If you are presenting a speech, the audience doesn't tell you when you can begin. You take the lead. This is a norm, that the person in the superior position takes the lead. If you violate this norm, you may find that your goal attempt will be unsuccessful.

In a more equal type of relationship, you and the listener probably take turns leading the interaction. You initiate the interaction sometimes, and your partner initiates sometimes. There is no norm that gives one person the lead.

Second, in a superior-subordinate type of relationship, the range of possible communication topics tends to be quite restricted. Topics are typically limited to the business that brings the individuals together. For example, with a teacher it is a norm to talk only about school and course-related topics. It is also appropriate to discuss other nonpersonal issues such as social and political topics. However, it is atypical to discuss personal concerns such as family problems or relationship problems. That is not to say that students and teachers never talk about personal topics. What we are saying is that unless the relationship has evolved into a kind of friendship or a counseling relationship, it is usually best to limit topics to nonpersonal ones when speaking with someone in an unequal relationship. Shortly, we will examine another way to categorize relationships, which will answer some of the questions you may have at this time. Keep in mind that at this point we are very roughly categorizing relationships as equal or unequal and discussing the general norms for communication for these two types of relationships.

Third, our language tends to be more formal and precise in an unequal relationship, whereas in an equal relationship it tends to be more colloquial. We tend to be more careful in choosing words when talking to superiors or subordinates than we are when talking to close friends and other peers. So it may be perfectly all right to greet your friend with "How the hell are you?" but this greeting would probably be frowned upon if you used it with a boss, a teacher, or even your parents.

As you can see from this discussion, there are some communication norms that differ for unequal and equal relationships. What we are suggesting is that you follow these norms in many of your communication encounters. But whether or not you follow these norms depends on other qualities of your relationship with the listener. Thus the second way in which you can categorize your relationships is how intimate or nonintimate they are, that is, how close they are. This gives you more information about how you should communicate with another.

Relationships can be placed on a continuum from very nonintimate to very intimate. Nonintimate relationships are ones in which you know little if any personal information about the other. There is no sense of closeness with the other, and you probably interact only when and if necessary. Your encounters with salespeople, many teachers, interviewers, employers, and various strangers can typically be categorized as nonintimate. Let us emphasize that it is possible to develop close relationships with people who are in authority over you or over whom you are in a position of authority. It is also possible, and indeed extremely common, to have very nonintimate relationships with peers. You probably have nonintimate relationships with most of your classmates and the people in your dorm or apartment building. Thus when you are assessing the nature of your relationship with a listener, you need to consider two dimensions as depicted by the following illustration:

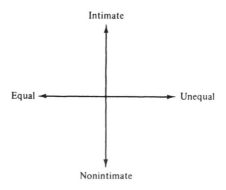

You should keep in mind that this illustration represents two continua, not discrete categories. However, we can use this illustration to examine four possible types of relationships.

First, a relationship with a listener or listeners may be high on intimacy and high on equality. An example is your very best friend. In this type of relationship, general norms are less likely to influence your communication than are the private norms or rules you have worked out.[2] Thus your concern should be more with how to make your communication appropriate for this person rather than with any norms of communication. So, if your friend and you have worked out a private rule that states that you cannot talk about religious beliefs, your concern should be with observing this rule if you want to maintain the relationship. These rules are often not stated explicitly but instead have evolved over the course of the relationship.

A second possible relationship is one that is high on intimacy and low on equality. An example might be a doctor-patient relationship or a therapist-client relationship. The relationship is unequal because one person is in a position of authority over the other because of his or her expertise and ability to help the other. The relationship may be very intimate because of the topics that must be discussed. In a relationship of this type, you need to be concerned with both the private rules that you have transacted for the relationship[3] and with following general norms for behavior. In particular, you should respect the unequal nature of the relationship and allow the superior to take the lead.

Third, you may be involved in a relationship that is low on intimacy and high on equality. Most of your relationships with peers probably fall into this category. In this type of relationship, you need to observe and follow the norms for interaction imposed by situational features. These relationships are ones in which you do not know the other, so your best bet is to begin by letting situational norms guide your behavior. For instance, if you meet a stranger at a school picnic, you should follow the norms for communication that you have determined are in operation through your situational analysis. This is because you have no information about the other on which you can base decisions about what is appropriate and inappropriate communication.

Finally, a relationship may be low on intimacy and low on equality, such as many employer-employee relationships or teacher-student relationships. In this type of relationship, your communication should be guided by both situational norms and the norms we have discussed for unequal relationships, such as allowing the superior to take the lead, formality in language, and restriction of topics.

Overall, a general rule of thumb is that the less intimate we are with the listener, the more we must rely on situational norms. The more intimate a relationship is, the more we need to observe private rules and norms. The more unequal a relationship is, the more we should observe the three general guidelines for communicating with a superior.

Now it is time for you to consider the nature of the relationship you have with the listener or listeners with whom you will attempt your first communication goal.

1.   List who your listener(s) will be: _____

2. Our relationship can be categorized as_____(high, moderate, low) on intimacy.

3. Our relationship can be categorized as_____(high, moderate, low) on equality.

4. Based on the nature of my relationship with my listener(s), there are things

that I *can do* when we communicate. These things include: _____

_____

_____

_____

5. Based on the nature of my relationship with my listener(s), there are things

that I *cannot do* when we communicate. These things include: _____

_____

_____

_____

If you have difficulty completing this activity, be sure to seek the help of your instructor because it means that you do not fully understand what we mean by the nature of your relationship with a listener and how that relationship influences your communication.

The Goals of the Listener

The second principal aspect of the listener that you must consider in order to be an effective communicator is his or her goals for the situation. In Chapter 4 we explained the purpose of realistic goal setting and how to prepare yourself to achieve your communication goals. It is important that you realize that your listener or listeners will also have personal communication goals. Your goal in presenting a speech may be to persuade your listeners to join your cause, but your listeners may simply want to be entertained. Your goals are not necessarily incompatible in this situation, unless you feel that you are not interested in keeping the listeners entertained. In any case, the purpose of assessing the listeners' goals for the situation is so that we can adapt our communication to help all parties involved attain their goals, at least partially. This, of course, cannot always be done, but it is what we should be striving to achieve.

How can you determine what another's goals might be? We would argue that you cannot *know*, unless you ask and the listener gives you an honest response. But that is not typically the approach to use. Imagine if a classmate began a conversation with you after class one day and then asked you, "So what are your goals for talking to me?" You might think the person fairly strange, or at least a bit pushy. There are times when such a direct approach is appreciated, however. There are times, for instance, when a teacher might ask a group of students what they hope to receive from a course. The problem is that people don't always know or can't verbalize what it is that they want. So a direct approach is not necessarily the answer.

Instead of trying to *know* others' goals, you will simply make *inferences* about those goals. Inferences are guesses that you make on the basis of the information that you have about a listener. When you make an inference, you are not just pulling possibilities out of the air; you are attempting to make an informed guess. Your inferences may be incorrect, and you may get into trouble if you act as if your inferences were the truth. When you make an inference about listeners' goals, you must always be prepared to alter it if you receive more information about the listeners that suggests that your initial inference was wrong.

In order to make inferences about another's goals, we can rely on two major elements of the communication process: the situation itself and all the information we have and can gain about the listener as a person. Let's look at how the situation can help us make inferences about listeners' goals.

Earlier we talked about the notion of situational norms, or expectations for behavior, that we can determine by observing many other features of the situation. All of that information about the situation is useful in this process of making inferences about listeners' goals because it suggests reasons why people are in the situation. For example, why do people attend parties and other social activities? Generally, people want to enjoy themselves, pass time pleasantly, and socialize. They want to talk to people and meet new people. By examining the nature or purpose of a situation, we can gather information about general reasons why people are there. Probably everyone at a party, for instance, has the goals of wanting to enjoy themselves, socialize, and so forth. *They may have other goals too,* but they certainly have these goals.

If you are a speaker at a publicized lecture, why are the listeners there? They are probably there because of an interest in the advertised topic or an interest in you as a speaker. Again, they may have other reasons for being there, but these are the two most likely reasons.

Information about a situation, then, helps you to make inferences about goals that probably everyone in the situation has. It does not tell you what goals individual A has, but it suggests possible goals that individual A *may have.* There are many times when that is the closest we can come to determining the listeners' goals for a situation. When that is the best we can do, we begin the interaction, trying to derive more information about the listeners as individuals and modifying our assumptions about goals as necessary. For example, suppose a classmate approaches you after class and begins a conversation. What does the situation tell you about that person's possible goals? Typically, students in the same course talk to one another because it is a nice safe environment in which to meet someone with whom they have something very obvious in common. They also talk to one another because they want to discuss their common experience of the course. Perhaps they are worried about an upcoming exam and want to see how others in the class feel about it.

By looking at the general reasons why students in a class begin conversations with one another, you can make the inference that those reasons apply to this person who has initiated a conversation with you. Suppose, however, that in the course of the conversation, the other person talks about how he or she is going to be missing many classes and is worried about keeping up with the course and getting notes. You now have some information that suggests one of the other's goals for the conversation: He or she may be interested in finding someone from whom notes can be obtained. Notice, however, that this inference may be incorrect. The person may legitimately be worried and simply want to express these feelings. But your best guess is that the person would like to make a contact in class from whom to borrow notes.

Now we come to the second major source of information about listeners' goals, and that is the listeners themselves. Knowledge of the situation provides general reasons why people are there. But in order to make guesses about particular listeners, we need to examine the information that we have about them. Much of this information comes from what another says and does during the interaction, which is why we must be prepared to change our inferences as we receive new information. We also make inferences on the basis of how a person looks and what the person wears, but this kind of information may be deceiving. The person's behavior and talk provide better information about goals.

Thus in assessing listeners' goals, you need to examine the situation for clues and then rely on any information you can gain about them. The more listeners there are, the more difficult it is to make inferences about individual goals. We'll discuss this more fully in the chapters on group discussion and public speaking.

For your first planned communication goal, think about the possible goals of your listener or listeners. You have already considered the situation and the nature of your relationship with the other(s), so you have some information to help you make good guesses. Remember, you may modify your guesses before you enter the communication situation and again as you begin the interaction. But at this point you are ready to make some initial inferences:

Some possible goals of my listener(s) for my first communication goal:

1. _____

2. _____

3. _____

4. _____

Before we move on to the final aspect of listeners that you need to assess, we want to reemphasize the importance of adapting your communication to help both you and your listeners achieve specific goals. Let's return to the example of the classmate initiating a conversation with you after class. Suppose you are correct in assuming that the person would like to be able to borrow your notes during the semester. And suppose your goal for the situation is also to have a contact from whom you can borrow notes. Perhaps you didn't even have this goal until you realized that it was the goal of the other. Notice the compatibility of your goals and those of your partner. This is a very simple situation in that you can agree to lend your notes and can request that the other do the same. If you both agree, you have successfully achieved your goals. If, however, you ignored the other's goals and said, "No I don't think you'd want my notes because I take them in shorthand and you won't be able to read them. But I sure would like to borrow your notes when I miss class," you are less likely to be successful. The other's goal has not been satisfied, and so he or she may say, "I prefer to find someone I can trade notes with."

There are times when our goals will not be so compatible with those of our listener. In such situations an attempt to adapt so that both partners' goals are at least partially fulfilled increases the chances of success. Suppose your goal for talking with a classmate is to meet someone new and initiate a new friendship, and his or her goal is to borrow notes. When this person approaches you after class, you figure this is a good opportunity to try to initiate further contact so that you can get to know the other better. In the course of the conversation you discover that his or her goal is to borrow your notes. Even though you and the other have different goals, the possibility exists that you may both be satisfied. You may agree to meet somewhere so that the other can copy your notes. That will provide you with the opportunity to get to know the other individual so that you can decide if this is a person with whom you want to spend more time. And it will satisfy the other's goal of getting notes. As he or she gets to know you better, he or she may decide that a friendship with you would be nice.

Notice that you could lose the opportunity to get to know this person better, and thus fail at your goal, if you said, "No, I don't like to lend my notes. But why don't we have lunch together this week?" The other could say that he or she was busy. By not making any attempt to satisfy the other individual's goals, you are not likely to have your goal fulfilled. We are not advocating that you always give people what they want so that your goals will be met—absolutely not. If you do not like to lend your notes, you should refuse the other's request. What we are saying, however, is that both or all people in a communication situation are looking to achieve their goals. They are not likely to help you achieve your goals if theirs are not satisfied to some extent or if there is little possibility that you will help them achieve their goals in future encounters.

The Needs, Interests, and Values of the Listeners

The final aspect of listeners that we should examine includes the needs, interests, and values of those listeners. We need to adapt our communication so that it is appropriate for our listeners' needs, interests, and values if we want to increase the likelihood that we will be successful.

When we talk about a listener's needs, we are talking about something different from his or her specific goals for the communication situation. A person has many needs, which he or she is always trying to fulfill. But some needs may be more important at a particular time than others. The goal is the particular outcome that an individual would like to see occur in a situation. The person's needs are the drives or appetites that he or she has, which may or may not be the same as his or her goals. A few examples may clarify this point.

A person may attend a lecture because he or she wants to find out more about a specific topic. That is the individual's goal for the communication situation. That individual comes to the lecture with a host of needs, such as to be comfortable, to be safe, and to affiliate with other humans. In this example the person's goal is not to fill a particular need, but the needs are present nevertheless. On the other hand, a person's need to affiliate with other people may motivate him or her to attend the lecture. In this case, the individual's goal for attending the lecture is to satisfy a need. Thus in any communication situation, a listener's sole reason for being there may be to satisfy a need. In that case the communication goal is need satisfaction. On the other hand, a person may enter a communication situation with a goal other than need satisfaction, but his or her needs will always be present to some degree. People still need food, even though their goal for attending a lecture is to learn. If the lecture lasts for four hours and they begin to get very hungry, their need for food may become activated and even more important than their goals.

Thus whenever you are in a communication situation, it is important to adapt your communication so that it takes the needs of the listener into account. Even though their primary reason for being there may not be to have a specific need satisfied, needs are ever present. If you ignore the needs of your listeners, you are likely to be less effective in achieving your communication goals, even if you attempt to help them achieve their goals. So, for instance, if people have come to your lecture with the goal of learning and you try to satisfy their goals by providing them with a great deal of information, you may fail to achieve the result you wanted because you ignore their needs. You give them so much information that they grow tired, hungry, and uncomfortable. They don't learn much because their attention is distracted, and you don't accomplish your goal of teaching because you have not satisfied their needs.

What are the needs of your listeners? We cannot give you a definite answer to that question. Various scholars have differing views about the needs that motivate people. Maslow, for example, felt that people have five basic needs: physiological, security, affiliation, esteem, and self-actualization.[4] You are probably familiar with Maslow's hierarchy of needs. Schutz claimed that people have three basic needs: inclusion, control, and affection.[5] People undoubtedly have all of these needs plus others. One way to help you determine the needs of listeners is to think of your own needs. Think of as many of your needs as you can. Your listeners will probably experience those needs too.

To make inferences about the specific needs a listener may have in a particular situation, you need to think about all of the information you have about the situation and the listener, just as you did in trying to make inferences about the other's goals. The process is the same for making guesses about needs. A general rule of thumb, however, is to adapt your communication so that you do not violate people's needs for safety, comfort, and self-esteem.

In addition to considering listeners' needs, we need to think about what interests our listeners. You can be sure that if you bore your listeners, you are not likely to achieve your communication goals. One of the best ways to keep the attention of listeners is to attempt to talk about topics that are of interest to the listeners as well as to yourself. You have probably been involved in conversations, for instance, where the topic was of little interest to you. You probably found your mind wandering and ended the conversation at the first possible opportunity.

The process of trying to assess a listener's interests is the same as trying to assess goals and needs. First, the situation itself may give you clues to the interests of the listeners. If their participation in the situation is voluntary, you can make some good guesses about their interests. For example, if people attend a speech voluntarily, you can be fairly sure that they have at least some interest in the topic. If a person attends a social event, you are safe in assuming that he or she has some interest in that event. Thus you can begin a conversation by talking about the event itself.

Second, you can find out about a person's interests by talking with them. Obviously, the more topics you explore, the more you can find out about someone's interests. If you bring up tennis, for example, and they say they don't play and don't ask you any questions about it, you can probably infer that they are not interested in the topic. The key is to observe their verbal and nonverbal responses as topics are brought up. If they seem to want to pursue a topic, by continuing to make comments and ask questions about it and by maintaining eye contact with you, it is safe to assume that they have some interest.

Finally, in conducting a listener assessment, you should think about the listener's values, which you discover in the same way that you discover goals, needs, and interests. A value is an evaluative orientation toward an issue or object: When you value something, it is important to you. When you hold a particular value toward an issue, you are positive toward it or negative toward it. Thus the value of freedom may be important to you and you feel that freedom is good. You may feel positively toward education and democracy. You may feel that euthanasia is immoral; that is one of your values.

It is important to consider our listener's values when we communicate. It is not so important that we and the others have the same values, although it may be easier to achieve our communication goals if we do. What is important is that we understand the others' values so that we can adapt our communication to the others. For example, if you are talking about euthanasia with someone who feels that it is perfectly acceptable, you may be more successful in achieving your goal of persuading him or her that it can be immoral if you first understand his or her orientation toward the issue. If you understand the other's orientation, you are in a better position to show that your orientation is more beneficial. We will consider this idea more fully in Chapter 8 when we look at public speaking.

Keep in mind that we are not telling you to be indecisive about your values or to change your values so that they are compatible with those of the listener.

We are saying that you need to take the listener's values into account when you communicate. By understanding the values of the other, you can make choices about what to say and how to say it that are likely to enhance the possibility of both of you achieving your communication goals.

The final step, then, in completing the listener assessment you have been doing for your first communication goal is to consider the listener's needs, interests, and values. Try to answer each of the following questions, keeping in mind that you will probably change some of these inferences as you begin interacting with the listener.

1.   Listener needs that are likely to be important in the situation: _____

_____

_____

2.   Probable listener interests: _____

_____

_____

3.   Listener values that are relevant for the situation: _____

_____

_____

The final topic we need to discuss is how to mesh the observations you make when you conduct a situation analysis and those you make in doing a listener assessment. The best advice we can give you is to view what you learn from situation assessment as providing you with information about what is generally appropriate. That is, it tells you about typical goals, needs, interests, and values of people there. It also tells you what the general rules or norms are for communicating in that situation. You need to begin your interactions with this information guiding your communication choices. The information you gain from listener assessment tells you more precisely how to adapt to the particular person you are talking to. Therefore, the more you get to know about a person, the better able you are to adapt your communication so that it is appropriate for that person. You should try not to violate situational norms in the process, however, as you adapt to a particular listener.

At this point you have carefully planned a goal analysis for your first personal communication goal. You have also assessed the situation and the listener(s). Go back to the goal analysis that you completed in Chapter 4 and make any changes that are necessary to improve your goal analysis based on your new understanding of the listener(s) and the situation. When you have completed that goal analysis, you probably should see your teacher, who will let you know when you are ready to go out and try to achieve that communication goal.

SUMMARY

In this chapter we have examined the processes of situation and listener assessment. Listener and situation assessment is a communication skill that is necessary in all types of communication encounters, from social conversations to public speeches. By analyzing the situation and the listeners, we can adapt our communication so that it is appropriate for the particular time and place in which communication occurs and appropriate for the specific listeners.

To conduct a situation assessment, we need to think carefully about and observe the following features of the situation: the nature or purpose of the situation, the physical location, the presence of others, and time. By analyzing these situational features, we are more likely to be successful in that situation because our speech will be appropriate for the situation.

To conduct a listener assessment, we need to consider carefully the nature of our relationship with the listener(s), the goals of the listener(s), and the needs, interests, and values of the listener(s). If our communication takes these aspects of the listener(s) into account, we stand a greater chance of achieving our personal communication goals.

three

UNDERSTANDING COMMUNICATION CONTEXTS

chapter 6

Communication in Social Relationships

CHAPTER OBJECTIVES

1. To understand needs that relationships fulfill.
2. To understand the role of perception in dyadic communication.
3. To understand various types of relationships and how relationship type affects communication.
4. To improve our attitudes in social relationships.
5. To reduce apprehension about social interaction.
6. To develop skills necessary for effective communication in social relationships.

INTRODUCTION

In Chapter 1 we examined three types of communication situations: dyadic, small group, and public speaking. In Part Three of this book we will take a look at these three types of situations in more detail. This chapter will focus on improving communication in dyadic (one-to-one) situations, with an emphasis on developing social relationships. The material in this chapter builds upon what you have learned so far, so it is important for you to review the material in earlier chapters if you need to. In Chapter 2 you assessed yourself as a communicator and discovered your strengths and weaknesses. In Chapter 3 you learned techniques to improve your attitudes toward yourself, toward others, and toward communication. You also learned ways to reduce the apprehension you may feel about communicating. Chapter 4 taught you the process of goal setting, and you learned how to conduct listener and situation assessments in Chapter 5. You now have the *general* techniques you need to improve as a communicator because the techniques you have learned thus far are necessary in any type of communication situation. In this third part, we will teach you the *specific* concepts and skills that you need for dyadic, small group, and public communication. And we will show you how to apply the general skills and techniques you have already learned.

You may have discovered in Chapter 2 that you have trouble communicating one to one in social situations. Go back to Chapter 2 to identify the specific weaknesses you have in the three areas of attitude, apprehension, and skill. Keep these areas of improvement in mind as you read this chapter and complete the activities.

In this chapter we will examine communication in one-to-one situations. We will consider why we need relationships and how to improve our attitudes, reduce our apprehension level, and improve our skills in one-to-one communication situations.

FUNCTIONS OF OUR RELATIONSHIPS

We all have a variety of types of relationships. We are involved in family relationships, friendships, romantic relationships, work relationships, and more. Weiss claims that different types of relationships satisfy different needs or fulfill different functions.[1] A friendship, for example, does not fulfill the same functions as a marriage relationship. On the basis of his research, Weiss derived five categories of functions that relationships can provide, and, in fact, he claims that we seem to need to have all of these fulfilled to experience well-being.[2] As we discuss these five types of relationship functions, think about the relationships you have now that fulfill each of the functions.

1. *Intimacy.* We need relationships in which we can express our thoughts and feelings freely. Relationships that provide intimacy involve a sense of trust and understanding, and the partners make themselves available to each other.
2. *Social integration.* Relationships that provide social integration are those in which people share ideas, experiences, and small favors. In these relationships the partners share similar concerns. A relationship with a classmate or someone with whom you work may fulfill this function.
3. *Opportunity to provide care.* In some relationships we have the opportunity to take care of another person, such as when a parent takes care of a child. This type of relationship often provides us with a sense of purpose and fulfillment because we are helping another individual.
4. *Reassurance of worth.* Some of our relationships make us feel that we are worthwhile and competent, that we are skillful at something. This is often true of relationships with coworkers and classmates, although our friends and families may fulfill this function.
5. *Assistance.* We need relationships in which the other can provide us with help, sometimes help over a long period of time. For most of us, it is usually family relationships that provide this function, although friends

and neighbors are sometimes willing to give us assistance over an extended period of time.

Other scholars offer additional reasons why we form relationships. Gerald Phillips and H. Lloyd Goodall, Jr., have written an enlightening book based on interviews and questionnaires that dealt with relating to people.[3] In the book the respondents tell their feelings about why people need relationships. They say everyone needs:

Someone to confirm his or her importance

To believe there is someone on whom they can depend for help and support

To have someone with whom they can spend special times

Someone with whom they can plan, scheme, and complain

Someone just to be with[4]

As you can see, there are many functions that are fulfilled by relationships. And different relationships fulfill different functions. So it is not necessarily important to have a large number of relationships. It is more important to have relationships that fulfill our needs.

TYPES OF RELATIONSHIPS

We have examined functions of relationships, and as we have noted, relationships are not all alike. They can differ in the functions they fulfill. Another way that relationships differ is in type. In Chapter 5 we talked about how the type of relationship you have with another can affect what you say and how you say it. This is part of listener analysis, and in this section we will examine this idea in more depth. Keep in mind the main point we are making: Understanding the different types of relationships we have will help us choose the most appropriate communication behaviors to enhance those relationships.

There are many ways to classify relationships, but we will look at two types of relationships, personal (interpersonal) and impersonal (noninterpersonal).[5] For example, the relationship you have with the checkout person at the grocery store is an example of an impersonal relationship. The relationship you have with your sister, your friend, or your sweetheart could illustrate the personal relationship. As Miller suggests, it may be more appropriate to think of these two types as ends of a continuum rather than as two distinct types.[6]

Four major differences distinguish the personal and impersonal relationship. First, in impersonal or noninterpersonal relationships we tend to relate to people according to their social role, as "the checkout person," "my physician," "my professor."[7] We do not adapt our communication to them as individuals but interact with them as we would with anyone in that role. In interpersonal relationships, we relate to the other as a person, as an individual with unique qualities.

Second, in impersonal relationships we make predictions about what the other is likely to do based on what we think other people in that group are likely to do.[8] For example, we might predict that a teacher will reprimand a student who fails to complete an assignment because that is what we would predict teachers in general to do. In our interpersonal relationships we are more likely to predict the other's behavior on the basis of what we know about the other as an individual. You know, for instance, that Chris enjoys horror movies. You might predict that if you ask Chris to see a horror film, your invitation will be accepted.

Third, we can distinguish between interpersonal and noninterpersonal relationships by the use of or deviation from norms.[9] In noninterpersonal relationships, we tend to rely on social norms or rules to guide our behavior. For example, in talking with a stranger at a party we would probably stick to light, fun topics rather than controversial topics. This is because there is a norm that typically operates in social settings such as this that regulates what topics are appropriate. In our personal relationships, on the other hand, we rely more on private rules that we develop with the other individual. We have already examined this idea in some detail in Chapter 5.

A final difference in the types of relationships we have is in the breadth and depth of the association.[10] The breadth of communication in a relationship refers to the amount and variety of information we share with another. The depth indicates how much we share with another and how intimate the information is. In impersonal relationships there is typically little breadth and little depth. That is, we do not talk about a wide variety of topics, and we do not talk about intimate information. In personal relationships we tend to talk about more topics and in more detail. There may, however, be someone that you call a friend with whom you discuss few topics but go into great detail about those topics. You probably do not feel as close to this individual as you do to someone with whom you are able to share many topics in depth.

This final difference between interpersonal and noninterpersonal relationships provides a means for trying to change a relationship to a more personal one. If we wish to lead an impersonal relationship to a more personal level, we should increase the breadth and depth of our communication with that person. We should be cautious in doing this, however, because the other person may not want to change the nature of the relationship. Through listener assessment, we should be able to get some idea of whether or not the other individual would like a closer relationship. Then all we can do is take a chance and observe the other's response. If the other person reciprocates, it may be an indication of a desire to move the relationship to a more personal level. It is important to realize that increasing breadth and depth needs to occur in small steps or stages. We cannot change a relationship overnight. Our attempts to talk about more topics in more depth should be made gradually. If we come on too strong all of a sudden, the other person may withdraw from the relationship.

IMPROVING ATTITUDES IN SOCIAL RELATIONSHIPS

In Chapter 3 we discussed how to improve our attitudes toward ourselves, toward others, and toward communication. We will now focus on improving attitudes toward communicating in relationships. Before we discuss ways to develop more positive attitudes, we'd like you to review the attitude assessment you completed in Chapter 2. Did you discover that you were self-accepting or that self-acceptance is something you need to work on? Since it has been found that self-accepting people tend to accept others, you probably need to strive for other-acceptance if you are not self-accepting. Did you discover that you hold some unreasonable beliefs about communication?

In this section we will discuss three ways to develop better attitudes about communicating in relationships. First, we'll briefly discuss self- and other-acceptance. Next, we'll look at the role of perception in communication. Finally, we'll discuss several misconceptions or unreasonable beliefs people often have about relationships.

Self- and Other-acceptance

To begin improving our attitudes toward communication in relationships, we need to convince ourselves to become more self-accepting and more accepting of others. Remember, self-acceptance is a choice, as is other-acceptance. You must make the conscious effort to choose not to evaluate yourself or others but instead to evaluate *behaviors*. You must continually tell yourself when you experience failures in relationships that you are not a failure as a person. Then you need to examine your behaviors to determine if there are any particular behaviors that contributed to the relational problems. It is those behaviors that you should judge and try to eliminate or change.

We have a tendency to blame the other person when a relationship has trouble or dissolves. By developing acceptance of others, we will find ourselves pointing to their behaviors, not their personal qualities, that contributed to the problems. We believe that it is very difficult to avoid placing blame when there are relationship problems. But we also believe that it is much more constructive to examine what both people *did* to contribute to any problems. By focusing on behaviors, we are more apt to learn from bad experiences because we will be able to point to specific actions that seemed to lead to failure. This does not mean that in a different relationship these same behaviors would necessarily cause problems, but we could monitor them more carefully in future relationships.

Thus the first way to develop a more positive attitude about relationships is to try to develop self- and other-acceptance. If you feel you need further review of this concept, return to Chapter 3, where we discussed it in greater detail.

Understanding the Process of Perception

A second way to improve your attitudes toward relating is to gain greater understanding of the process of perception and its role in relationships. When two people communicate, they perceive themselves, each other, and the situation differently. We need to learn to accept these differences. Understanding the process of perception and how we attribute meaning will help us to understand and accept differences.

Perception is defined by Emmert and Donaghy as "the process of organizing random stimuli received from the environment about us, transforming them, and attaching meaning to them."[11] In other words, when we perceive, we are actively trying to make sense out of the stimuli around us. Perception involves selection, organization, and interpretation.[12] By selection we mean that people choose to pay attention to certain aspects of a situation or certain behaviors. Because we are presented with so many objects, words, behaviors, and so on, we tend to select those that are intense (the loud voice), those that are repeated, and those associated with our needs, interests, and goals (for example, we notice food more readily if we are hungry).

We also tend to organize our perceptions so that they make sense. If you were at a party and saw someone make several phone calls and run outside, you would probably try to put those perceptions together into some sort of story. You would undoubtedly connect the phone calls with running outside because we tend to organize perceptions so that we can attach meaning to them.

Interpretation is the third part of perception. Our interpretations of what we perceived are influenced by our past experiences, our expectations, what we know about people, and so forth. If you have been at a party before where someone made several phone calls and left, and later you found out that the person was having car trouble, you might interpret the present situation in the same way.

How we select, organize, and interpret stimuli is influenced by our attitudes. That is why it is so important to have positive attitudes toward communication and toward ourselves and others. If you feel that people do not like you, you may be apt to perceive a compliment as a sarcastic comment. If you are inclined to think other people are selfish, you are likely to perceive their actions as selfish even when they are not.

We have no way of knowing if our perceptions are correct or incorrect. In addition, a variety of perceptions held by different people may all possess some degree of truth. But we can be sure that individuals will perceive the same instance differently. Let's try an experiment to show you how different two individuals' perceptions of the same situation can be.

With a partner, go to a crowded area and observe an individual for five minutes. Be sure the person is not aware that you are observing. You and your partner should each complete the following form, completing only items 1 through 10 at this point. Approach the individual, explain the experiment, and ask for his or her responses to the first ten items. Afterward, complete items 11 through 13. These last items are reserved for later comparison with your partner. Compare your perceptions with your partner. What differences were there in your perceptions? To what might you attribute those differences? Was there a difference between your attitude toward the observed individual and your partner's? If so, why might that be?

Person Perception Form

1. Age _____

2. Height _____

3. Weight _____

4. Marital status _____

5. Major _____

6. Favorite type of music _____

7. Religious affiliation _____

8. Favorite TV shows _____

9. Favorite pastimes _____

10. Political affiliation _____
11. Attractiveness (Rate from 1 to 10, with 1 = very unattractive and 10 =

very attractive) _____
12. Likability (Rate from 1 to 10, with 1 = not likable to 10 = very likable)

_____

13. Possibility of being a personal friend (Rate from 1 to 10 with 1 = no

possibility to 10 = extremely possible) _____

What is it that influences the way we perceive people and situations? First, there are psychological influences such as our attitude toward self and others, our apprehension level, the mood we are in at the time, our memory of past situations and people, our personalities, and stereotypes we hold. Second, there are physical influences on the process of perception. For example, if we are hungry and tired, our perceptions of the same person or the same event may be different than they would be if we were satisfied and rested. Our capacities to see, hear, taste, and smell can also affect our perceptions, as can our physical location in a situation.

Unfortunately, we often make some mistakes in the process of perception.[13] The following generalizations are usually true:

We are influenced by what is most obvious.

We cling to first impressions, even if wrong.

We tend to assume that others view things as we do.

We tend to favor negative impressions over positive ones.

We tend to blame people for their misfortunes.

A good way to check your perception of an event is to consider three things about the situation so that you can try to avoid the common mistakes in perception. First, think about what actually occurred. What did you see, hear, touch, smell, or taste? Try to be descriptive, not evaluative. Second, think about the meaning that you attached to the event. How are you interpreting what you saw, heard, or felt? Third, check the accuracy of your interpretation. Ask yourself if there is anything that you saw, heard, felt, smelled, or tasted that confirms your interpretation of the event. If there is no direct evidence for the meaning you have attached to the situation, accept the possibility that your interpretation could be incorrect.

We need to use perception checking in our social relationships. For example, instead of making assumptions about the behavior and feelings of others, check out your perceptions with them. Instead of saying, "You were late for our date. I know you don't want to see me anymore," say, "You were late for our date. I have a feeling that you are not eager to see me anymore. Is this true?" Notice that in the second case you are checking your perception with the other. You are acknowledging the possibility that your perception could be wrong.

In addition to using perception checking in our social relationships, we also need to check the attributions we make about why others do what they do. When we perceive another person's behavior, we typically try to understand the causes of that behavior.[14] For instance, we almost always wonder why a friend shouted at us angrily or why a teacher who is usually cheerful seemed so depressed one day.

In searching for the causes of behavior, we typically assign one of two causes: situational influences or personality influences. An example will clarify this distinction. Suppose a classmate fails an exam. You are likely to attribute this failure to a lack of intelligence, a flaw in the person. If *you* failed the exam, however, you are likely to say that it was because of a variety of situational influences—you weren't feeling well that day, you didn't have time to study, the exam was unfair, or the like. This is what you are likely to do when the behavior is ineffective in some way, such as failing an exam.

On the other hand, suppose a classmate wins a scholarship. This time you will probably attribute this to luck, knowing the right person, or other situational influences. If *you* won the scholarship, however, you would undoubtedly attribute it to your intelligence and hard work, aspects of you as a person.

Knowing the ways that we typically attribute causes to the behavior of ourselves and others allows us to check our tendencies to make those attributions. Just as our perceptions can be inaccurate, so can our attributions. Checking our attributions can help social relationships. If, for example, a close friend stops calling you as much and doesn't seem as warm and friendly, your natural inclination might be to think, "Pat is turning into a very unfriendly person." You attribute Pat's behavior to a personal flaw. By knowing that you are doing this, you can stop yourself. You can think, "I wonder if something is bothering Pat. Maybe he is in trouble." In other words, you can search for situational causes of Pat's behavior, which are often easier to accept and deal with. By attributing Pat's behavior to situational rather than personality causes, you are more likely to act in a supportive manner. This will help to maintain the relationship. Accusing Pat of becoming an unfriendly person will only lead to an argument and perhaps bring about the end of the relationship.

Thus we can improve our attitude toward communicating in relationships by understanding the processes of perception and attribution. By understanding how our perceptions can be inaccurate and how we attribute cause to the behavior of others and ourselves, we can increase our tolerance for others' behaviors and try harder to understand them. Knowing that we might be wrong may produce a more supportive and nonjudgmental attitude, which is likely to show through in our behavior toward others.

Misconceptions About Communication in Relationships

The third way that we can improve our attitude about relating is to try to change any unreasonable beliefs we might have about communicating in relationships. Mark Knapp describes five misconceptions people have about communicating that can have a negative impact on their relationships.[15] We believe that these misconceptions represent unreasonable beliefs. As you read these, think about whether or not they are misconceptions that you have accepted, and put an *X* next to those that you feel you have accepted. If there are any that you hold, you need to try to change them into reasonable beliefs by using the ABC model of reasonable thinking that we explained in Chapter 3. What this involves is identifying your unreasonable beliefs (as we are asking you to do here) and then disputing those beliefs to show why they are unreasonable.

_____ 1. *The belief that people are consistent.* We have a tendency to think that other people are consistent, and we want them to be consistent. You *may* have found yourself saying to another, "But you used to love me. Didn't you mean it?" We all find ourselves wanting others to be consistent because it helps us make predictions about them and helps us know how to act.[16] However, people change and situations change, so being inconsistent is very natural. It is important to be able to tolerate some inconsistency. Otherwise, it is very difficult to maintain satisfying relationships.

_____ 2. *The belief that meaning is simple.* We often believe that the words someone says have a simple meaning. As Knapp puts it, we think, "Well, you said it so you must have meant it!"[17] As we have already discussed in Chapter 1, communication is a process of assigning meaning to verbal and nonverbal symbols. In a communication situation there are many cues to which we can attach meaning, not just the words. And our own feelings, moods, experiences, and so forth affect the meaning we attach. So in order to communicate more effectively, we must recognize that meaning is not simple and that we often intend several meanings.

_____ 3. *The belief that communicators are independent.* We often have the habit of seeing our behavior as independent of another's behavior rather than seeing our behavior as connected. Thus we hear people say, "I don't know why she left. I didn't do anything wrong." When we see ourselves as independent from another, we fail to realize that relationship problems are created by both people. It is not all one person's fault if there are problems. If you do not accept this belief, you are more likely to ask what each of you did to contribute to the problem.

_____ 4. *The belief that causes are obvious.* As we have stated, people have a tendency to attribute causes to their own and others' behavior. And we are often guilty of assuming that our attributions are correct. As Knapp puts it, we may say to another, "You can't fool me. I know why you said that."[18] We do not always know why we do what we do, so causes are not as obvious as we sometimes think. And even when they may appear to be obvious, we could be wrong.

_____ 5. *The belief in finality.* A final misconception that we often accept is that issues and relationships can be finished completely. When a relationship "ends," it may actually never end in the partners' minds. And when we decide that something is settled, it probably is not completely settled. As Knapp points out, we often act as if something is finished so that we don't have to put as much time and energy into it.[19] But by trying to be finished with an issue, we are usually only burying it temporarily, and it is likely to resurface later.

REDUCING APPREHENSION IN SOCIAL RELATIONSHIPS

Now that you have begun work on improving your attitude in relating, you can also work on reducing any apprehension you might feel about interacting one to one. Before we discuss the specific techniques that you can use, return to Chapter 2 and examine your PRCA-24 score for dyadic situations. Note whether it is high, moderate, or low. If your score is high, you should try the relaxation procedure that we described in Chapter 3 and will review in this section. If your score is moderate or low, you may want to use the shortened version of the relaxation procedure as described in Chapter 3.

Regardless of your score, we all experience apprehension when interacting with others in at least some situations. If you rarely experience tension in one-to-one situations, you may not need to spend as much time on this section of the book, although you may find it helpful in reducing that occasional anxiety. For those of you who frequently or always seem to feel apprehensive in relating to others, keep in mind that your level of apprehension can be influenced by your attitudes and skill level. So in addition to reducing your tension with the help of the techniques offered in this section, you may experience a reduction in apprehension by working to improve your attitude and skills.

First, you can learn to reduce your apprehension by practicing the relaxation technique described in Chapter 3. Remember that apprehension is a *learned* response to a situation, and it can be unlearned. In the relaxation approach described in Chapter 3, you begin by learning to relax your body completely. Once you master that, you begin to imagine the items on a hierarchy until you are able to relax as you imagine them. By repeating this process until you can remain relaxed throughout the hierarchy, you can learn to experience relaxation instead of tension in one-to-one situations.

To use this technique, you must construct a hierarchy of items for relating to others. You can refer to the public speaking hierarchy on pages 64–65 to help you. Remember that to construct a hierarchy you start with items that are the least anxiety-provoking and move to those that are the most anxiety-provoking. Instead of thinking of one-to-one situations in general, you might need a hierarchy for talking to authority figures such as teachers, bosses, and advisers. Or you may need a hierarchy for meeting new people in social situations. Make as many hierarchies as you need. They all do not need to be done now. At this time you should construct one hierarchy for some type of one-to-one situation that presently causes you apprehension. Work on scrap paper until you have it complete; then write it here.

My Hierarchy for Relating

1. _____

2. _____

3. _____

4. _____

5. _____

6. _____

7. _____

8. _____

9. _____

10. _____

With the hierarchy completed, you need to go back to the muscle relaxation instructions on pages 63–64 and practice relaxing. Once you feel that you can relax completely, you are ready to begin using the hierarchy. Begin by trying to imagine yourself in the situation listed first in the hierarchy. Does it make you feel tense? If so, forget about it and go back to trying to relax. When you are feeling relaxed again, try once again to imagine yourself in the situation. If you can do so without feeling tense, you are ready to move to the next item on the hierarchy. Repeat this procedure until you can remain relaxed as you imagine each item on the hierarchy. When you can do this, you are ready to tackle another hierarchy if necessary.

In Chapter 3 we also described a shorter version of this relaxation procedure. You may want to try working with that shortened procedure if you are not very apprehensive about dyadic situations or if you do not have sufficient time to follow the complete procedure.

A second technique for reducing apprehension in one-to-one situations is to use the goal-setting method that we discussed in Chapter 4. This involves setting a small, fairly easy goal for yourself, such as "I will talk to a stranger at the party for at least three minutes" or "I will ask the salesperson for the price on an unmarked item." Once you have set the goal, prepare the entire goal analysis, specifying criteria for success and the steps you will need to carry out the goal. Then go out and try the goal, being sure afterward to evaluate your success by examining your *behavior* and comparing it to the behavioral criteria that you had written.

Practice the technique of goal setting for a one-to-one situation. Perhaps you can select your first goal by referring to the top item on your hierarchy. Write that goal here:

My goal for a one-to-one situation: _____

_____

Now decide on the specific time and place in which you'll carry out the goal.

Time: _____

Place: _____

List your criteria for success. If you need this reviewed, return to Chapter 4.

1. _____

2. _____

3. _____

4. _____

5. _____

List the steps that you will take to prepare for the goal.

1. _____

2. _____

3. _____

4. _____

5. _____

Finally, list the steps you will take to carry out the goal.

1. _____

2. _____

3. _____

4. _____

5. _____

After you complete the goal, go back to your criteria for success and determine how well you performed. If there are criteria that you did not meet, be sure to figure out what you might do differently the next time. Then you are ready to set a second goal.

This technique is effective in reducing apprehension for a number of reasons. First, it breaks situations into small, manageable goals. So, for instance, if you have trouble talking to strangers, this general situation can be tackled by breaking it into small goals. You can begin with a short conversation with a stranger after class and move to more difficult situations. With each successful situation, you will feel your apprehension lessen and your confidence build.

Second, the goal-setting technique helps us focus on behaviors, which are more easily managed than feelings. Instead of worrying about how you will feel in a situation, you will concentrate on how you will behave in a situation. You know that you can more easily make yourself behave in specific ways than you can make yourself feel a particular emotion. Concentrating on your behaviors will increase your confidence in your ability to do what you want to do.

Finally, the goal-setting technique can reduce tension by ensuring that we are carefully prepared for a communication situation. The technique forces us to do a listener and situation assessment and to plan the steps we will take to prepare for and carry out the goal. This thorough preparation will reduce some of the uncertainty of the situation and thus increase our confidence.

By using the relaxation technique and the goal-setting technique, you should find that over time your apprehension level will decrease. If you discover new forms of relating that cause you anxiety, you will have the tools you'll need to try to reduce that tension.

IMPROVING THE SKILLS OF RELATING

In this final section we will be concerned with the specific skills involved in communicating in relationships. The development of effective skills will not only aid in the maintenance of relationships but may also help to reduce apprehension and increase confidence. Before you read about and participate in activities to build your skills, return to Chapter 2, where you assessed your dyadic communication skills. Review that section of Chapter 2 so that you can focus on the particular areas in which you feel you need improvement. In this section we will discuss six skill areas that are important in developing and maintaining relationships.

Developing Interpersonal Trust

Johnson suggests that the development of trust is very important in our interpersonal relationships.[20] Trust in relationships begins with acceptance of self and others. This acceptance allows us to take risks with others, and the development of trust begins with the taking of risks. If that risk is confirmed, that is, if the other person shows us support and accepts the risk we have taken, interpersonal trust will develop. If, on the other hand, the risk we take is met by disconfirmation and rejection, the beginnings of interpersonal trust will be destroyed.[21] For example, suppose you have been talking with a classmate each day before and after class, and you decide to try to initiate some activity with that person outside of class. You try to move the relationship to a more personal level. When you suggest to the other that you get together for a movie or a bite to eat, if she or he responds in a cooperative, supportive way, you are on the road to developing trust. Even if that person says he or she works nights and can't get together, you will still feel a sense of trust if the person says so in a way that makes you feel good about having made the offer. If, however, that person ridicules you for the offer, trust may be destroyed, and you will probably find it difficult to continue even a casual relationship.

Expressing Ideas Effectively

A second interpersonal skill that Johnson says is important is the ability to express ideas effectively.[22] This means that we need to be able to say what we want to say clearly and accurately. This entire book is devoted to helping you improve your ability to communicate, so we don't need to spend much time discussing that idea here. But the point we want to stress is that the ability to communicate clearly is critical in building relationships because they are often so emotion-laden that there is potential for misunderstanding and conflict. By choosing words carefully to express what we want to say and adapting them to our listener, we can reduce the chance that conflict and misunderstanding will occur. The following suggestions may help you to express your ideas more effectively:

1. *Own your feelings.* [23] This means that you make it clear what messages reflect your thoughts, feelings, and actions. You take responsibility for your thoughts and feelings rather than blaming others for them. For example, instead of shouting, "You are really hard to get along with," you should say, "I find it difficult to get along with you. I feel like we argue too much." The second statement makes it clear that it is *you* who feels this way. The first statement sounds like an overall judgment of the other that is likely to provoke a defensive reaction.

2. *Use description.* [24] Describe events and behavior instead of evaluating them. When we evaluate, we often put the other person on the defensive. For example, telling another that he or she is inconsiderate implies a judgment that is likely to create defensiveness. It is better to describe the behavior that you think is inconsiderate. You might say, for instance, "You were late in meeting me today and last week." This is less likely to provoke a defensive reaction than saying, "You are always late. You just don't care about me." In the first case you are being descriptive whereas in the second case you are being evaluative.

3. *Ask if your message is being understood.* [25] It never hurts to ask another person to state what he or she thinks you have been saying. Think of the times you have given people directions and they misunderstood you. You would have found this out had you asked the person to repeat the directions back to you.

4. *Explain your idea in several ways.* [26] Teachers know that different ways of explaining the same idea will reach different types of students. That is why they often repeat and rephrase an idea, using several examples instead of just one. This will help you communicate more clearly too. Use examples, analogies, and multiple ways of explaining an idea. It is a mistake simply to keep repeating the same words when someone does not understand because both of you will only get frustrated.

5. *Be sure your wording is appropriate to the listener.* [27] In Chapter 5 we talked a great deal about adapting your message to your listener. That idea is important enough to repeat here. Use language that is appropriate for the nature of your relationship and your listener's knowledge, experience, interests, attitudes, and values.

To increase your understanding of accurate, clear expression of ideas, look at each of the following statements, and decide how they could be rewritten to make them clearer. Then rewrite the statements as you have changed them on the lines provided.

1. A young man asks his girlfriend, "Why can't you ever be anyplace on

time?" _____

_____

2. At the fraternity meeting, Chris said to Tom, "Tom, you're talking too

much." _____

_____

3.   "You shouldn't have bought me such an expensive gift," Jennifer said to

her best friend, Cathy. _____

_____

4.   "Do we have to eat so late?" a wife asks her husband. _____

_____

_____

5.   Your friend tells you, "You are really great." _____

_____

_____

Communicating Confirmation

A third important interpersonal skill is the ability to communicate confirmation
of the other. Our messages tell the other person how we perceive them and our
relationship with them.[28] Likewise, their messages tell us how they perceive us.
For example, the statement "I'll make the decision; you don't know enough about
the issue" communicates that the other person is seen as not informed enough
to make a decision and needs to have the decision made in his or her stead.
Obviously, this statement is not likely to please the other because it is belittling.

The most satisfying interpersonal message we can hope to receive is total
confirmation; the most damaging may be that of disconfirmation.[29] Confirming
messages are those that are supportive, that recognize the other person's ideas and
feelings as valid, and that make the other person feel good. Confirming does not
mean agreeing. It means supporting other people in a way that shows an understanding of their ideas and feelings.

When we receive disconfirming messages, we tend to feel as if we do not
exist, our behavior and feelings are unimportant, our identity is ignored or put
down. In the decision example the message is disconfirming because it communicates to the other that his or her input into the decision is not wanted and is
unimportant.

Test your understanding of confirming and disconfirming messages by reading the statements that follow. Put a _D_ next to those that you think are disconfirming and a _C_ next to those that are confirming. If you are uncertain about
any of them, discuss them with your teacher.

_____ 1.   A parent says to a child, "When you grow up you'll understand."

_____ 2.   A group member makes a suggestion, and no one in the group
              responds.

_____ 3. One friend says to another, "I don't agree with you, but I respect your position."

_____ 4. An employer says to an employee, "When I want your suggestion, I'll ask for it."

_____ 5. A counselor says to a client, "Don't put yourself down for your feelings. You are entitled to the feelings you have."

Self-disclosure

Unless another person can get to know us, our likes and dislikes, joys and sorrows, and unless we can get to know them, we will not develop a personal relationship. This "getting to know you" is accomplished through mutual self-disclosure. Self-disclosure means providing another with information about oneself that the other could not obtain otherwise. It does not necessarily mean revealing your deep, dark secrets, although if you did, that would be self-disclosure. It means telling another about your thoughts, feelings, experiences, and other details about yourself. The ability to self-disclose appropriately is a fourth interpersonal skill that you need to develop.

To build satisfying relationships, there must be some self-disclosure. You cannot get close to another person if neither of you ever reveals anything about yourselves. Luft has found the following to be characteristics of self-disclosure:[30]

It is a characteristic of an ongoing relationship.

It occurs reciprocally.

It is timed to fit what is happening.

It concerns what is going on within and between persons present.

It moves by small increments.

One way to think of these characteristics is to consider them guidelines for effective self-disclosure. This means that we should engage in self-disclosure in our ongoing relationships. Some people seem to fear self-disclosure and avoid it. It is difficult to have relationships with those people because the relationships can't get more intimate without mutual self-disclosure.

Second, we should observe our self-disclosure behavior and that of others to determine if it is indeed reciprocal. When you tell your friend something, does he or she respond by self-disclosing? Do you self-disclose when others disclose to you? If self-disclosure is not reciprocal, it may mean that it is poorly timed or inappropriate for the relationship. This leads to the third guideline for self-disclosure.

When we self-disclose, we need to make sure that it is appropriate for the time, place, and listener. We have all had experiences in which a stranger has approached us on a plane or bus and told us intimate details of his or her life. We all can recognize the inappropriateness of this. Self-disclosure with someone we know is not always appropriate either. Think about what you learned about situation and listener analysis. The timing of your disclosure is important, as is the place. If the content of the self-disclosure is very intimate, it should be reserved for a private place where there are no others present who could possibly overhear. And we would pick a time when our friend was free to talk, not when he or she was running off to a class. We can't give you a list of specific rules for what is appropriate and inappropriate. We can, however, advise you to assess the listener and the situation carefully to make your judgments about when and what to self-disclose.

Finally, self-disclosure should move by small increments. That is, we should take time to let another get to know us. There is no need to reveal everything about yourself the first time you and another begin to open up. This is likely to drive the other person away because it is too much too soon. We like to open up with another gradually as trust develops.

To develop your self-disclosure skills, we ask you to participate in the following activity. We do not want you to run out and self-disclose. Instead, we want you to keep a journal for one week. In that journal, each day at least once, you should record the following information each time you initiate a self-disclosure or someone initiates self-disclosure with you:

1. How would you describe the nature of your relationship with the other?
2. When and where did the self-disclosure take place?
3. Was self-disclosure reciprocal?
4. What was the content of the self-disclosure? How intimate was the information revealed?
5. Was the self-disclosure appropriate for the time, place, and nature of the relationship? If not, why not?
6. Is there anything you could have done to improve the quality of the self-disclosure?
7. How did you feel about this interaction with the other?

This journal is for your personal use, although your teacher may ask you to turn it in as an assignment. In either case, you should use it to monitor your self-disclosure skills.

Becoming an Effective Social Conversationalist

A fifth important interpersonal skill is the ability to initiate, maintain, and end social conversations and to use your voice effectively in conversation. Before we examine the specific activities this involves, try the following exercise. Choose someone whom you think is a good conversationalist. This person should be someone that you know or can readily observe. Plan a time to observe that person in some social situation such as at a party, in the dorm, or in the dining hall. Carefully watch what that person does. How does this person approach others? How does he or she initiate conversations? What kinds of topics does he or she bring up? What does he or she do verbally and nonverbally to maintain the interest of the other person? How does he or she end conversations?

As soon as possible, write down the answers to these questions to record your observations. Now make three lists. The first list should be the things that he or she did that you think were effective. The second list should contain the behaviors he or she did that you do not think were effective. The third list should contain the ineffective behaviors that you observed that you think you also do and the effective behaviors that you observed that you think you also do well. You now have a list of your strengths and weaknesses as a conversationalist to add to the checklist you completed in Chapter 2. As you read this section, try to focus on the ideas and activities that will help you improve your weaknesses. Perhaps set a goal and write a goal analysis for a social conversation, carry out the goal, and write a goal report to evaluate your success.

Let's look at some basics of effective social conversation. Dorothy Sarnoff, Broadway singing star and speech consultant, offers ten secrets of conversation in her book *Speech Can Change Your Life.* [31]

1. *Stimulate others.* Try to use the techniques for gaining and maintaining attention that we discuss in Chapter 8 on public speaking. Humor, stories, vivid language, and the like help you gain attention in a conversation, not just a public speech.
2. *Edit.* Avoid rambling, repeating, or overstating a point. Say what you want to say, but don't drag it out.
3. *Avoid "I" disease.* Ask the other what he or she thinks, does, and feels rather than talk just about yourself. We all like to talk about ourselves, but you will not keep another involved in a conversation if you do not give him or her a chance to talk.
4. *Don't interrupt.* You should wait until another is finished before you interject your thoughts or reactions. Try to make your responses relevant, and don't jump in to finish the other's sentences or stories.
5. *Avoid boring topics.* What is boring to one person is thrilling to another. If you are careful in your listener analysis, you will have a much better idea of what the other person considers boring. If you are not sure, bring up a topic and watch for the other's response. If he or she does not seem to add much to the topic or does not seem enthused with a topic, drop it and move on to something else.
6. *Don't offend.* Again, listener and situation assessment will help you determine what might be offensive to another person. When in doubt, be cautious in your choice of language and topics.
7. *Don't gossip.* There is nothing wrong with a little light gossip, but if you have to gossip about people in order to keep a conversation going, you need some brushing up on your conversation skills. There are plenty of other topics to talk about. By gossiping you run the risk of offending the other person, ruining your reputation, and ruining the reputations of the people about whom you are gossiping.
8. *Don't argue.* This doesn't mean not to express disagreement. However, in most situations conversation is meant to be enjoyable, and you'll put a damper on it if you use conversation to convert people to your social, religious, or political ideals. A good conviction can be explained without getting angry. So if you and another do get involved in a conversa-

tion in which you find yourself arguing ideals, do so for the enjoyment of it, leaving anger out of it.

   9. *Include others.* Try to make others feel a part of the conversation by using eye contact and observing and responding to their reactions.

  10. *Listen.* Don't pretend to listen—actually listen to what others say. If the topic doesn't suit you, you can always try to change it.

Let's move now to specific techniques for starting, maintaining, and ending conversations. Keep in mind, however, that the ten general guidelines for effective conversation we just discussed apply at all points in the conversation.

Initiating Conversations   There is no magic to beginning a conversation with someone. As you read the techniques we offer, you'll discover that they are fairly mundane in the sense that they are commonly used. Sometimes people, especially those who fear initiating conversations, think that they have to come up with a creative opener to get people to want to talk with them. Sometimes creative openers can be cute, but they are a risk that is not necessary to take. Most people most of the time use standard openers to initiate conversation. We recommend that you use these. They are predictable to people. If you say, "Nice day we're having today," the other person knows how to respond. They are not thrown off and left speechless. Moreover, standard openers are the norm for starting conversations. How else could you start a conversation? "Hello. What's your position on abortion?" The other will think you are doing a survey or you're a bit strange. Remember when we talked about the breadth and depth of communication? It is inappropriate to strive for depth as a way to open a conversation because trust has not been built and the other might question your motives.

So instead of trying to be creative in starting a conversation, try to use any of the following. The one or ones you select will depend on what you feel comfortable with and what is appropriate for the situation and the listener.

   1. *Introduce yourself.* People sometimes start conversations by saying, "Hi. I'm Jerry, your new neighbor," or some form of introduction. This technique works well in opening a conversation because it is a cue to the other person that you'd like to engage in conversation. One problem with it is that it does not create a topic to continue the conversation (unless you choose to discuss the topic of names).

   2. *Request assistance.* You have undoubtedly been approached by people who have asked you what time it was or when the bus was due to arrive. This is a second common way to start a conversation. After you ask for the assistance or the information, however, have a follow-up question or comment to keep the conversation going. Otherwise the person is likely to give you the information you request and say nothing else.

   3. *Ask a question about some situational feature.* This is probably one of the most useful ways to begin a conversation. You pick out some aspect of the situation to ask the other person about, such as, "Isn't this one of the best parties you've ever been to?" or "How old do you think this house is? It's incredible!" This technique is very effective because it can always be used. You always communicate in a situation, so by observing the situation, you can select some feature to discuss. Also, the feature is visible to the other person, so he or she can respond easily. Finally, by asking a question, you draw the other into the conversation because a question demands an answer. If you simply make a comment, the other person does not necessarily have to respond. But it is a norm that when you are asked a question, you respond to it, even if you do not feel like talking.

4. *Give a compliment and follow it up with a question.* [32] If you compliment someone, you will probably make them feel good about themselves, and they are more likely to want to engage in conversation. You might say, for example, "I love your necklace. Where did you get it?" When you use this opener, be sure that you are sincere. Do not say you like or admire something if you do not because your insincerity might show through. Also, don't overdo your compliment because you might make the other feel uncomfortable. One reason this technique is not always effective is that some people have trouble accepting compliments, and awkwardness may result when you try to open a conversation this way.

These four ways of initiating a conversation are not the only possible ways, but they are commonly used and generally effective. Take a minute to think of some other methods for starting a conversation, and list them here:

1. _____

2. _____

3. _____

Practice using various techniques for beginning conversations until you find ones that seem to work for you. Remember, though, that you need to assess the situation and the listener to help you make your decision about what is appropriate.

Maintaining Conversations   Sometimes students report that they do not have too much trouble starting a conversation but that they do not know how to keep it going. They wonder what topics to bring up or what to do when there is a lag in the conversation. There are several techniques you can use to keep conversations going.

1. *Use open-ended questions.* We suggest using open-ended questions instead of closed questions because they provide you with more information that can then be used to keep the conversation going. For example, you would want to use the open-ended question "What did you think of the basketball game?" instead of the closed question "Did you like the basketball game?" To the second question you are likely to get a yes or no answer, which then puts you in the position of having to ask another question. The yes or no answer doesn't do much to keep things going. On the other hand, the open-ended question forces the other person to say more than yes or no. The other's response provides you with more information that you can then follow up on.

Take a minute to rewrite the following closed questions so that they become open-ended:

1.   "Did you watch that special on TV last night? Wasn't it great?" _____

_____

2.   "Do you like being a computer science major?" _____

_____

3.   "Do you smoke?" _____

_____

Use caution in asking questions, however, because you do not want your conversation to become an interview. You need to make comments and ask questions to have an effective conversation.

2. Answer a question and follow up with a question. Sometimes conversations become like interviews because one partner fails to take the initiative in bringing up topics or asking the other partner questions. When that happens, the conversation sounds like this:

PAT: So where are you from?

CHRIS: Pittsburgh.

PAT: (after awkward pause) What's it like there? I've never been there.

CHRIS: It's OK. There are a few good things to do.

PAT: (after awkward pause) What do you like to do there?

Notice that Chris doesn't ask any questions of Pat. After Chris tells Pat that he is from Pittsburgh, he should ask Pat where she is from. This is what we mean by answering a question and following up with a question. This technique makes the conversation flow more smoothly and prevents it from being one-sided.

3. Get topic choices from the situation. A third technique that you can use to keep conversations going is to comment on and ask questions about situational features and activities. In any communication situation there are people, objects, and activities about which you can talk. If you are at a party, you can always bring up the topics of food (if there is any served), entertainment, who is there, what people are doing, and the actual setting of the party. If it is in honor of a special occasion, such as a birthday or Christmas, that presents additional topics. This is a very effective technique for maintaining conversations because it can always be used.

4. Follow through on what has already been said. The final technique for maintaining conversations is to follow through on topics that have been brought up. For example, if you meet someone who says he is a nurse, you can always follow through by asking questions about that. "How do you like the nursing profession?" "Where did you go to school?" and "What got you interested in the career of nursing?" are just some of the questions you can ask. So when you find out something about the other person, don't just drop it and search for a new topic. Try to make each topic go somewhere by following up on it. You will find that if you do this, you will not have a difficult time coming up with topics to keep things going.

Ending Conversations   Ending conversations is very similar to initiating them in that in both cases we tend to rely very heavily on standard lines. Again, this is because they are predictable and the other can respond to them easily. And norms have been developed for ending conversations. Typically, people end conversations politely so that both people feel good about having conversed. Also, they tend to give forewarning that they are going to end a conversation soon instead of cutting off abruptly. The forewarning can be either verbal or nonverbal, or both. For instance, you can look at your watch or ask what time it is. Then when you end the conversation, the other will know that you were about to do this. Or you can say, "I'm going to have to get going in a few minutes." Then you continue the conversation for a minute or so and you take your leave. The particular technique you use to forewarn the other that you want to end the conversation is not important. Use your situation and listener assessment to guide your decision, and try to use a technique that is appropriate for both.

Some of the common, polite techniques people use to end conversations are as follows:

1. *Explain that you have someplace else to go.* We often end conversations by saying that we have to catch a bus, attend a class, or go to an appointment. At parties and social situations, we tell people that we need to speak to someone else or haven't had a chance to mingle. This technique is polite because it justifies ending the conversation. Imagine if you were at a party and someone ended a conversation with you by saying, "I'm finished talking with you now," and walked away! You would probably find it strange because you are so used to people providing a reason for ending a conversation.

2. *Express your enjoyment of the conversation.* How many times have you said to someone, "It has been nice talking to you. I hope to see you again sometime soon"? This is another common method for ending a conversation. Instead of giving a reason for leaving, you simply let the other know that you have enjoyed talking. This method also makes the other person feel good about the conversation.

3. *Use a combination of the two methods.* Frequently people end conversations by providing a reason for leaving and expressing their enjoyment of the conversation. Can you think of any other common ways to end conversations? List them here:

1. _____

2. _____

3. _____

A final point we need to make about ending conversations is that you need to be aware of the difference between temporary and permanent closings. A temporary closing conveys the message that you want to see the other person again. For example, if you meet someone at a party that you would like to interact with again, you could say, "Since we're both tennis players, maybe we could play a game this weekend. How's Saturday for you?" The other person can accept your offer, refuse it altogether, or change the offer. But your closing remarks communicate a desire to see the other again.

A permanent closing says that you do not want to or will not be able to see the other again. For example, if you meet someone at a party and end a conversation by saying, "It's been nice talking to you. Bye," you will be sending the message that you will not be talking again. An exception to this is if the person you are talking to is someone that you see often or are very likely to see in the future. But if you are talking with a stranger for the first time, be sure that you decide whether you want to use a permanent or temporary closing, and use the appropriate type. If you say, "See you around" to someone that you are not likely to see, you will communicate a lack of interest in getting together again.

To practice your social conversation skills, try some of the following activities described by Philip Zimbardo, author of *Shyness: What It Is, What to Do About It:*[33]

1. Practice making telephone calls.

   Call information for a friend's telephone number.

   Call a movie theater to ask show times.

   Call a local department store for a price.

2. Try to talk to one new person a week.

   Go to places where you feel comfortable and strike up conversations.

   Go to places with friends and meet their friends.

3. Practice telling stories.

   Remember interesting stories you hear and practice telling them.

   Collect stories of interesting things that happen to you.

In addition to being able to initiate, maintain, and end conversations, being a good conversationalist involves using our voices and bodies expressively. Perhaps when you completed the self-assessment form on dyadic communication skills in Chapter 2, you checked using your voice effectively as an area in which you need improvement. You may feel that you would like to be a more interesting conversationalist. Most of the skills we have discussed so far in this chapter focus on improving the *content* of your communication, but we can become more interesting speakers by improving the *delivery* of our ideas as well. Chapter 9 discusses how to use your body and voice to communicate your ideas more effectively in a public speaking situation. Those techniques can be applied to the dyadic situation too. Thus if you are concerned not only about what you say when engaged in conversation but also about how you say it, you should find the information in Chapter 9 helpful.

The main point we would like to make here is that in a social conversation situation, we usually do not need to be as expressive in the use of our voice and gestures as we typically need to be in a public speaking situation. In public speaking, the speaker does most if not all of the talking, so he or she usually has to exert much more effort to maintain the listeners' attention. One way in which the speaker does this is to use both voice and body expressively and often dramatically.

In social conversation, both participants are involved in talking and listening, so it isn't necessary to try to be extremely expressive and dramatic. That doesn't mean that we don't need to try to use our voices expressively, but it means that we need to be careful that we adapt to the situation. We don't want to sound as if we are giving a speech to an audience of 100 when we are conversing with only one person.

One of the best ways to learn how to be appropriately expressive in social conversation is to observe others whom you consider to be skillful in this area. Try to model your behavior after theirs.

Listener and Situation Adaptation

The sixth interpersonal skill that we will discuss, and in many respects the most important skill, is listener and situation adaptation. In discussing the other five skills in this chapter, we referred continually to the concept of making communication choices that are appropriate for the situation and the other participant. In Chapter 5 we described a systematic approach to analyzing both the situation and the listener. We suggest that you review that chapter if you feel uncertain about what is involved in this skill.

In applying this skill to communicating in relationships, there are two main points we need to make. First, attention to the other person may be more important than attention to situational aspects. We are not saying to ignore the situation, but we are suggesting that in our relationships, we need to concentrate on adapting to the other. If, for example, you normally do not display affection to a close friend in public places, you may choose to give that friend a hug because you sense that he or she is in need. Thus you would be adapting more to the other individual than to the particular situation in which you meet. We feel that greater adaptation to the other is crucial in the development and maintenance of relationships.

Second, as our relationships become close, we rely less on social norms and more on private norms and rules to guide our communication behavior. We have already discussed this idea in Chapter 5, but we think it bears repeating. The implication of this idea is that in our personal relationships, we need to give priority to the private rules we have worked out with the other rather than to the social norms for a particular situation. Thus, although it is appropriate to discuss sports in a restaurant, if you and your partner have agreed not to discuss sports when you are out for dinner, you should observe the private rule rather than the social norm. Again, this is important to maintaining personal relationships.

Earlier we discussed the differences between personal and impersonal relationships. In impersonal relationships, we need to rely on social norms to guide our communication behavior because typically we have not worked out any private rules.

SUMMARY

In this chapter we have examined functions served by relationships. We need relationships that provide intimacy, social integration, opportunity to provide care, reassurance of worth, and assistance.

Our relationships can be broadly categorized as personal (or interpersonal) and impersonal (or noninterpersonal). In impersonal relationships we relate to people in their social roles, whereas in personal relationships we relate to the other as an individual. A second difference between the two types of relationships is that in impersonal relationships we make predictions about what the other is likely to do on the basis of what we think people in that group would do. In personal relationships we make predictions on the basis of what we know about the other as an individual. Third, our behavior in impersonal relationships is guided by social norms, but in personal relationships it is guided by private rules. Finally, the breadth and depth of our communication is greater in personal relationships.

We then considered ways to improve attitudes about communicating in relationships. It is important that we develop self-acceptance and other-acceptance and that we understand the process of perception if we are to improve our attitude. In addition, there are five misconceptions about communication in relationships that we need to avoid to have a more positive attitude. These misconceptions are the belief that people are consistent, the belief that meaning is simple, the belief that communicators are independent, the belief that causes are obvious, and the belief in finality.

In addition to attitude improvement, we discussed techniques for reducing apprehension about communicating in relationships. These techniques include systematic desensitization and goal setting.

Finally, we discussed six skills that are important in dyadic communication. These skills are developing interpersonal trust, expressing ideas effectively, communicating confirmation, self-disclosure, becoming an effective social conversationalist, and listener and situation adaptation.

chapter 7

Group Discussion

CHAPTER OBJECTIVES

1 To understand the components of the group discussion process.

2. To improve attitudes about communicating in small groups.

3. To reduce apprehension about small group communication.

4. To improve skills for effective participation in groups.

INTRODUCTION

In Chapter 6 we discussed communication skills that are important in interpersonal relationships. Although there are more people involved in group discussion, many of those same skills can be applied to the small group situation. In addition to these skills, we will focus in this chapter on specific skills that are needed for effective participation in the small group. We will also discuss how to improve our attitudes and reduce apprehension about communicating in groups.

Before you continue reading this chapter, look at the self-assessment you completed in Chapter 2. Specifically, examine your PRCA-24 group score and the checklist you completed assessing your skills for group discussion. D..s your PRCA-24 score indicate a low, moderate, or high amount of apprehension about speaking in groups? Is your overall skill development level satisfactory, and are there any specific areas in which you need improvement? You will want to keep these areas in mind as you read this chapter and work to improve as a communicator in groups.

We will begin by discussing the definition of a group, and then we will look at the three components of the group discussion process. Next we will examine ways to improve attitudes and reduce apprehension about speaking in groups, and we will conclude by detailing six skills that are necessary for effective participation in a small group.

WHAT IS A GROUP?

Before we examine the components of the group discussion process, we need to provide a definition of a group. Although at first glance it might seem simple to define *group,* it is actually a somewhat slippery concept. We know, for example, that a group involves more than one person, but how many people do we need to have a group? And if we could decide on that, the next question we would have to confront is, What do those people have to be doing in order for us to call them a group? If several people are standing in the hallway between classes and none of them are talking to each other, do those people constitute a group?

The definition of a group that we propose provides an answer to those two questions. This definition is a slight variation of Shaw's definition of a group.[1] A group is three or more persons "who are interacting with one another in such a manner that each person influences and is influenced by each other person."[2] We have changed Shaw's definition of a group from two or more persons to three or more persons because we have already defined the dyad as two persons interacting. Thus for our purposes a group must have three or more persons. Note that by accepting this definition, several people standing in a hallway not interacting with one another would not be a group. For an aggregate of people to constitute a group, they must be together for the purpose of interacting and influencing one another. They cannot just be in the same physical space.

In this chapter we will be concerned with the small task-oriented group. Groups are formed for a variety of purposes. There are therapeutic groups and social groups, but we will focus our discussion on groups that form to solve problems, make decisions, gather information, or complete some project.

How many people do we need for a group to be considered small? Just as defining *group* is troublesome, so is defining *small group.* Although different experts express varying opinions, we define a small group as one that consists of three to ten members. On the basis of our own work in groups and in teaching students about groups, we have noticed that groups with more than ten members have special problems that are usually not found in groups with fewer members. The number ten is an arbitrary cutoff point, however, so many of the concepts that we discuss in this chapter could certainly apply to larger groups.

Based on this definition of a small task-oriented group, how many such groups do you belong to or have you belonged to in the recent past? List those groups here:

1. _____

2. _____

3. _____

4. _____

5. _____

You may decide to use the groups to which you presently belong as the basis for some communication goals. We will discuss this further later in this chapter.

THE GROUP DISCUSSION PROCESS

We have already examined the notion that communication is a process in that it consists of a complex set of components that are interdependent. Each individual involved in communication is influenced by the other and influences the other, and thus what each person says and how it is said is influenced by the interaction. As a type of communication situation, group discussion is also a process. In this section we will examine the various parts of that process and how those parts are interdependent. By understanding the elements of the group discussion process, we can gain a greater appreciation for its complexity. And as a consequence, we can perhaps be more understanding when a group is fraught with problems and may even be better equipped to provide remedies for those problems.

Various scholars have provided models of group discussion. The model we are presenting draws upon other models, particularly those of Brilhart[3] and Tubbs.[4] In this model there are three major components of the group discussion process: (1) what the group has from the outset, (2) how the group functions with what it has, and (3) what the group produces by the completion of the process.

What the Group Has from the Outset

When a group is first formed, before the members even begin interacting, that group has potential assets and liabilities. That is, the group has characteristics that have the potential either to help the group or to hurt it. For example, when the group is formed, it may be given resources such as a budget, secretarial help, and a meeting place. These resources have the potential to have a positive influence or a negative influence on the group. If, for instance, the meeting place has many distractions, it may detract from the group's efforts. Thus this first component of the group process refers to all of the characteristics that the group and its members have initially. There are four primary characteristics that we will consider.

Members   First, and perhaps most important, from the outset a group has its members. Those members bring with them attitudes, values, skills, experiences, needs, interests, personality characteristics, knowledge, and so on, all of which have the potential to influence the group in a positive or negative way. Let's look at how some of these member characteristics can affect the group.

First, the attitude a member has about working in groups and in this group in particular can be either constructive or destructive. You have probably been involved in groups in which some members seemed to have a poor attitude about the group. In particular, they seemed to feel no sense of responsibility toward the group.[5] They did not contribute much; showed up late, if at all, for meetings; and did not do their share of the work. Our attitude toward the group, then, is translated into behavior that either helps the group or detracts from its success.

Another aspect of group members that is of particular interest to us is their apprehension level about communicating in groups. There may have been groups in which you experienced a great deal of apprehension about speaking, or perhaps you generally feel uneasy about participating in groups and obtained a high score on the PRCA-24 group subscale. The level of communication apprehension experienced by group members can have a detrimental effect on their behavior in groups. Some researchers have found that apprehensive group members participate less in groups and show less interest in the discussion.[6] Some have found that the apprehensive member is likely to be evaluated negatively by other group members and is less likely to emerge as group leader.[7]

A third aspect of group members that has the potential to influence the group is their attitude toward others.[8] Members who trust others and who are not defensive will probably have a positive influence on the group. Since group members have to work together to produce some outcome, members must rely on one another to do their share of the work and to contribute ideas and information to the group. This requires that members trust one another and that members do not get defensive about their ideas.

Fourth, how open-minded or closed-minded members are has the potential to influence the group.[9] You may have been in a group in which there was a member who would make comments such as "I've heard all I need to hear" or "There is only one way to do it." Comments like these reflect an attitude of closed-mindedness. Groups are likely to be more successful when members are open to new ideas and new information. After all, the major value of having a group rather than an individual work on a task is that with more people there are likely to be more ideas, information, and approaches to problems.

Members' skills is a fifth factor that can affect a group. If members are highly skilled in the areas needed for a particular task, the group has greater potential to be successful than a group in which the members are not skilled. Unfortunately, groups are not always formed on the basis of members' skills. You have probably been in groups in which none of the members knew how to type or use a computer when both of these skills were necessary for completion of the group task.

We could continue listing aspects of the group members that have the potential to influence the group process, but we have already mentioned some of the most critical. The point here is that everything about the members can affect the group process. Thus from the outset the members have the potential to affect the group in either a positive or negative way, depending on how the group functions. This idea will be explored in greater detail when we examine the second component of the group discussion process.

Purpose or Task of the Group   Groups are typically formed to achieve some purpose or to perform some task. Thus a second characteristic that a group has from the outset is its purpose or task. The nature of that purpose or task can have a tremendous effect on the group process. It provides a goal for the group and structures the group's activities, needs, and communication.

All of this assumes that group members are clear about the group's task or purpose, but this is not always the case. You may have even been a member of a group in which you were not sure what the group was supposed to be doing or why it existed. This is a fairly common problem in groups,[10] so common, in fact, that Phillips, Pedersen, and Wood argue that one of the first items on a group's agenda should be to determine what the nature of their task is.[11] We agree with this advice and will discuss it in more detail later in this chapter.

Group Size   The actual size of a group is a third characteristic that affects the group from the outset. The larger the group, the more difficult it is for the group to function as a single unit rather than as several smaller units.[12] This may be because it becomes increasingly difficult for all members to interact with one another. This may also explain why having an effective leader may be more important for a group as size increases.[13] The group needs an individual who can coordinate the efforts of all of the members and serve as a liaison for them. The amount of time each member participates tends to decrease as the size increases, and the distribution of member participation tends to become more uneven.[14] In a larger group, a few people may dominate at the expense of the rest of the members. As a consequence, members in larger groups tend to be less satisfied with the group and tend to experience more tension than members in smaller groups.[15] For someone who experiences apprehension about communicating in groups, this apprehension is likely to increase as the size of the group increases. Thus we can see how the size of a group has the potential to affect the group process either positively or negatively.

Environment of the Group   In this book we have emphasized how much the actual situation in which communication occurs can affect an interaction. The same is true for group discussion. The place in which a group meets can detract from its performance or can enhance it. In Chapter 5 we discussed the aspects of a situation that can have an effect on communication. Those same situational aspects apply here. The size of the room, distractions, and how the setting is organized all enhance or detract from a group's performance. If there are many distractions, it is difficult for a group to concentrate on its task. This often happens in classroom groups when five or six groups are trying to carry on meetings in the same room. Even if members can hear one another, which is not always the case, the presence of other groups can serve as a distraction. Members may feel greater competition when other groups are present or may simply be interested in what other groups are doing.

The size of the room can have an impact on the group process, as can any other features of the setting that interfere with the comfort of the group members. A room that is too small may become unbearably warm and may force members to have to sit very close together. A room that is too large, on the other hand, can also have a detrimental effect on the group. Members may spread out in the room, increasing the physical distance among them. This can result in members feeling uninvolved in the discussion and less close in their relationships with other members.

Finally, the organization of the setting may have a positive or negative effect on the group. Perhaps you have been involved in group meetings in which members were awkwardly arranged, with some members sitting back from the group. Usually those members are almost completely excluded from the interaction. The way in which group members arrange themselves, either by choice or because of the organization of the setting, can have a tremendous influence on group discussion. The seating pattern can affect the pattern of who talks to whom in the group and who emerges as group leader.[16] Seating patterns are often categorized as centralized or decentralized. A centralized seating arrangement is one in which one individual is in a position that allows him or her to control the flow of discussion. The traditional classroom is an example of a centralized seating arrangement. The teacher is in the central position and controls the discussion. Meetings of large groups are often run this way. Decentralized seating arrangements do not have a seat or position that allows an individual to direct the flow of communication. A circle is an example of a decentralized arrangement in that no one is in a position to direct communication. All members can talk to one another fairly easily. For the small task-oriented group in which you are likely to be working, a decentralized seating arrangement is probably the best because it typically results in higher satisfaction among members.[17] This may be because this seating arrangement allows for more equal participation.

Thus the members, purpose, size, and environment are characteristics that a group has from the outset that have the potential to influence the group in positive or negative ways. As we will see in the next section, whether these characteristics exert a good or bad influence on the process depends in part on what the group does.

How the Group Functions

The second major component of the group discussion process is what the group does with what it has or how it functions. This component is made up of a number of subprocesses that we will examine. Before we look at these specific processes, let's look at an analogy that illustrates what we mean by the first two components of group discussion and their interrelationship.

Suppose you have invited people over for dinner and you have decided to cook a wonderful meal for them. The quality of the meal that you create depends on what you start out with, that is, the ingredients, the utensils, the recipes, and the cookware. You need the right cookware and utensils, quality ingredients, and good recipes to prepare a good meal. This is like the first component of the group discussion process, what the group has at the outset. Having the right cookware, utensils, recipes, and ingredients, however, does not guarantee that you will create a fantastic meal. You must prepare the food well in order for the meal to be a success. Thus not only what you have to start with but also what you do with those things will determine what you create. This is also true of group discussion. Having skilled members, an appropriate size, a clear purpose, and an environment conducive to work does not guarantee that a group will be successful. What the group does with what it has will also affect the quality of the outcome. This is what the second major component of the group discussion process consists of, the processes that the group uses to produce the desired outcome. Let's look at seven of these processes.

Communication   Of the greatest concern to us is the process of communication. Groups accomplish most of what they do by talking; that is how they share insights, evaluate ideas, offer opinions, provide information, and make decisions. The quality of that communication is related to the quality of their performance.[18] Hirokawa and Pace, for example, found that effective groups, as compared to ineffective groups, carefully evaluated opinions and assumptions introduced by members and accepted only those that appeared valid, tested alternative solutions using criteria that they had determined were appropriate, and based their final decisions on assumptions that were accurate and reasonable.[19] This and other research suggests that what group members talk about and how they talk about it has a tremendous influence on the group's performance. In the final section of this chapter we will discuss the skills that group members need in order to improve the quality of the group's communication.

Procedures   The procedures that a group follows will affect the quality of their outcome. Perhaps you have been in groups in which there seemed to be no order to the discussion. The group seemed to have no method for arriving at solutions or completing the task. As a result, there was a lot of frustration among members as the group was sidetracked and backtracked and wasted hours. Just as we need to plan a route when we take a trip, a group needs to plan procedures to take it to its destination, which is the final product. If groups plan procedures and follow them carefully, departing from the procedures when necessary, they are more likely to be both efficient and effective. In the final section of this chapter we will offer a standard procedure that problem-solving groups can follow.

Member Behaviors and Roles   In addition to the communication behavior of members, other member behaviors have an effect on the group process. If members arrive late for meetings or don't show up at all or if they are unprepared, do not make contributions, or do shoddy work, the quality of the group's outcome will suffer. We have all been members of groups in which this kind of behavior occurred, and we were painfully aware that the quality of the group's performance was negatively affected.

Group members' behavior tends to become somewhat predictable over time. Each member enacts behaviors that are consistent. So, for example, Pat can be counted on to arrive on time, to be prepared, to take charge and get the group going, to make sure that procedures are followed, and to determine that everything that needs to be accomplished is completed. We might call this a leadership role. By role we mean behaviors that are consistently performed by a group member and come to be expected of that member.

Roles that group members take on can have a positive or negative influence on the group. Roles that are beneficial to the group are generally classified as task roles and maintenance roles.[20] Task roles are those that are enacted to help the group achieve its goal of completing some task. If Chris consistently initiated ideas in the group, we would say that Chris was performing a task role. Maintenance roles are those that are designed to help maintain good relationships among group members. Jackie's consistent attempts to be humorous at tense moments in the group's interaction would constitute a maintenance role. Both task and maintenance roles can be beneficial to the group. Groups involve more than just working on some task. They involve interpersonal relationships among group members. Thus members who try to help maintain smooth relationships are making a contribution to the group that is as valuable as helping the group accomplish its task.

Power Distribution and Status   As groups develop over time, a kind of pecking order usually emerges.[21] Some members are seen as more valuable than other members; that is, they have higher status in the group. This has an effect on the group in a number of ways, particularly on the group's communication patterns. High-status members typically initiate and receive more communications than low-status members.[22] Thus high-status members appear to have more influence in the group and may be more satisfied with the group as a result. It is not clear, however, whether some members talk more because of their status or whether they develop high status because they initiate more communication. All we know is that there is a relationship between status and communication patterns in groups.

Just as members of a group differ in status, they also differ in terms of power, which is the ability to influence other members. Usually, members with high status have high power and those with low status have low power. Thus power also affects the group's communication patterns such that the more powerful members send and receive more communications than less powerful members.[23]

Discrepancies in status and power can have a detrimental effect on the group. Low-status members may become frustrated with their inability to influence group decisions and are likely to become very dissatisfied with the group. As a consequence, the quality of the group's outcome may suffer.

Norms   A fifth group process that affects a group's performance is the development of norms. As Shaw defines them, norms are "rules of conduct established by the members of the group to maintain behavioral consistency."[24] Groups may not explicitly set up norms; that is, they may not openly discuss rules for behavior. Norms are more likely to evolve over time, just as our individual habits evolve over time. In your own experience with groups, you have probably noticed that groups develop consistent patterns of behavior. They may meet in the same place at the same time, they may begin and end meetings in the same way, and they may have established procedures that they follow consistently.

The norms that a group develops can enhance or detract from the group's outcome. If the group allows tardiness, poor preparation for meetings, disruptions, and so on, the group is likely to perform poorly. In addition, if some group members are not willing to accept norms, there can be problems in the group. For example, if a group establishes a norm that members should arrive on time at meetings, members who refuse to abide by that rule are likely to stir up conflict in the group. You may have been in groups in which there were members who violated group norms, creating conflict within the group. If this conflict becomes extreme, the group may split into factions of a few members each. A group that is divided is probably not going to be very successful at accomplishing its task.[25]

Cohesiveness Perhaps you have been involved in a group in which the members got along, liked and respected one another, and worked well together. Members identified with the group and felt like they were part of a team. This is referred to as cohesiveness. Groups vary in the extent to which they are cohesive. You may have been a member of a group that you felt was not cohesive at all. There is some evidence that a moderate amount of cohesiveness has a positive effect on a group's performance and that too little or too much cohesiveness may detract from a group's final outcome.[26] Groups with too little cohesiveness can become divided into factions, and those with too much may agree too easily and go along with the group rather than critically evaluate ideas.

Conflict The final process that influences a group's performance is how the group members handle conflict. Conflict refers to any disagreement within the group and is usually categorized into two types. First, there is conflict over ideas, which is healthy in a group. Groups need to examine critically ideas generated by members. This naturally involves conflict. The consequence of conflict over ideas should be better group decisions because these decisions will have been carefully analyzed and evaluated. If group members readily accept the first idea offered, it is less likely to be a good idea.

The second type of conflict is personality conflict, which is directed at a person rather than an idea. We have all been in groups in which two members seemed to argue constantly with each other in a way that made it clear that the conflict was personal. Statements like "Where'd you get that idea? You've got to be crazy if you think that would work" reflect personality conflict or at least poor management of conflict.

If groups establish a norm of disagreement over ideas and if members are able to handle conflict without becoming defensive and hostile toward one another, conflict will have a positive effect on the group's outcome. When conflict revolves around personalities and results in the splitting of the group into factions, it will have a detrimental effect on the group's performance.

From this discussion of these seven subprocesses that are part of the group discussion process, we can see that how the group functions has a tremendous impact on the group's outcome. So not only do the characteristics of the group at the outset affect the final outcome, so do these processes.

What the Group Produces

The third major component of the group discussion process is the group's outcomes, or what the group produces. By group outcomes we mean several different consequences of the group process. First and most obvious are the solutions, decisions, products, or recommendations that the group generates as a result of its work. A special type of small group that is often formed is the problem-solving group. The end product of a problem-solving group's efforts is a set of solutions designed to remedy a problem. But what is a problem? Brilhart suggests that a problem has three components: an undesirable present situation, a goal, and obstacles to achieving that goal.[27] For example, suppose the president of your college forms a committee of students and faculty to deal with the problem of cheating on exams and papers. The undesirable present situation is that some students are involved in cheating. The goal the group might wish to set is to eliminate or reduce the amount of cheating on campus. But there are obstacles to the attainment of that goal. For example, there is the difficulty of catching all of the students who are cheating; students are often unwilling to point out fellow students who are cheating. There are faculty members who are afraid of wrongly accusing a student of cheating. Problem solving, according to Brilhart, is "the procedure undertaken to overcome the obstacles in order to move from the undesirable present situation to the goal."[28] Later in this chapter we will discuss a procedure called the Standard Agenda that small groups can use to solve problems.

Another group outcome is the level of satisfaction of the members. You may have been involved in group projects in which you felt very satisfied by the end and in others in which your level of satisfaction was very low. A third group outcome is the interpersonal relationships among members.[29] Perhaps through the group process you have made a friend or an enemy. Finally, our personal growth may be a group outcome.[30] We may have learned about ourselves, about others, about working in groups, and so forth. Even if the more tangible outcomes such as the final reports were not of high quality, if there is personal growth, the group process has been successful to some extent.

As you can see from this discussion, group outcomes involve much more than the actual decisions or solutions. Throughout this section of the chapter we have emphasized how the other two components of the group process model can affect the group outcomes. Thus you can see how these three components are interrelated.

IMPROVING ATTITUDES AND REDUCING APPREHENSION

Throughout this book we have discussed the importance of positive attitudes toward self, others, and communication. We have presented techniques for improving attitudes in these areas and for reducing apprehension about communication. In this section we will briefly discuss those concepts as they apply to the group discussion situation.

By now you have been working on achieving self- and other-acceptance. Just as this is important in communicating in relationships, it is important in the group process. By accepting others, we may be better able to focus our comments and disagreements on ideas rather than on people and their personalities. This can reduce the possibility of destructive group conflict. And by accepting ourselves, we can concentrate on evaluating our behaviors as group members and on improving behaviors that do not enhance the group process.

As you recall, we have also emphasized the importance of a positive attitude toward communication. Many people claim that they hate working in groups. In fact, one researcher coined the term *group hate* to refer to negative attitudes about the group process.[31] Think about your own attitudes toward working in groups. What, if anything, do you dislike about working in groups? List your answers here:

1. _____

2. _____

3. _____

4. _____

5. _____

If you listed any reasons you dislike working in groups, think about whether or not those things are always true about working in groups. Are any of the reasons you listed true in only some groups? Our point is that many of the reasons people cite for hating the group process are not inherent in that process. For example, if you dislike groups because not everyone participates equally and some people seem to have no influence at all over the group's decisions, is that something that always occurs in groups? Of course not. Based on our discussion of the three components of the group process, you can see that the power distribution is a result of the group's interaction. In some cases it may be very uneven and cause conflict and member dissatisfaction. In other groups the power may be relatively equal. Thus many of our negative attitudes about groups come from the faulty assumption that all groups are alike and that if there was a problem in one, the same problem will exist in any group. The best way to combat a negative attitude about the group process is to understand that process and realize that each group is unique. Some group experiences will be fantastic, and others will be tedious.

But regardless, the outcome of personal growth may make the experience worthwhile, even though we may not feel that way at the time.

At the beginning of this chapter we asked you to look at your PRCA-24 score on the group subscale. Was that score high? If so, in addition to improving your attitude and developing your skills at group discussion, there are two techniques that may help reduce your apprehension about communicating in groups. These are the relaxation technique that we presented in Chapter 3 and the goal-setting method discussed in Chapter 4.

We presented a long and short version of a muscle relaxation technique in Chapter 3. To review the short version, read page 66. You can use that muscle relaxation technique to try to relax before entering into group discussion situations. For the long version you remember that we paired the muscle relaxation with items on a hierarchy arranged from least anxiety-provoking to most anxiety-provoking. In Chapter 6 we asked you to create a hierarchy for communicating in social relationships. At this time we would like you to create such a hierarchy for group discussion situations. Begin by deciding on a type of group discussion situation. Perhaps you are currently working on a class project or are a member of a student government group. You can go back to the list of groups to which you belong that you generated at the beginning of this chapter to help you select a type of group for this hierarchy. To create the hierarchy, work on a separate sheet of paper first. Think of situations involved in the group process that make you feel apprehensive. Put those that make you feel most apprehensive near the bottom and those that make you feel least apprehensive at the top. Try to produce about ten items in your hierarchy. Just to stimulate your thinking, here are a few sample items:

1. I am on my way to school to meet my group.
2. I am sitting in our meeting room waiting for other group members to arrive.
3. I am listening to other group members present ideas.
4. I am listening to another group member ask me for my opinion.
5. I am offering my opinion to the group.

It is important that you create your own hierarchy because a situation that causes one person to be anxious may present no problem for another person. When you have completed your hierarchy on scrap paper, write it here:

1. _____

2. _____

3. _____

4. _____

5. _____

6. _____

7. _____

8. _____

9. _____

10. _____

In addition to this relaxation technique, a second technique to help you reduce apprehension about communicating in groups is goal setting. As you know, goal setting does much more than help reduce anxiety. But it can alleviate anxiety by helping you to prepare thoroughly for communication situations. To use goal setting, as you recall, you must specify some small, realistic goal for yourself. Your goal might be "I want to offer at least two ideas during my group's meeting" or "I will present the research that I did for our project to my group." To set a goal, you must think of a particular group situation in which you will be involved. You have already thought of these when you created your relaxation hierarchy. For one of those situations, think of a specific goal that you would like to accomplish, and write it here:

Goal for group discussion: _____

_____

Complete the goal analysis for this goal following the procedures outlined in detail in Chapter 4. Remember to specify criteria for success and the steps you will take to prepare for and implement your goal. Write these on another sheet of paper. You may want to consult your teacher if you have any problems. Once you have completed the goal, you need to assess your behavior in that situation. Remember, to do this you look back at your criteria for success and determine which ones you accomplished and which ones you did not. By following this procedure, you can see in which areas you need further improvement for your next group discussion goal.

IMPROVING SKILLS IN GROUP DISCUSSION

The general skills of goal setting and listener and situation analysis are important for all types of communication situations, and group discussion is no exception. In this section we will briefly discuss listener and situation analysis applied to the group discussion situation, but we will also examine skills specific to group discussion. And as we mentioned earlier, the skills that we looked at in Chapter 6 for improving communication in social relationships can also help you to improve as a group member. In this section we will focus on six specific skill areas for improving effectiveness as a member of a small task-oriented group.

Following an Orderly Procedure

When we talked about the components of the group discussion process, we emphasized the point that groups are more likely to be successful if they follow some orderly procedure. By following some standard procedure for problem solving or decision making, groups are less likely to get bogged down in unnecessary work. They are also going to have more success at keeping to the task and being thorough in completing that task.

Phillips, Pedersen, and Wood offer a procedure for group problem solving called the Standard Agenda.[32] To improve your skills as a group member, you should learn this procedure. If the groups to which you belong do not use any procedure, you might want to introduce this one.

There are six steps or phases of the Standard Agenda. The first phase is called "understanding the charge." The basic objective of this phase is for the group to determine what their charge or task is and what their final outcome is supposed to be. This is the phase in which the group members figure out what they are trying to accomplish as a group and when it is due.

Phase 2 is understanding and phrasing the question. At this stage the group needs to analyze the problem it is trying to solve. Members are interested in defining the nature of the problem, its symptoms, and, if possible, its causes. Suppose, for example, that with your group you decide to study the problem of students getting closed out of classes during registration time in order to devise solutions to that problem. The question the group needs to ask in phase 2 is "What exactly is the problem?" Perhaps students are getting closed out of courses because not enough sections are offered, because students are registering when they are not supposed to, because departments are understaffed and cannot offer classes frequently enough, or because class sections are being kept small because there are few large classrooms on campus. Notice that there are many reasons why students might be getting closed out of classes, all of which would call for different solutions. Thus in this phase the group must try to determine what the specific nature of the problem is and what is causing it. At this point the group's decisions are tentative because they have yet to do their fact-finding.

Phase 3 is the fact-finding stage. In this phase group members need to determine what information they will have to gather. They will have to collect information from a variety of sources, including the library, interviews with experts or relevant people, and possibly surveys. Once the group gathers its information, members must summarize it and draw conclusions about the nature of the problem, its symptoms, its causes, who is affected by it and to what extent, and how the problem has been handled elsewhere.

In our example of students being closed out of courses, the group would have to gather a great deal of information. Members might have to interview the registrar to find out if there are any records indicating the number of students who are closed out of classes, whether he or she believes there is a problem, and, if so, what is causing it and what can be done about it. It is unlikely that there are any records of students getting closed out of courses, and thus the group might have to plan and conduct a survey of students. Members may find out that there really is no problem after all or that the problem is not big enough to warrant action. Or the group may find out that the problem is not what they thought it was and may need to rethink the nature of the problem. If the group discovers that there is a problem through their fact-finding, it should be in a better position to devise solutions.

Phase 4 involves setting criteria and establishing limitations. The group must generate standards or criteria by which it will judge the quality of its solutions. This is similar to what you did in goal setting, when you established criteria for judging your level of success in achieving your goal. By setting up criteria for judging solutions, the group is in a better position to evaluate the alternative solutions that are generated by the group.

In addition to creating criteria, in phase 4 the group also identifies the limitations within which it must work. There are various kinds of limitations that restrict possibilities for solutions. For instance, groups often work within financial limitations. They may have a limited budget or no budget at all. Thus they must generate solutions that fit within their financial limitations. A second type of limitation is the legal limitation. Often there are laws or regulations that could affect a group's choice of solutions. Solutions must not violate any laws. Third, there are moral limitations. As a group tries to solve a problem, it must try to generate solutions that are morally acceptable. In phase 4 the group needs to identify what constitutes a morally acceptable solution. Finally, there are logistic limitations. No matter how great a solution sounds, it is no good if it cannot be feasibly implemented. Thus the group needs to consider all of the practical issues that would be involved in implementing a solution. It must consider the resources it has, the personnel, the time limits, and so forth.

By the time the group reaches phase 5, discovering and selecting solutions, it will have done a great deal of work. But it will also be in a very good position for selecting solutions because it will understand the problem, will have gathered information, and will have set criteria and established limitations for solutions. In this phase, then, the group tries to generate alternative solutions. Members then compare those alternatives to the criteria and limitations and select the solution or solutions that best meet those criteria and limitations. This may involve combining two or more solutions to devise the one that is most appropriate.

The final phase is preparing and delivering the final report. When the group has generated solutions, its work is not done. It must put its results into a final report, to be written, presented orally, or both. One way we can suggest for organizing the report is to follow the steps of the Standard Agenda. That is, divide the report into sections that correspond to the first five phases. That way the group will be sure to be thorough in presenting its report. Remember, though, that the report must be persuasive. You must convince those in authority that the problem is as you say it is and that the solutions you have suggested are the best ones.

Suppose, for example, that you have been asked by the president of the student government to work on a committee charged with investigating and developing solutions for the parking problem on your campus. At the first meeting of the committee, you suggest that the Standard Agenda for problem solving be used, and the committee members agree.

You begin with phase 1, understanding the charge. What would your group do to complete this phase?

1. _____

2. _____

3. _____

Remember, this first phase involves determining exactly what you are being asked to do as a group. What is your task? What are you supposed to turn out? A written report? When is it due? Who gets it? Will the committee make an oral presentation? To whom? When? These are the kinds of questions the committee needs to try to answer before they begin trying to solve the problem they have been given. Without answering these questions, the group has a much greater potential to stray from the task or to waste time because of a lack of direction.

Once your committee has completed phase 1, you are ready to begin phase 2, understanding and phrasing the question. What would your group need to do in this phase?

1. _____

2. _____

3. _____

Since your objective in this phase is to define the nature of the problem, its symptoms, and if possible, its causes, your group would need to consider several questions. What is the nature of the parking problem? Is it insufficient space, poor location, or both? Is it a problem for students, for faculty, for staff, for the handicapped, or for visitors? Does the problem occur on a daily basis or just when there are special events on campus?

Notice that your committee may not have answers to all of these questions. This is where phase 3, fact-finding, comes in. Since the first step in this phase is to determine what information is needed, think of the kinds of information your committee would need in this case. We have already suggested that your committee would need to know who was affected by the problem, when, and what the nature of the parking problem is, but what are some other kinds of information you think your committee might need?

1. _____

2. _____

3. _____

4. _____

5. _____

In addition to those that you just listed (although you may have listed some of these), your group should find out how many parking spaces are available, who is in charge of parking arrangements, how many people are registered to park on campus, how parking spaces are allocated, and if there is a problem of unregistered cars taking the spaces that have been allocated. Finally, the committee may want to investigate how parking problems have been handled at other campuses that are similar to yours.

How might your group go about finding this information? Be as specific as possible as you list suggestions. For instance, rather than listing "interviews," list the people your committee should interview. You don't need to list their names, just their positions. Be sure to see your teacher for help if you have difficulty with this.

1. _____

2. _____

3. _____

4. _____

5. _____

Once your group has gathered the necessary information and drawn conclusions about the parking problem, you are ready for phase 4, setting criteria and limitations. As we explained, in this phase your committee's task is to determine criteria or standards by which you would judge your solutions and to identify limitations within which you must work. Let's begin by considering criteria for judging your solutions.

To create criteria, think about what you want your solution to accomplish. Write your criteria using "The solution should. . . ." For example, for the parking problem on which your group is working, one criterion you may want to write is "The solution should provide more spaces for handicapped students." Another possibility is "The solution should provide a means for handling the problem of illegally parked cars." Note that the criteria your group generates *depend* on what your group has discovered about the problem. For example, suppose your committee discovered that the problem involved handicapped students. Then you would want to write a criterion such as the first one we suggested. Even though you have not actually completed the fact-finding for this problem, list some other possible criteria to make sure that you understand how to write them.

1. _____

2. _____

3. _____

Again, if you have difficulty with this, you should see your teacher for help.

Once your group has listed the criteria to be used in evaluating solutions, you should list the limitations within which you must work. Limitations restrict possibilities for solutions. If your committee has been given no budget, you must devise solutions that do not cost anything, or you must include as part of your solutions ways to raise money to implement those solutions. If your group has been given a large budget, then you can consider solutions that require financial resources. In addition to financial limitations, we also discussed legal, moral, and logistical limitations. In devising solutions for the parking problem, can you think of any legal, moral, or logistical limitations?

1.   Legal: _____

2.   Moral: _____

3.   Logistical: _____

Talk with your teacher if you have trouble writing these, but remember, we have given you a hypothetical case, and so you do not have all of the information you would have at this point if you were working on an actual problem. Thus, it may be more difficult to identify limitations than it would be if you had actually completed all of the phases discussed thus far.

At this point your committee is ready for phase 5, discovering and selecting solutions. You are in a much better position to create solutions than you were when the group was first formed because you have a wealth of information about the problem, and you have criteria and limitations to guide you. Just as the criteria you write depend upon the information you have about the problem, so too the solutions you devise depend upon that information. If, for example, you discovered that a parking problem occurred only when there are special events on campus, you would come up with very different solutions than you would if you discovered the problem occurred on a daily basis. Once your group has generated a list of possible solutions, be sure to check them against your criteria and limitations to help you select the best solutions. If, for example, you have written the criterion, "The solution should provide more spaces for handicapped students," your committee needs to make sure that your solutions meet that standard.

If your committee did a good job in phase 1, you would already know what form your final report should take, when it was due, and who was to get it. Thus, in phase 6, preparing and presenting the final report, your committee would focus on the preparation of a persuasive report. That report should explain the nature of the parking problem, who is affected, when they are affected, and all of the other pertinent information your group has gathered. Your report should list and explain your criteria and limitations, and then present your solutions. It is important that you defend your choice of solutions by showing how they meet the criteria and fit within the limitations. If you simply present your solutions without providing a rationale for your choices, the person reading or hearing the report may not be convinced that the solutions your committee suggests are the best. If your group has done a thorough job in solving the problem, you will have much more information about the problem than the person to whom you present that report. Your group must demonstrate that you have a great deal of information about the problem by including it in the report.

By following this procedure, your group is probably going to be much more thorough in its problem solving. And the more familiar you are with the procedure, the more you can guide your group through it if other members are not acquainted with it. Learning the Standard Agenda and following it can greatly enhance your effectiveness as a group member.

Preparing for Meetings

A second skill area that is important for group discussion is preparing for meetings. You may have been in groups in which members showed up for meetings unprepared, and as a consequence, the group took much longer to accomplish its objectives or had to schedule additional meetings. A major contribution that you can make is to arrive at group meetings prepared. This does not just involve doing whatever you were assigned or volunteered to do. There will be plenty of meetings in which there will be no required preparation, but you can still prepare. At the very least, as group members we need to think about the issues the group is discussing prior to the meeting and jot down our thoughts and opinions. By doing this we are likely to be much better prepared than most of the other group members, perhaps even all of them. Notice how this can contribute to your confidence. And it will also do a great deal for the value the other group members place on you as a member.

A second way to prepare for meetings involves more time than the first. In this case you not only think about the group issues and jot down ideas, but you also do some fact-finding on your own or do any other group tasks that need to be done. The only caution we have here is that you not try to take on everything yourself. If you do, you are likely to resent other group members for not working as hard as you, and they might resent you for trying to take over the group.

Expressing Ideas and Opinions

Groups cannot make much progress if members do not offer ideas and opinions. Thus a third area in which you can improve to become a more skilled group member is in offering opinions and ideas. There are a few points that we can make to help you do so more effectively.

First, we all like to have our ideas accepted and praised and may experience everything from mild embarrassment to outrage when our ideas are criticized or rejected. However, in the group situation we must learn to think of ideas as the property of the group, not of a particular individual. If we continue to think, "This is *my* idea," or "That is *your* idea," we are likely to get angry and defensive when our ideas are rejected. Thus we are suggesting that when you offer an idea, you think of it as something that now belongs to the group to analyze and either accept or reject. Try not to think of it as your personal property.

Second, when you offer ideas and opinions, you need to do so tentatively. That does not mean that you should not be confident in your ideas, but it does mean that you should realize that it is the responsibility of the group to explore alternative ideas and select those that are most appropriate for the task at hand. You may have been in a group in which a member offered an idea and then was not willing to reject it after the group had reached the decision that it was inappropriate. We must be willing to reject our own ideas when better ones are offered. That means that all ideas and opinions must be offered as possibilities, not as the only worthwhile suggestion or the only way to do things.

Third, in offering ideas and opinions, we need to provide support for them. We cannot persuade other members that our ideas are good if we do not show them why they are good. Saying "Well, that's what I think because that is my opinion" is not a convincing argument for getting the group to accept an idea. We must back up our opinions with evidence, such as that obtained in fact-finding. In persuading a group to accept a solution, we can demonstrate how it meets the criteria and limitations as a way to support it.

Cooperation

To be an effective group member, it is essential that you realize that it is a cooperative enterprise. If you are competing, it is with people or groups outside your group. Cooperation does not mean agreeing when you don't mean it or accepting poor ideas so as not to hurt someone else's feelings. It does, however, mean that group members must put group goals ahead of their own individual goals. You may be in a group to make a new friend or to pass the time, but you must put the group's goal ahead of your goal. In many cases you might be able to satisfy your own goal by helping the group accomplish its goal. This is the same idea that we presented when we discussed listener assessment. We explained that we are more likely to achieve our personal goals when we help other individuals achieve their goals. The same applies here. By helping the group accomplish its task, you might be able to make not just one new friend but a few of them. If, however, you do not contribute to the group task but waste group time trying to socialize to accomplish your goal, you may find yourself with several enemies instead.

Cooperation also involves respecting other group members and their ideas, even if you do not agree with them. In more concrete terms, this means that you must listen to other members, not interrupt them, and monitor your communication with them. You may decide that an idea is the most ridiculous one you have ever heard, but you must refrain from making that comment and state your disagreement more politely. Insulting another member may only bring the other group members to that person's defense, perhaps even resulting in the acceptance of the idea that you thought was so absurd.

To be cooperative means that you take responsibility within the group. This means doing your share of the work and meeting any other responsibilities that the group demands. Simple things like attending meetings and arriving on time can contribute much to a group's success. Perhaps you have been in groups in which poor attendance at meetings caused much frustration and low-quality outcomes. It is amazing how much more smoothly the group process can proceed if all members meet their basic responsibilities to the group.

Leadership

When we mention leadership as a skill area necessary for effective group participation, you may think, "I'm not the leader type." Although you may not typically
emerge as the sole leader of a group, and you may not want to, we would argue
that all group members should learn leadership skills. We believe that all group
members can exercise leadership in the group without necessarily being seen or
designated as *the* leader. In this view, leadership is seen as a set of functions or
behaviors that can be performed by any group member.[33] From this point of view,
then, all members have the potential to exert leadership if they perform the
behaviors that constitute leadership. Just what are those behaviors?

Earlier we said that group roles can be divided into two types: task roles
and maintenance roles. The same is true of leadership functions. Let's look at both
types of behaviors that members can perform.

First, leadership involves helping the group establish its goals and objectives, not just overall, but for each individual meeting of the group. By assisting
the group in deciding what needs to be accomplished, a group member can make
a significant leadership contribution to the group. In this way the group will have
a focus to help keep it on track.

A second behavior that can be performed is keeping the group on track. You
have probably been in groups in which members would begin discussing topics
that took the group away from its task. Although this can alleviate boredom and
tension at times, too much of it can produce frustration and low-quality work.
Thus the member or members who try to direct the group to stay on track are
exercising task leadership.

A third task function that provides leadership in a group is summarizing.
Many times groups discuss topics for a long period of time. The group may reach
a point where members are not sure how everything they have discussed fits
together, or they may lose sight of the issues they have already examined. A very
valuable function that a member can perform is to summarize at various points
in the discussion. This helps remind members which issues have been covered and
how those issues fit together.

Fourth, group members may make sure that a decision has been made.
Perhaps you have been in a group in which no one ever officially reported what
the group had decided. Instead the group went along assuming that everyone had
the same understanding of the decisions that had been reached. In addition,
everyone assumed that silence on the part of members indicated agreement. In
these groups we often hear members saying later, "I don't think that is what we
agreed on." A leadership contribution that any member can make is to stop the
group at various points in the discussion and ask, "Have we reached a decision
here? Does everyone agree with it? OK, let's write it down." In this way a group
can keep track of the decisions it has made and can try to make sure that all
members actually do agree with the decisions.

This list of task leadership functions is by no means exhaustive. The basic
idea is that any behavior that helps keep the group making progress on its task

is a task function. Not every task function is necessarily leadership, but by assisting the group in accomplishing its task, you will be a more effective group member regardless of whether or not all of your behaviors can be seen as leadership.

Leadership behaviors that fall in the maintenance category are behaviors that help to maintain harmonious relationships among group members. Again, the list we provide will not be exhaustive, but it should give you some ideas about how your behavior can lead the group toward better interpersonal relationships.

A first maintenance function is mediating in conflicts. There will be times in group discussion when two or more members disagree and the group seems to be going nowhere. An important leadership behavior that a group member can perform is to mediate the conflict. This involves taking charge and stopping the members from talking while you try to identify each individual position on the issue. You should also point out areas in which those in conflict actually agree and try to identify clearly the precise areas of disagreement. By intervening in the process, you may be able to prevent the discussion from degenerating into personality conflict.

A second maintenance leadership behavior is making sure that all members have an opportunity to express themselves. You may have been in a group in which you felt that other members dominated the discussion and prevented you from voicing your ideas and opinions. As a group member you can exercise leadership by making statements such as "Before we hear from you, Pat, let's hear from someone who has not had a chance to speak on this issue. What is your opinion about this, Chris?"

Third, all group members can help maintain smooth relationships among members by offering praise and encouragement. Often in groups we are quick to criticize members' ideas, but we are not so quick to praise them. Although you do not want to overdo this because your praise could come to be seen as insincere, you should encourage members to participate by telling them when you think an idea or piece of work has been valuable.

These three maintenance behaviors should stimulate your thinking about ways to help the group develop better relationships among members. Instead of trying to memorize lists of task and maintenance leadership behaviors, you need to improve listener and situation assessment skills so that you can identify what the group needs and try to provide it. That brings us to the sixth and final skill area for improving communication in groups.

Listener and Situation Assessment

We have stressed the importance of trying to assess the other's needs, goals, values, and interests so that we can adapt our communication to the other in our interpersonal relationships. This same skill is necessary in the group discussion situation, and it may be even more difficult to adapt our communication in the group situation than in the dyadic situation. Quite simply, this is due to the number of participants in the group situation. Instead of trying to assess the goals, needs, and interests of one individual, we are trying to assess those of three or more individuals. And to complicate matters, we are also trying to ascertain what the group as a whole needs, its goals and interests. All of this makes the task of listener assessment much more difficult.

In earlier chapters we also discussed situation assessment and the importance of adapting our communication so that it is appropriate for the situation. In Chapter 6 we emphasized the point that in our close relationships we usually generate private rules for interaction and so do not have to be as concerned about public norms. In the group situation, private rules are also developed and need to be attended to. But groups are usually part of an organization and have been given their task by a person in authority. Thus we also need to be concerned with public norms for behavior, particularly norms for that specific organization. All of this makes situation assessment of a group very complicated.

To improve your skills at listener and situation assessment in group discussion situations, you need to continue to try to be systematic in your observations. You should try to observe each of the following:

1. What are the goals of the group as a whole? What are the goals of the group for this meeting? What are the needs of the group at this time?
2. What are the particular goals and needs of the individual members? Are they different from the group goals and needs? Are they compatible or incompatible?
3. What are the private norms for behavior in our group? Which ones seem to be most influential in the group?
4. What are the public norms that operate in this specific situation? Are there any organizational norms or rules that we must abide by as a group? What are these?

After trying to answer all of these questions about your group, you will need to consider how you can adapt your behavior so that it is appropriate for your specific group situation. This will involve making choices about what is most important at the particular time. Sometimes you may decide that it is more important to try to meet the needs of an individual member than it is to meet the needs of the group, although the two are not necessarily incompatible. There may be times when you choose to ignore a group norm in order to abide by an organizational rule. Unfortunately, we cannot give you the right answers about what to do when. All we can teach you to do is to be aware of these various listener and situational features so that your choices are informed. Adapting to the group situation takes experience. The more groups in which you work, the better you will be able to communicate appropriately and effectively within them.

SUMMARY

In this chapter we have examined the three major components of the group discussion process. The first component, what the group has at the outset, consists of the members and their attitudes, their apprehension level, and their skills, the purpose or task of the group, the size of the group, and the group environment.

All of these are characteristics that the group begins with, and they all have the potential to affect the group in a positive or negative way. Whether their influence is positive or negative depends on the second major component of the process, which is how the group functions. If the group functions in ways that enhance the chances of success, it will be using what it has from the outset in a positive manner. This second component involves several processes: communication within the group, the group's procedures, members' behaviors and roles, the distribution of power and status, the development of group norms, cohesiveness, and the management of conflict. How the group functions in these seven areas can either detract from or enhance the group's performance. The final component of the group process is what the group produces, or its outcomes. Group outcomes can take several forms. First are the solutions, decisions, or products created by the group; a second outcome is the level of satisfaction among members; third is the interpersonal relationships among members; and finally is the personal growth of group members. The quality of the group outcomes depends on the other two components of the model: what the group has to work with from the start and how the group functions.

Next, we considered ways to improve attitudes and reduce apprehension about communicating in groups. The best way to combat a negative attitude about working in groups is to understand the process and realize that each group is unique. This can lead to a better attitude because we have a tendency to think that all groups suffer from the same problems. By understanding the components of the group process, we can see that there is nothing inherent in working with groups that is problematic. Whether group experiences are wonderful, mundane, or stressful depends on what the group has from the outset and how it functions.

We examined two major ways to reduce apprehension about communicating in groups. The first way is to practice the relaxation technique explained in detail in Chapter 3. The second method is to use goal setting as an approach to groups. Goal setting helps us prepare for situations very thoroughly and systematically, which can provide us with a great deal of confidence.

In the final section of this chapter, we discussed six skills that are important in group communication. These skills include following an orderly procedure, preparing for meetings, expressing ideas and opinions, cooperation, leadership, and listener and situation assessment.

chapter 8

Preparing a Public Speech

CHAPTER OBJECTIVES

1. To understand the concept of public speaking as extended conversation.
2. To learn about three types of public speeches.
3. To develop the skills involved in speech preparation.
4. To complete the steps of preparing for a first speech.

INTRODUCTION

In these final two chapters we will be examining the public speaking situation. Although you may think of presenting a speech to your class when we mention public speaking, we mean any communication situation in which one person is speaking to many. Thus trying to persuade a board of directors to accept a proposal, informing a group of employees about a new company policy, or presenting a report generated by a small group to a department head are all examples of public speaking. At this point in your lives you may not think that you will be doing any public speaking in the future, but you will probably discover that your job does involve speaking to a group of coworkers or superiors. As people move higher in the ranks of an organization, they typically find that their job requires increased communication of a variety of types. There are always meetings to run, subordinates to inform, or superiors to persuade. And in many instances this involves public speaking.

The thought of presenting a public speech is frightening to most people. In fact, in a survey reported in *The Book of Lists,* the number one fear reported by those surveyed was public speaking![1] So if you face the prospect of giving a speech with apprehension, you are in good company. Take a look at your PRCA-24 score for public speaking in Chapter 2. Is your score high, moderate, or low? If it is low, you will want to concentrate your efforts on improving your public speaking skills as we take you through the next two chapters. If your score is high or moderate, you will want to work not only on your skills but also on reducing your apprehension and improving your attitude. We will discuss techniques of reducing apprehension and improving attitudes in Chapter 9. In this chapter we will focus on the skills that are necessary for improving as a public speaker.

Therefore, you should examine the skill checklist for public speaking that you completed in Chapter 2. You can find that list on pages 42–43. Are there any specific skills involved in public speaking on which you need improvement? Is your overall skill development level satisfactory? You may have found that public speaking represents your weakest skill area. This is probably due to two main reasons. First, you may have not had any training in public speaking. It is difficult to be effective at something for which one has had no training. If you were never taught how to ski or make wine, you would probably have a difficult time trying to do it well. A second reason why public speaking may be the area of communication in which you need the greatest improvement is because you lack experience. People can be trained to play tennis or read music, but if they do not practice those skills, they are likely to become rusty. Thus if you have had a few opportunities for public speaking, you probably have many specific areas in which you need improvement in order to be an effective public speaker.

In this chapter we will begin by discussing the concept of public speaking as extended conversation. Then we will discuss three types of public speeches. Finally, we will take you through the steps of preparing a speech in order to help you develop the specific skills involved in the preparation of a public speech. In Chapter 9 we'll focus on how to deliver the public speech, reduce apprehension, and improve attitudes.

PUBLIC SPEAKING AS EXTENDED CONVERSATION

This concept originated with James Winans in the early part of this century. Winans argued that public speaking is enlarged conversation.[2] What he meant is that presenting a public speech is like having a conversation with a group of people. Thus many of the principles of effective conversation can be applied to the public speaking situation, but they need to be enlarged. For example, we can maintain attention in conversation by displaying our enthusiasm for what we are saying. We display enthusiasm by our gestures, body movement, voice pitch and rate (our voices become higher-pitched and we speak more rapidly), and facial expressions. To maintain the attention of an audience during a speech, our display of enthusiasm needs to be enlarged so that it can reach to the back of the room. This may involve speaking louder and using even greater vocal expression, bigger gestures, and more movement. We need to be careful not to overdo it, though, just as we shouldn't overdo it in conversation.

If we think of public speaking as an extension of conversation, we are more likely to speak *to* our audience rather than *at* them. You have probably been to presentations in which you felt that the speaker was really conversing with you. You felt that the speaker was sincerely interested in conveying a message to you and to each and every person in the audience. On the other hand, you may have seen speakers who did not seem concerned with conveying a message. They were either trying to get the speech over with, were simply going through the motions, or were so tied to notes or a manuscript that they did not come across as really trying to communicate with the audience. When we carry on conversations, we generally do not talk at people. We try to share our thoughts and feelings with them. We are less concerned with saying everything perfectly than we are with communicating our messages. We need that same conversational quality when we present a public speech.

In conversation we typically adapt what we say and how we say it to the particular person with whom we are speaking. For instance, we don't talk about the intimate details of our lives with strangers, nor do we tell our friends only the most superficial information. We change, depending on who the other person is. We are also prepared for anything in a conversation. We are willing to drop a topic that seems to be going nowhere or to ask questions when the other seems interested in a subject. In other words, we are flexible or adaptable in conversation.

To be effective speakers, we need to be adaptable in the public speaking situation too. When our audience becomes restless, we need to try to recapture their attention, even if it means straying from our plans. If the audience looks confused, we might need to insert an additional example or define a term. We must adjust to what our audience is doing, just as we adjust to what the other is doing in a social conversation. We cannot just plow ahead with our plans, regardless of audience reaction. We would not continue raising questions or making comments about a topic when our conversational partner was very obviously disinterested. Why would we want to do that in a public speaking situation?

It is true that we enter public speaking situations much more prepared than we are for social conversation situations. We are not suggesting that you try to give a speech without preparing an outline and notes. But we are suggesting that you need to be flexible. Your notes are a guide to give organization to your presentation, but you need to be able to make changes in your plans, based on your audience's reaction. That is what we mean by using a conversational quality or style when presenting a speech.

The idea of public speaking as extended or enlarged conversation also implies that what is appropriate or effective for one audience may not be for another audience. Just as it would be absurd for a person to plan a conversation to be used no matter who the other individual was, it is absurd to think that a speaker can plan a speech without considering the specific audience. Throughout the speech preparation process, we need to consider our audience's goals, needs, values, and interests. We will discuss this idea in detail later in this chapter when we apply the concepts of audience and situation analysis to the public speaking situation.

Thus we believe that you can begin to enhance your effectiveness as a public speaker by thinking of public speaking as extended conversation. If you accept this metaphor, you can begin speaking with the same kind of conversational quality you use during a conversation with one other person. You will be more prepared than you might typically be for a social conversation, but you will adapt to the responses of your audience as a skier moves and turns to adapt to the trail with its bumps and curves.

TYPES OF SPEECHES

One way that speeches can be categorized is on the basis of their primary purpose. We can discuss speeches that are designed to inform, to persuade, or to entertain. In this book we will be concerned primarily with the informative speech, although we will also discuss the persuasive speech and the entertaining speech.

The Informative Speech

The purpose of an informative speech is to present information in an understandable manner. We want the listeners to learn something from our presentation. We may want to teach them how to develop film, the history of ballet, or tips for playing poker.

To present effective, informative speeches, speakers must carefully define what it is that they are trying to convey to the audience. Speakers are likely to be more effective at helping the audience understand their ideas if they can narrow down the topic rather than overload the listeners with information. We will examine this idea later when we talk about selecting a topic and a specific purpose for a speech.

It is also important that an informative speech be clearly organized with clear transitions between ideas so that the audience can follow the speaker's train of thought. If they can't see how the ideas in the speech fit together, they will probably not remember much of what the speaker said, nor is the speaker likely to achieve the immediate purpose of helping the audience understand some ideas. We will teach you how to organize a speech later in this chapter and discuss how to use transitions between ideas.

Third, an informative speech must be adapted to the listeners so that it is appropriate for their level of knowledge. In addition, the speaker must show them why the information is important for them to learn or related to their lives in some way. Even if the speech is organized and clear, the speaker cannot teach the listeners anything if he or she cannot motivate them to want to listen to the speech. One of the best ways to motivate the listeners is to show them how the speech topic can help them or is of value to them. We will discuss this idea further when we look at audience and situation analysis applied to the public speaking situation.

Verderber suggests eight principles the speaker can use to help the audience understand and retain the information presented in an informative speech.[3] The information in the speech should be

1. Relevant to audience experience (for example, interest a college class near midterms with information on how to study effectively)
2. New to the audience (interest the audience by telling them about some interesting events that took place in their town 100 years ago)
3. Startling to the audience (tell the audience about the frequency of child abuse right in their own town)
4. Presented humorously (strengthen a speech on juggling by saying, "I am going to show you how not to juggle three balls; that's when I drop one of them.")
5. Associated with familiar ideas (tell an audience about some shopping tips for satisfied purchasing)
6. Described visually (use colored swatches of cloth and volunteers to show how certain colors are more becoming to some people than to others)
7. Repeated during the speech (summarize each point; repeat your purpose several times)
8. Well organized (put main ideas in logical order; have a clear introduction and conclusion)

We will be discussing these ideas in the section of this chapter on preparing the speech so that you will be better able to use them as you prepare your own speech.

To help you begin thinking of topics for an informative speech, let's look at four types of informative speeches:[4]

1. *Speeches about objects.* The speaker describes some object, which is anything that is visible and stable in form. You could describe a violin, a park, a statue, or your favorite building.
2. *Speeches about processes.* This type of speech includes the steps in some process, such as how to make dandelion wine, how to groom a dog, or how to operate a restaurant. The purpose is to inform the audience about how to make something, how to do something, or how something works.
3. *Speeches about events.* The speaker describes something that happened or something about to happen. Topics could include a cross-country race, a historical event, or the opening of the new civic center.
4. *Speeches about concepts.* This speech describes abstract ideas, theories, or principles. Buddhism, patriotism, and evolution are examples of topics for informative speeches about concepts.

In this chapter we will be asking you to complete the steps necessary to prepare for an informative speech. To begin considering possible topics, take some time to list topics you could discuss for the four types of informative speeches.

Objects: _____   _____

_____   _____

Processes: _____   _____

_____   _____

Events: _____   _____

_____   _____

Concepts: _____   _____

_____   _____

The Persuasive Speech

A persuasive speech is given to try to influence the audience's thoughts, feelings, attitudes, or actions. When we present a persuasive speech, we are trying to do more than help the audience understand ideas. We are trying to alter the listeners in some specific way. Perhaps we want to persuade them to think about what freedom means to them (speech to alter thoughts), to feel guilty for wasting food (speech to alter feelings), to agree that a new tax plan is inadequate (speech to alter attitudes), or to stop smoking (speech to alter actions). In all cases we are trying to change our listeners.

Like the informative speech, the persuasive speech must be clearly organized, use clear transitions, and have a specific purpose. Moreover, it must be adapted to the listeners' knowledge level. And the speaker must show the audience that what he or she is proposing is beneficial to them in some way. For example, if the speaker is trying to persuade the audience that a new tax plan is inadequate, the speaker must show the audience how the plan will fail to help them or will affect their lives in some negative way. By doing this the speaker is more likely to be able to convince the listeners to agree with the point of view expressed in the speech.

In preparing for a persuasive public speech, speakers must analyze their audiences' position on the issues they are advocating. Without knowing this it is very difficult, if not impossible, for speakers to adapt their speeches to their audiences. Therefore, the speaker must try to determine if the audience is favorable, neutral, or unfavorable to the speaker's position. To determine this, the speaker uses audience analysis techniques as we discussed in Chapter 5 and will discuss further in this chapter. The speaker will use techniques that are adapted to the position held by the majority of audience members. For example, suppose you gave a speech in your speech class advocating that students not take speech classes. What do you think the position of audience members would be? Although there could be a few students who agreed with you, probably most of them would be somewhat unfavorable to that position. (If the course had not been handled very well by the teacher, most of the students might agree with your position, which you could determine through audience analysis.) In the typical case, however, students would probably disagree with you because by agreeing with your argument they would have to admit to themselves that they were wasting their time and were foolish for enrolling in speech class.

Knowing that your audience was unfavorable to your position would help you plan strategies for presenting your speech. Ehninger, Monroe, and Gronbeck suggest that you would have to approach your subject gradually, trying to convince your audience to listen to you.[5] You would have to try to maximize what you have in common with audience members, offer strong proof for your arguments, and show them that you are interested in the same end result they are.[6]

In addition to determining your audience's position on your topic and planning strategies for handling your speech, you need to think about how you will organize your speech. A classic method of organizing the persuasive speech is Monroe's Motivated Sequence.[7] This involves five major steps:

1. *Attention.* Gain the attention and interest of the audience to the topic.
2. *Need.* Show how the problem affects the audience.
3. *Satisfaction.* Explain a solution that will satisfy the audience.
4. *Visualization.* Vividly show the audience how the solution will help them.
5. *Action.* Tell the audience exactly what they should do to bring about the solution you propose.

Notice that by organizing a persuasive speech with Monroe's Motivated Sequence, we are certain to show our audience how they will benefit by the proposal we are advocating.

Let's look at an example of using the motivated sequence to persuade an audience of college students to avoid driving when they have been drinking alcohol:

ATTENTION:	Provide some startling statistics of the number of alcohol-related traffic fatalities among college-age people in this country.
NEED:	Provide information about the number of alcohol-related automobile accidents in the area in which the audience members reside; give examples of college students who had been involved in automobile accidents in which a driver had been drinking; explain how likely audience members are to be involved in an alcohol-related traffic accident.
SATISFACTION:	Explain that the only solution is not to drink and drive; discuss alternative modes of transportation such as public transportation, taxicabs, and special community programs that provide transportation for persons who have been drinking alcohol.

VISUALIZATION: Discuss the consequences of drinking and driving, focusing on what can happen to the victims of drunk drivers and the victims' families; discuss the legal penalties for drunk driving and the long-term consequences of an arrest record.

ACTION: Tell the audience not to drink alcohol and drive; tell them to stop their friends and family members from drinking and driving.

The Entertainment Speech

There are times when a speaker's purpose is to entertain the listeners. Usually an entertainment speech is presented at some special occasion such as an awards banquet, an annual company dinner, or the meeting of some club or organization. Usually entertainment speeches are humorous, and they are always light and enjoyable. It is not important that the audience leave having learned new ideas or having been changed in some way; it is more important that they enjoy themselves during the speech.

To present an effective entertainment speech, we need to adapt our speech to the audience and to the occasion. In fact, one of the ways in which we may make a speech humorous is by drawing upon experiences, people, or situations that our listeners have also experienced. Many famous comedians talk about the most mundane topics in a humorous way. They may make jokes about how people behave in a grocery store or on a beach. Part of what makes these jokes funny is that we have experienced these situations and can relate to what the comedian is discussing. The entertaining speaker needs to do the same thing. He or she must try to help the audience see the humor in their experiences. In addition, there may be humor in the situation in which the speaker is presenting the speech or in the occasion that brings the listeners together. The speaker should try to use this common experience as a way to entertain the audience.

In this section we have briefly examined informative, persuasive, and entertainment speeches. By talking about them separately, we may have given you the impression that they do not overlap. They do. When we present an informative speech, we may have to persuade the audience that our topic is worthwhile, and we may have to entertain them to maintain their attention. As we try to persuade an audience to agree with our position, we often have to provide new information about the topic. Thus, rather than thinking of these as three distinct purposes, it is better to consider them three primary purposes of speeches. As a speaker, you need to decide which is your primary purpose. This will give your speech a focus, but you should realize that you may have secondary purposes as well.

IMPROVING PUBLIC SPEAKING SKILLS

Now that we have considered the ways in which public speaking is extended conversation and have discussed three primary purposes of speeches, we will begin taking you through the stages of preparing a speech. As you become skilled at each stage of speech preparation, you will be on the road to becoming a more effective public speaker. We will cover some additional skills in Chapter 9, so keep in mind that in this chapter we will look only at the stages of preparing the speech. But to become a skillful speaker, we need to be able to follow the steps of preparing a speech and to be able to do so with skill. For a speech to be effective, it must have good content and be delivered well. Our emphasis in this chapter is on helping you learn how to prepare the content of the speech.

Stages in Preparing a Speech

Before we look at the specific stages of speech preparation, there are some preliminary points we should make. First, although we will discuss the stages in a particular order, you will find that you often have to repeat some earlier steps based on decisions that you make in later stages. You may also find that there is overlap among the stages. For instance, one stage we will discuss is audience and situation analysis. You will discover that throughout your speech preparation you will need to assess your listeners to make sure that the choices you are making are appropriate for them. Second, the stages we are presenting can be followed to prepare an informative, persuasive, or entertainment speech, although our emphasis will be on the informative speech. Finally, as we take you through the steps of speech preparation, we will ask you to begin trying to prepare a speech. You will undoubtedly be giving speeches in your speech communication course, so you may find this preparation useful immediately. However, even if you will not be presenting a speech in the near future, you will probably gain a greater understanding of the stages if you attempt to prepare a speech as you read this material. Let's look at the nine stages of speech preparation.

Stage 1: Choosing a Speech Topic   Our choice of speech topic is of great importance because it not only affects the audience's response to us and the speech, but it also affects the way we feel about presenting the speech. Many beginning speakers select topics that they are not satisfied with and are very uncomfortable when it comes time to present the speech. In fact, a poor choice of speech topic can greatly increase the apprehension we might feel about a particular public speaking situation. Thus it is important to start thinking about a topic as soon as you know you have to present a speech, unless, of course, the topic is assigned to you. Even if your topic is assigned, you'll find that you have to make decisions about how you will approach that topic and what specifically you will and will not include. So an early start in thinking about your topic is a good idea anyway.

There are three guidelines that we can use to help select a speech topic. First, begin by thinking of topics that you have knowledge about because it is very important that the topic you select be one with which you are familiar. It is not a good idea to run to the library in search of some new topic. We tend to feel much more confident when we speak about a subject about which we have a great deal of knowledge. So begin making a list of topics you feel you know a lot about.

A second guideline we can use is to think of topics in which we have interest. We are more likely to feel enthusiastic about presenting a speech on a topic that we are interested in, rather than one in which we have little or no interest. You should go back to your list of topics about which you have knowledge and consider which ones you are most interested in.

A final guideline for selecting a topic is to consider which ones are appropriate for the listeners and the situation in which you'll be giving the speech. We have considered the idea of listener and situation assessment in Chapter 5, although we have not yet applied the concept to the public speaking situation. We will do that in some detail in stage 3 of the speech preparation process, but you should already have some idea of what we mean by the concept. The topics we select for speeches must be capable of being adapted to our audience and the speech situation. For example, can we adapt the topic we have in mind to the time limit we have? Can we adapt it to the level of knowledge our listeners have about the topic? Is it appropriate for the classroom setting? These are just some of the issues that we need to consider when deciding if our topics can be adapted to the listeners and the speech situation. After we discuss this in more detail later in this chapter, you may need to reconsider your topic choice.

With these three guidelines in mind, take some time now to think of some possible speech topics. You will need to decide on a specific topic in order to complete the remaining activities in this chapter. Begin by listing topics about which you have some knowledge. These could be subjects you learned about through coursework, reading, or personal experience. Your hobbies and extracurricular activities may serve as excellent topics. List some possible topics here, including any of those that you listed on page 172. (Try to list ten topics because the longer your original list, the more possibilities you will be able to consider.)

1. _____

2. _____

3. _____

4. _____

5. _____

6. _____

7. _____

8. _____

9. _____

10. _____

Now, keeping the second guideline in mind, go back and put an asterisk (*) next to the topics about which you have the greatest interest. Think of which ones you would be most excited about sharing with others. You may find that many of them fit that description because very often the things we know a lot about are the things in which we have the greatest interest.

Finally, consider each of the topics with the asterisks and put an X next to those that you feel can be adapted to the audience and the speech situation. Which ones do you think are most appropriate for the classroom situation?

If you have more than one possible topic, make a decision as to which one you will speak about. If you feel equally good about all of them, perhaps ask your teacher or a classmate to help you decide. List your final topic choice here:

My speech topic: _____

Stage 2: Writing a Specific Speech Purpose   At this point the speech topic you have selected may be very broad. There is a good chance that you will have a time limit for the speech you will be presenting in class, perhaps five to ten minutes. Thus you need to take your rather broad topic area and narrow it down so that it can be covered in the time allotted. Also, you need to decide exactly what it is that you are trying to accomplish by presenting your speech. What is it that you want your audience to know or think or feel or do? You need to be specific about what you are trying to accomplish in presenting a speech, just as you need to be precise about your goals in other communication situations. In Chapter 4 we discussed the importance of clear goals for communication because they help us choose behaviors. If we do not know what we want to achieve, it is almost impossible to choose communication behaviors that are likely to be effective. If we know what we want, we will have a better idea of how to try to accomplish that objective. You will find that by clearly defining your speech purpose, it will be easier to plan the speech than if you were unsure about your objective.

To plan a speech purpose, we begin by deciding what our *general* purpose is. Earlier we discussed informative, persuasive, and entertainment speeches. That is what we mean by your general speech purpose. Is it to inform, to persuade, or to entertain? Typically, your teacher will assign the general purpose by requiring an informative, persuasive, or entertainment speech. If your teacher has given you the choice, we suggest that you plan an informative speech. We feel that preparing an informative speech is somewhat less difficult than preparing a persuasive speech and that it is more difficult to present an effective persuasive speech than an effective informative speech.

Once you have your general purpose, you need to plan your specific purpose. This should be written as one complete sentence, emphasizing what it is you are trying to accomplish with your audience. Let's look at some examples for an informative speech:

I want my audience to understand the steps involved in developing film.

I want my audience to understand three features to consider when buying a tennis racquet.

I want my audience to know the parts of a 35-mm camera.

Here are some examples for a persuasive speech:

> I want my audience to agree that the proposed new mall will create serious traffic problems in the community.
>
> I want my audience to donate blood next week when the Red Cross Bloodmobile is on campus.
>
> I want my audience to feel guilty about wasting food in the dining halls.

Notice that in all of these examples, we have specified the response we are seeking from the listeners. Not only are we clear about what we are trying to accomplish with our audience, but we have also narrowed down our topic. For example, you may have decided to talk about tennis because you know a lot about it and are very interested in it. But the topic of tennis is much too broad and must be narrowed down. By writing the specific purpose "I want my audience to understand three features to consider when buying a tennis racquet," the broad topic has a specific focus. A speaker would now know exactly what to include in the speech. The speaker would discuss three features of tennis racquets and what to look for in terms of those features when purchasing a racquet.

The specific purpose is a statement that we write for our own use. We do not say it to the audience, although we may tell our audience our purpose in the introduction to our speech. But we are asking you to write a specific purpose for each speech that you do because we feel it helps speakers to prepare a clear speech. How can a speaker do a good job of organizing a presentation if he or she does not know what the objective of the speech is?

For the topic you have selected for your first speech, write three specific purposes, beginning each with "I want my audience to. . . ." Then you can decide on the one you will select for your speech. Remember, unless your teacher has instructed otherwise, write specific purposes for an informative speech:

1. _____

2. _____

3. _____

If you know now which one you will choose as your specific speech purpose, put an asterisk next to it. If you are unsure, you may want to ask your teacher for some help in choosing.

Stage 3: Assessing the Listeners and the Situation   At this point, although you have already been thinking about the audience and the speech situation, you need to be more systematic in your assessment. At the end of this section, you may decide to change your specific speech purpose to make it more appropriate for the audience and the situation, or you may discover that you have made a good choice. Let's begin by discussing audience analysis.

Our purpose in assessing our audience is to try to learn as much as we can about our listeners so that we can plan a speech that is appropriate and adapted to them. There are three major questions that we need to try to answer about our audience. First, we need to answer the question "How much *knowledge* does my audience have about this subject?" Perhaps you have heard a speech in which the speaker talked over your head. You just didn't have the knowledge necessary to understand the speech, and the speaker did not adjust the speech to your level. The opposite problem can happen too, in which the speaker assumes little or no knowledge on the part of the audience when they actually are knowledgeable. In this case the audience ends up being bored because they are receiving no new information or they may feel insulted by the speaker's assumption. As speakers we must attempt to determine how much knowledge our listeners have.

A second question we need to answer is "How much *initial interest* does my audience have in this subject?" Here we are trying to assess the amount of interest the listeners have in our topic before we begin the speech. If we determine that the audience is not interested in our topic, we will have to use more techniques to gain attention throughout our speech. We will discuss techniques for gaining attention later in this chapter.

The third basic question we are trying to answer is "What is the *attitude* of my audience toward this topic?" We can discuss attitudes as favorable, neutral, or unfavorable, realizing that this represents a continuum rather than distinct attitudes. Thus an audience could be extremely unfavorable, mildly unfavorable, and so forth. When preparing for a persuasive speech, it is especially important to assess the audience's attitude not only toward the topic but also toward the specific position you are advocating. For example, if we determined for our speech on donating blood that our audience was largely favorable to donating blood (our topic), we might discover that the listeners are unfavorable to donating *their own* blood (our specific position on the topic). For an informative speech, we still need to consider attitudes toward our topic because they can either enhance or detract from our ability to inform our audience. For instance, if your topic is deer hunting and your purpose is to inform your audience about techniques of deer hunting, audience members with an unfavorable attitude toward the topic might psychologically shut out your speech, either by not listening to you or by thinking about why they object to hunting, and as a consequence shut you out during the presentation. Regardless of the type of speech, we need to consider our audience's attitude toward our specific topic.

How does a speaker go about trying to answer these questions? We need to try to gain as much information about our listeners as possible, such as age, sex, education level, occupation, religion, and so on because on the basis of this type of information we can make *inferences* about their knowledge about, interest in, and attitude toward our topic. By inferences we mean *informed guesses* because we cannot know that we are correct, but we are also trying to find out about our listeners rather than just taking a wild guess to answer these three questions. Remember that we are trying to describe our audience as a group, not the individuals within that group. For example, you may describe your classmates as mostly sophomores, between the ages of 18 and 20, mostly middle-class, and so forth, but there are likely to be people in the audience who do not fit that description. As speakers we cannot try to understand each individual in the audience because that would be impossible. So we must try to understand the group, what that group is like, and make decisions about our speech based on the characteristics of that group. If our audience consists mostly of people aged 18 to 20, we may decide that they have little knowledge of retirement plans. That doesn't mean that no one in the audience has much knowledge of retirement plans, but as a group they are not likely to have much knowledge because they are probably not yet concerned about the issue of retirement.

Thus what we are trying to do in listener assessment is to describe our audience as fully as possible in order to try to answer the three basic questions outlined earlier. Where do we obtain information about the audience? It depends on the situation. Let's look at a couple of examples to clarify this point.

Suppose a speaker is invited to present a speech to a local organization comprised of women in the field of communication. Just by knowing that the organization is for women in communication, the speaker has some very important information. He or she would want to select a topic in the field of communication but would not want to select a basic or simplistic aspect of communication. Thus just by knowing the organization to be addressed, a speaker can gain a great deal of information about the audience. In addition, the speaker can always ask the individual who proposed the speech for information about the audience. How large will the audience be? Will there be both men and women in the audience? What specific areas within business communication are they involved in? How old are they? Where are they from? By asking questions about the audience, a speaker can collect valuable information to answer the three basic questions.

Suppose you have to present a speech in class. How can you go about answering the three questions about knowledge, interest, and attitude of your audience? You are probably enrolled in a college class and know whether the class is all male, all female, or mixed. From the course number you can often make a good guess about the year in college of most of the class members. Is it a sophomore class, for example? Is it open to students of all levels? Depending on the type of school it is, you may be able to determine where the listeners come from. If your school is a community college, the class members most likely come from your community. If it is a state university, the students are probably from various parts of the state. If it is a private college, they may come from many areas of the country, although they are likely to be from areas immediately surrounding the school. You may also be able to determine the majors of students enrolled in the course or can at least ask the teacher for this information. Thus for a speech in class, you already have some information about your audience on which to base the answers to the three questions. To make certain that you understand this concept of listener analysis, try to answer the three questions about your audience (your classmates) on the speech topic you have selected. Make sure you think of your specific speech purpose, not the general topic you selected. If you have trouble with these questions, be sure to see your teacher for help. Otherwise, these answers are to help you with your speech preparation.

1.   How much knowledge does my audience have about my topic? _____

_____

2.   How much initial interest does my audience have in my topic? _____

_____

3.   What is my audience's attitude toward my topic? _____

_____

In addition to assessing your listeners, you need to assess the situation in which you will be presenting the speech. In Chapter 5 we discussed this concept in general. Now let's look at how it is applied to the public speaking situation. Three aspects of the situation must be considered in order to design a speech that is appropriate.

First, you need to think about the nature or purpose of the speech. Why are you presenting a speech? Are you fulfilling a class assignment? If yes, you have to make certain that your speech meets the requirements of that assignment. For example, if you have been assigned to present an informative speech and to use visual aids, you must be sure that your general purpose is informative and that you actually use visual aids. If you do not fulfill the assignment, your audience's expectations will be violated. Are you presenting a speech at a graduation ceremony? If so, you need to think about what topic is appropriate for the occasion. For example, a graduation speaker who talks about a research project he or she has been involved with violates audience expectations. The speaker at a graduation ceremony is expected to talk about the future of the members of the graduating class and their accomplishments. If the speaker talks on another topic, the listeners, instead of listening, sit and wonder when the speaker will talk about the graduates and their future. Thus as a speaker you need to think about the purpose of the speech situation or the occasion for the speech and make sure that your topic is appropriate.

Second, you need to consider the physical setting and how it might influence your presentation. Always try to look at the room where you'll be speaking in advance of the speech so that you can become familiar with it and see what facilities are available and how it is set up. You need to consider the organization of the setting. How are the seats arranged in location to the speaker? Is the speaker very distant from the audience or close to them? Is there a table, desk, or podium separating the speaker from the audience? Is there a stage on which the speaker is supposed to stand? By considering these issues, you will have a better sense of what to do to establish the kind of relationship you want to create with the audience. For instance, if you want to maintain a sense of formality and some distance from the audience, you should physically stand away from the audience and behind the podium. If you want to establish a closer relationship with the audience, you should perhaps step in front of the desk or podium to be physically closer to the audience. In essence, you should try to organize the setting so that it is conducive to the type of relationship you want with the audience and to the type of atmosphere you want to create, such as formal or informal.

In addition to considering the organization of the setting, you need to think about the comfort of the room. Are the chairs comfortable? Is the temperature too hot or too cold? If the room is uncomfortable in any way, you will have a harder time maintaining the attention of the audience. Moreover, if you talk very long, the audience may start to get resentful. If the room is uncomfortable, you need to try to keep your presentation as brief as possible, and you may even want to mention that you are aware of the listeners' discomfort due to the temperature or the chairs. Just by acknowledging that the audience is uncomfortable, you can show concern for the listeners.

In examining the location of the speech, you need to consider possible or likely distractions. Is there an air conditioner that is too loud, or can you hear noises from adjoining rooms? If there are some potential distractions and a room change is impossible, you might want to mention the distractions to the audience when those distractions occur. Sometimes a humorous remark about the distraction can do much to relieve the tension created by the distraction and to build rapport between the listeners and the speaker.

The third aspect of the situation you should observe is the time of day of the speech and the time allotted for the speaker. As we discussed in Chapter 5, if a speech is to be given late in the evening or very early in the morning, the speaker must plan techniques to help maintain attention. The speaker can always remark about the time of day because this can show the audience that the speaker is aware that they are tired. Audiences are pleased when the speaker shows concern for them.

You also need to be careful about sticking to the time allotted for the speech. If you are assigned to give a five-minute speech in class, be sure that you do not go over five minutes. You have probably been in situations in which the speaker went on long past the time allotted and found yourself getting very restless and maybe even annoyed. A simple thing like remaining within the allotted time can do much to enhance an audience's respect for a speaker.

Thus, in conducting a situation analysis, you need to be aware of the occasion or purpose of the speech situation, the physical location for the speech, and the time of the speech. For the informative speech that you are preparing for your class, answer each of the following questions to analyze the speech situation. By answering these questions, you will be able to see some of the aspects of the situation that you will need to adapt to as you plan and actually deliver the speech.

1.   What is the purpose of the speech situation? What is the assignment you

have been given? _____

_____

2. Where will the speech be presented? _____

3. Describe how the setting is organized and where the speaker is in location

to the audience. _____

_____

4. How comfortable is the room? Are the chairs comfortable? How about the

temperature of the room? _____

_____

5. What time of day will it be when you deliver your speech? How much time

have you been allotted to speak? _____

_____

6. What facilities are available? A lecturn? A blackboard, chalk, and erasers?

_____

One last point we want to mention is that speakers should conduct a situation assessment in advance of the speaking day if possible, as we are asking you to do. Even with advance planning, however, the speaker must always check out the situation immediately prior to the speech and make any last-minute adjustments if necessary. For instance, someone may have rearranged the chairs in the room, and the speaker must consider how to adapt to that change or actually put the chairs back in the order he or she desires.

Stage 4: Writing the Residual Message Now that you have completed your initial listener and situation assessment, you are ready to reconsider your specific speech purpose. Make any changes in it that you feel are necessary. For example, suppose that through your audience analysis you decided that your audience already has quite a bit of knowledge about your topic, but your specific purpose is to provide them with basic information about it. You may want to rewrite the purpose statement so that it focuses the speech on a more advanced aspect of the topic.

Once you have your specific purpose set, you need to write a residual message,[8] also called a thesis statement. This is your main point, the one idea you want your audience to remember if they forget everything else about your speech. The residual message is usually very close in wording to the specific purpose, but the major difference is that the residual message is a statement that the speaker says to the audience. Let's look at an example. Suppose your specific purpose is "I want my audience to cut down on the number of cigarettes they smoke." There are a number of different main points that you could select to try to achieve that purpose. Here are some possible residual messages you might have:

> Cutting down the number of cigarettes you smoke may add years to your life.
>
> By cutting down the number of cigarettes that you smoke, you will have extra money in your pocket for other things.

Notice that these are two different residual messages that could both be used in a speech with the purpose of persuading the audience to reduce their cigarette smoking. The speaker would select one of these, each of which would produce a speech with a unique focus. In the first case, the speaker would emphasize the health hazards of smoking. In the second, the speaker would focus on the amount of money the smoker spends on cigarettes and what that money could be used for. The residual message that you select will give focus to your speech. Everything that you include in the speech should help develop that residual message. Ideas that do not support that residual message should be left out of the speech because they may confuse the audience about what your point is. You have probably heard speeches in which you were unsure of the speaker's point. The ideas included in the speech are supposed to build on one another to lead the listener to the main point or the residual message.

At this time, write the residual message for the speech you are planning. After you prepare your outline for the speech, you may need to change it, but a tentative residual message can help guide you in preparing the actual speech.

Specific speech purpose: _____

_____

Residual message: _____

_____

If you are having trouble writing a residual message or specific purpose, ask your teacher for help.

Stage 5: Generating Ideas and Researching the Topic   You are now at the point where you are ready to begin generating ideas for your speech. What ideas will you include? To answer that question, you need to begin by thinking about what you already know about your specific topic. Jot down ideas you have. Don't worry about putting them in any particular order yet. At this stage you are trying to generate a lot of ideas. In the next stage you can be concerned with organizing them.

Once you feel that you have listed all the ideas that pertain to your topic, you will want to do some research on that topic. In listing ideas you may have discovered areas about which you have little knowledge. These are areas you will want to brush up on through research. By researching your topic, you will feel more confident that you will be able to answer questions from the audience. And you will probably find some new ideas or examples that may increase your excitement about the topic.

Material for a speech may be gathered from many sources. You have probably written term papers as a student. The kinds of sources you used for your papers can be used to generate ideas for a speech. One source you should consider is other people. By speaking to others who have knowledge on the topic, you can gain not only additional information you might not have known but also a new way of looking at the topic. You might be able to get some interesting quotations to use in your speech or some humorous anecdotes. By talking to others who have knowledge of the topic, you may also become more enthusiastic about the speech because you will be learning about the topic. When others are enthused about a topic, we tend to feel more excited about it too.

Another source of material for your speech is written material. This includes a variety of sources such as books, newspapers, encyclopedias, yearbooks, dictionaries, periodicals, and almanacs. You have probably made use of many if not all of these sources in writing papers.

Try to select the most recent sources for most topics because they will contain the latest developments or recent facts. That does not mean that you should completely overlook older sources, however. It simply means that you need to be sure that some of your sources are recent.

Also, in researching your topic, be sure to look for anecdotes, examples, statistics, or quotes for your speech. You will need to build these items into your speech to make it clear and interesting, as we will discuss in stage 7.

Before you continue with the stages of the speech preparation process, take some time to generate ideas for your speech. You should also do some research on your topic so that you will have many ideas to work with in the next stage.

Stage 6: Organizing the Speech   Once you have ideas for your speech, you need to decide which ones to include and how you will organize them. In this section we will be concerned with organizing the body of the speech. Later we will consider the introduction and the conclusion.

There are many advantages of careful planning and conscientious outlining when preparing a speech. The outline enables the speaker to do the following:

1. Check the organization and logic of ideas
   a. Locate instances of disorganization
   b. Locate instances of illogic
   c. Determine whether there is enough supporting material in the speech
2. Determine if the main points stand out clearly
3. Remember the speech

The main advantage for the listeners is that they will be able to identify the speaker's residual message and follow the logic of the speaker's ideas. If an audience cannot understand how ideas fit together in a speech, they may not even bother trying to listen to the speech. You must make the job of listening easy by presenting a speech that is clearly organized.

Before you prepare your outline, you must think about how the main points you want to make in your speech are related to one another. You need to decide on a sequence of ideas that makes sense. There are seven sequences you can use to organize your main points.[9] As you read these, try to figure out which sequence would work best to develop the residual message you have written for your first speech.

1. *Time.* Certain speeches are about the steps in a process, how something has changed over time, or the history of a person, place, thing, or idea. When we want to talk about ideas over time, we use the time sequence. We put our main points in chronological order or the order in which they should occur. For example, suppose our speech is about how to make lasagna. We might want to order our main points as follows:

Decide what ingredients we need

Buy the ingredients

Prepare the sauce

Prepare the ground beef

Cook the lasagna noodles

Layer the noodles, meat, sauce, and cheeses in the pan

Bake for one hour

Notice that we have organized our speech into the steps in the process of making lasagna. The main point to remember about using this sequence is that we must keep our steps or ideas in the proper order. If we jump around, we will confuse the listeners.

2. *Space.* Sometimes a speech is about how something is comprised of parts, such as the parts of an automobile engine or the sections of an orchestra. In these cases, we need to plan as our main points the parts of the thing we are trying to describe. In many cases, we don't have to worry about which part we start with, as long as we discuss all of the main parts. If, however, we want to explain how to use the object by explaining its parts, we would need to discuss the parts in a particular order. Suppose, for example, that we wanted to explain how solar heating works. To do this we would want to discuss the components of the solar heating system and how they work together. If you are planning to give a speech about some object or system that consists of several parts, you would use a space sequence, with the major parts as your main points.

3. *Classification.* Suppose that you want to give a speech about types of dogs or types of wines. In this case the various types would represent your main ideas, and you would organize your speech using the classification sequence. If we were going to give a speech on the various options one can select as a communication major, we would use this sequence with the following main points:

Mass communication

Organizational communication

Interpersonal communication

You use a classification sequence whenever you are talking about types, kinds, or categories. The types or categories represent your main points. Just be sure that your categories are mutually exclusive. You do not want them to overlap because your audience will be confused. For example, in discussing common household pets, you would not want your categories to be dogs, cats, birds, and parakeets. In this example, the overlap is obvious, but it is not always quite that obvious, so you need to make certain that your categories are exclusive.

4. *Analogy.* We may want to show our listeners how two things are similar, and in these speeches the major similarities represent our main points. For example, suppose that you want to explain how two universities are very much alike. You decide that they are similar in terms of programs offered, the campus, and the student body. You would organize the main points of your speech like this:

University X	*University Y*
Programs	Programs
Campus	Campus
Student body	Student body

As you presented the speech, you would discuss the programs at University X, then those at University Y, focusing on the similarities. Then you would move to the second major similarity, the campus, and so forth.

5. *Contrast.* A fifth sequence for organizing ideas for a speech is the contrast sequence. This is actually the same as the analogy sequence, but here you are trying to show differences between two things. For the example of the two universities, you would organize your main points exactly as shown, but this time you would be pointing out how they are different from each other.

6. *Cause-effect.* A sixth choice a speaker has for organizing ideas is the cause-effect or effect-cause sequence. We use this when we want to show the relationship between events or conditions. For example, if we wanted to present a speech on the problems that the building of a new mall would create, we would use a cause-effect sequence. The cause would be the building of the mall, and the effects would be the various problems it could produce. In using a cause-effect sequence, the speaker must provide evidence that there is indeed a relationship between what he or she posits as a cause and the effects.

The effect-cause sequence is used less frequently, but it may be most appropriate for your particular speech purpose. When you use this sequence, you typically describe or mention some existing condition and then discuss what you see as the causes of that condition. For example, you may want to call your audience's attention to a problem on campus, such as a lack of student involvement in campus life. Most of the body of your speech, then, might concern the causes of student apathy on campus. In many cases, when speakers use the effect-cause sequence, the audience is acutely aware of the existing condition. The speaker does not need to spend much time describing the condition. Instead, he or she emphasizes the causes of that condition. As in the cause-effect sequence, the speaker must provide sufficient proof for arguments about causal relationships.

7. *Problem-solution.* Often speakers discuss problems and how those problems can be solved. Perhaps the speech you are planning involves a problem and solutions. If so, this last sequence is the one you might want to use to organize your main ideas. If the audience is likely to be very aware of the problem, you may not need to say much about it, but may instead focus much of your talk on the solution or solutions. In cases, however, where the audience is not aware of the problem, the speaker must first demonstrate that a problem exists before offering solutions.

Thus to prepare an outline for a speech, we need to think about the relationship among our main points and decide which of the seven sequences best fits our ideas. Then we need to organize our ideas according to the appropriate sequence. Having an outline is meaningless if there are no logical connections among ideas. The audience must see the logic of the outline, how the ideas are related to one another. Choosing one of the sequences will result in an outline with clear relationships among main points.

In preparing our outline, we need to use indentation and the correct symbols to indicate which ideas are main ideas, which are subordinate, and so on. We use the following symbols and format in an outline:

I. Roman numerals are for main points.
   A. Capital letters are for first-level subpoints.
      1. Arabic numerals are for second-level subpoints.
         a. Lowercase letters are for third-level subpoints.
            (1) Arabic numerals in parentheses are for fourth-level subpoints.
               (a) Lowercase letters in parentheses are for lowest-level subpoints.

In creating the outline, we need to make sure that each statement has a corresponding symbol. Also, if we have one entry at a given level in our outline, we need at least one more entry at the same level. For example, look at the first-level subpoints in this partial outline:

I. There are five basic positions in classical ballet.
   A. First position
   B. Second position
   C. Third position

D. Fourth position
E. Fifth position

The capital letters represent subdivisions of the first main point represented by the Roman numeral I. If we had only a capital A, it would mean that we had divided our main idea into subpoints but then failed to discuss all of the subpoints. It would be like the following, which is incorrect:

I. There are three parts of a speech.
   A. The introduction

It makes no sense to subdivide a main point and then talk about only one of the subpoints. And if there is only one subpoint, it is really just a restatement of the main point. So you can use this as a general rule: Whenever you use a symbol in an outline, there must be at least one other symbol of the same type in the outline under that main point. The beginning of the outline should look like this:

I. Here is your first main point.
   A. Here is your first subpoint.
      1. This would be a subpoint of A.
      2. This is another subpoint of A.
   B. This is a second subpoint of the main point in I.
II. Here is your second main point.

Let's look at a sample sentence outline so that you can see exactly how it is put together. This outline will be for the body of the speech. We will discuss the introduction and conclusion later in this chapter.

I. The first step involved in grooming a dog is preparing for the bath.
   A. First, the groomer cuts the unnecessary hair off the dog.
   B. The groomer then uses powder to pull the excess hair out of the ears.
   C. Then the groomer cuts the nails.
II. The second steps involves the least amount of time. It involves washing the dog.
III. The third step involves preparing the dog to go home.
   A. First, the dog must be brushed out under the blow dryer.
   B. Second, the dog must be trimmed with scissors to remove all the little hair.
   C. Some groomers then paint the dog's toenails.
   D. Finally, the groomer puts a bow in the dog's hair and sprays it with cologne.

Notice that this outline uses a time sequence of ideas. The speaker would discuss the three major steps in the process of grooming a dog. It makes sense to talk about the steps in the order in which they need to be done, and in fact, it would probably confuse the audience if the speaker discussed the steps out of order.

At this point you already have written your residual message and have generated ideas for your first speech. Take some time now to try to prepare an outline for your speech. Begin by looking over your main ideas and deciding which of the seven sequences best fits your ideas. Write that sequence here:

Sequence: _____

Now prepare your outline on a sheet of paper. It may take quite a bit of work to complete the outline, but this is a very important step in the process of preparing a speech and should be done correctly. If you are having trouble outlining your speech, be sure to ask your teacher for help.

Stage 7: Preparing Supporting Materials   Once you have an outline of your main ideas and subpoints, you are not yet done with the body of the speech. You need to add supporting materials to bring those ideas to life. You have probably noticed that there are many places in this book where we have said, "for example." That is a reference to supporting materials. They are details that serve three main functions. First, they provide an explanation for your main points. They make your main points much clearer to your audience. Second, they provide evidence for your ideas. In persuasive speeches it is especially important to have support for the claims we make. We cannot say, for example, that the new mall will cause traffic problems without supplying evidence for that claim. The final function of supporting materials is that they make the speech more interesting and relevant to the audience. By presenting a story or an example, a speaker can grab the attention of the listeners. There are eight types of supporting materials that you can use as a speaker.

   1. *Examples.* An example is a single instance used to develop a generalization. If you said to someone, "I have traveled a great deal," and then you named one place you had been to, you would be providing an example. Examples may be real—that is, things that actually happened—or they may be hypothetical. We are usually better off using real examples because they can be more persuasive, but hypothetical examples can arouse a great deal of interest. We have used many hypothetical examples in this book. We have frequently made statements such as, "Suppose you have been invited to present a speech to a local organization." These are hypothetical examples in that they did not happen, but they could happen.

   2. *Illustrations.* Illustrations are longer examples or stories. People love to hear stories. Perhaps you have heard speeches in which the speaker said, "When I think of that, I'm reminded of a story. . . ." This probably caught your attention and made you want to listen to the speaker to find out what happened. We need to be careful that our stories are relevant to the point we are making, however. Otherwise, the audience will wonder why we told them.

   3. *Statistics.* Statistics are numbers that we can use to clarify a point or provide evidence for a claim. To use statistics effectively, there are several guidelines that we need to follow. First, we need to use current statistics. If they are outdated, it will be easy for our listeners to disagree with us. Second, we need to make sure that our statistics are from reliable sources. If the listeners question

the source, they will undoubtedly question the statistics. Third, we need to phrase the statistics in simple, understandable terms. It is usually better to provide percentages or round off numbers than to present the specific numbers. You should only present the specific numbers if it is essential that the audience know the exact figures. A fourth guideline is that we should use statistics sparingly. Too many numbers will confuse and bore the audience. Fifth, if we must use many statistics, it is best to put them on a visual aid so that the audience can follow them. We will discuss visual aids in detail in Chapter 9.

4. *Quotations.* Quotations can add color and variety to a speech. Often a quote can provide evidence for a claim we are making. At other times it can simply grab attention or move the listeners emotionally. We need to make sure that we cite the source of our quotes and that we use quotes that are relevant to the points we are making.

5. *Comparisons.* Comparisons show the similarities between two ideas or things. We may use literal comparisons, such as when we say that the hailstones were as big as golf balls. Or we may use figurative comparisons, as when we say that a person was as fast as lightning. Comparisons are especially useful at making a completely foreign idea or thing understandable to the audience.

6. *Definitions.* There are times when speakers use key terms that they must be sure the listeners understand. For example, a speaker who is talking about modern dance must define *modern dance* because many audience members may not know what the speaker means. Definitions may be presented as formal dictionary definitions, or they may be phrased in terms of the speaker's interpretation of the word or idea.

7. *Descriptions.* Descriptions paint pictures in the minds of listeners and add dimension to ideas. A speaker who is discussing an impressive football play can describe that play in detail so that the audience can understand it and why it was impressive.

8. *Visual aids.* Nearly any speech can be enhanced by the use of visual aids. We will discuss the types and use of visual aids in Chapter 9, but we want you to realize that visual aids are also supporting materials.

We can offer several suggestions for using these supporting materials. First, make sure that you have some supporting material for each point in your outline. You want to make each point understandable and vivid for the audience. Second, use a variety of forms of support. The more types of support you use, the more interesting your speech will probably be to many types of listeners. Some people are particularly impressed by statistics, while others love stories. A third suggestion is that the supports need to be adapted to the audience. Use local examples, if possible, or ones that the listeners can identify with. If, for example, you are discussing the problem of drunk drivers, it is best to use an example of an accident that occurred in your area as a result of drunk driving rather than an example from a distant city.

In the speech you are planning, you need to work in the supporting materials you will use. To do this, go back to your outline and to the rough notes you have about your topic. The rough notes you have contain the research that you did on the topic and may provide you with some examples, statistics, quotes, and so on. You need to plan these into your outline to make sure that each of your points is supported. Take some time to do this now. You may need to return to the library or other sources of information to obtain more materials.

Stage 8: Planning the Introduction and the Conclusion   It is important that the speaker prepare the introduction and the conclusion after the body of the speech has been thoroughly planned. Once the body is prepared, the speaker can plan an introduction that is accurate and relevant and a conclusion that provides a good summary. Let's look at the specific elements of the introduction and the conclusion.

The introduction should include five specific parts. First, the introduction should gain the audience's attention to the topic. Thus the speaker needs to plan an attention-getting device to open the speech. There are a number of techniques that you can use. Situation analysis will help you decide which to use.

1. *Humor.* A joke, a humorous reference to the occasion or the surroundings, or an anecdote is a good way to get attention. People enjoy humor, and the speaker who uses it will be off to a good start. Be sure that it is relevant to the speech or the situation and that it is not offensive. Your listener and situation assessment should help you here.

2. *Story.* A story is an excellent way to gain attention because it involves the listener in a plot. The listener wants to hear what happened. Just make sure that the story is relevant, appropriate for the audience, and not too long.

3. *Startling statement.* A dramatic statement that startles the audience is an effective attention-getting technique. We need to be careful not to shock our listeners or offend them, however. The statement "The number one fear of Americans is public speaking" would probably be startling to listeners and would thus be an effective way to open a speech about public speaking apprehension.

4. *Quotation.* A quotation can be a very effective way to gain attention as long as it sets the proper mood and is clear and forceful. The speaker should be careful not to choose a quotation that is too long, because it could gain the audience's attention only to lose it.

5. *Visual aid.* Often a visual aid can gain an audience's attention. A student presented a speech on sign language, for example, and began the speech by signing. She used herself as a visual aid. Any of the types of visual aids we will discuss in Chapter 9 can be effective.

You can probably think of other ways to gain attention that would be appropriate for your speech. Just be sure that your attention-getter is adapted to the audience and the situation and sets the right mood for your speech topic.

The second part of the introduction is common ground with your audience. You need to show your audience how your topic relates to them, is important to them, or is interesting to them. You cannot just assume that the listeners will see the relevance of your topic to their lives, and so you must try to show them this right away. Your attention-getter may grab them, but if they do not think the speech is important to them, they may hear little beyond the attention-getter. Thus you must think carefully about how your speech can be made relevant to your listeners and be sure to make that connection for them in the introduction. For some topics, depending on the audience, it will be fairly easy, and in other cases it will take some work. For instance, if your speech is about retirement plans and your audience consists of college students, you will have to convince them that thinking about retirement plans is something they should do right now. Perhaps a way to do this is to suggest that their parents are probably nearing retirement age and that with the information you will be presenting, they may be able to help their parents.

The third component of the introduction is the statement to establish credibility. Credibility refers to your trustworthiness and expertise. You must convince your listeners not only that you know what you are talking about but also that you can be trusted. To establish your expertise, you can tell your audience about your personal experience with the particular topic or cite sources you have read or interviewed. It is not quite so easy to establish your trustworthiness. You must have your audience's best interests at heart. If you do, you are likely to come across as sincere and concerned about the listeners.

Fourth, the introduction should contain your residual message. If this is the one idea you want to leave with your audience, you must be sure to state it clearly. One place to do this is the introduction. By stating the residual message, you let the audience know what you are trying to convey through your speech.

Finally, the introduction should contain a preview of the body of the speech. If, for example, you are going to discuss the five positions of classical ballet, you would state that to your audience. You might say, "Today I'll discuss the five positions in classical ballet: first, second, third, fourth, and fifth." This lets your audience know what ideas you will be discussing and the order in which you'll discuss them. By providing a preview, you reveal your organizational plan for your listeners, making it easier for them to see how your main points are connected.

Now that you are familiar with the five parts of the introduction, take some time to plan the introduction for your speech. When you have it planned, outline it on the lines provided:

Introduction

1.   Attention device: _____

_____

_____

2.   Common ground: _____

_____

_____

3.   Credibility: _____

_____

_____

4.   Residual message: _____

_____

_____

5.   Preview: _____

_____

_____

Many speakers seem to think that their conclusion is unimportant and put little time into preparing a good one. Others don't seem to think a conclusion is even necessary and end their speeches by saying, "That's it," or "That's all I have to say." This is a poor way to end a speech. Remember, the conclusion is the final part of the speech and therefore gives the last impression of the speaker. It is important that the conclusion be as exciting as the introduction. The conclusion should accomplish three main tasks:

1. It should focus the listeners' attention on the residual message.
2. It should leave the listeners in the desired mood.
3. It should convey a sense of completeness so that the speaker does not have to tell the audience that the speech is over.

To accomplish these tasks, the conclusion must contain a restatement of the residual message and a summary of the main points covered. You don't want to use the same wording for your residual message, particularly in a short speech, because it is too repetitive. The audience may think, "She already said that." You want to restate the residual message in a slightly different way so that you can try to make sure the audience gets your main point, and at the same time you can make that message interesting to the listeners.

The summary should be brief, but it should review the main points covered. So, for example, if your speech was on the steps of developing film, you would want to review the steps to make sure that your audience understood them. If your speech was about fielding strategies for softball, you would want to review those strategies.

The summary and the residual message are the two main parts of the conclusion, but there are some additional techniques you can use as long as you keep the conclusion brief. There is nothing as frustrating to an audience as a speaker who says, "In conclusion . . .," and then continues talking for 20 minutes. One additional component you might want in the conclusion is a final attempt at achieving common ground with your audience. In your introduction you related your topic to your listeners, showing them why it is important or relevant to them. This is an effective technique for the conclusion because it can help leave the audience in the mood that you desire. Moreover, it can restimulate their interest in your topic.

A second technique you can include in the introduction is to return to your attention-getter. If you used a quotation in your introduction, for instance, you could end your speech by saying, "So remember the words of . . ." and reread the quotation. Or you could restate the point of the story you told. By returning to the attention-getter, you give your speech a sense of completeness and do so in an interesting manner.

You are now ready to plan the conclusion to your first speech. You will need to think about the order of the parts to the conclusion. You do not necessarily have to begin the conclusion with the summary or the residual message. We will provide spaces for these two parts and additional ones, but you might want to reorder the parts of the conclusion so that they are most effective for your specific speech.

Conclusion

1.   Summary: _____

_____

_____

_____

2.   Residual message: _____

_____

_____

3.   Additional techniques: _____

_____

_____

_____

Stage 9: Inserting Transitions   At this point you have your speech just about complete. You have a complete outline with main ideas, subpoints, and supporting materials. You have the introduction and conclusion prepared. The final stage in preparing the speech is to insert transitions, which are words, phrases, or sentences that show the listeners when we are finished with one point and moving to the next. Not only do transitions let the audience know when we are moving to a new point, but they also show the audience the relationships among our points. For example, if we say, "Now that you have gathered all the materials you need, you are ready to move to the second step of making candles," notice that this transition lets the listeners know that we are finished talking about step 1 and are ready to move to a new point. It also lets them know how that next point relates to the first one. It tells them that the next point is step 2 in the process. We could just use the words "My next point is . . .," which would let the listeners know we were moving to a new point, but this would not let them know how the two points are related.

There are two special types of transitions we can use in a speech. First, there are internal summaries. When a speaker feels that the audience needs a review of what has been said so far before the speaker can go on to a new idea, the speaker may use an internal summary. This involves statements such as "Now that you have decided what type of tennis player you are and have determined the type of racquet that best meets your needs, you are ready to shop around to find the right racquet." The speaker reviews what he or she has covered before moving on to new material. These are particularly useful in longer speeches because the speaker gives the audience a great deal of information.

Second, we can use internal previews. The last part of the introduction is a preview of the body of the speech, but there may be times when a speaker needs to remind the audience of where the speech is going. For example, after discussing a problem in detail, the speaker might want to preview the solutions that will be discussed. These become more necessary as the length of the speech increases.

At this time, then, you should complete the outline for your speech by inserting transitions between each of your main points. You will also need a transition to the first main point and to your conclusion. You may have a number of subpoints for your main points that also need transitions. Try to choose transitions that not only let the listeners know when you are moving from one point to the next but that also let them know how the ideas are connected.

SUMMARY

In this chapter we have been concerned with preparing for the public speaking situation. We began by presenting the idea of public speaking as extended conversation. By this we mean that we need to think of the speech as a conversation with many people. This will help us adopt a conversational style of speaking, which we believe is effective for most types of speaking situations and is especially appropriate in the classroom. Just as we adapt to the responses of the other in casual conversation, as speakers we need to adapt to our audience. We need to convey the sense that we are talking to or with our audience rather than talking at them. We are more likely to do this if we think of a speech as a conversation with our listeners rather than as a formal situation in which we read to the audience with no deviation from our plan.

There are three major types of speech purposes. We may simply want to inform our audience, present them with new information. Or our objective may be to persuade the listeners to change their feelings, beliefs, or actions. Finally, in the entertainment speech, our purpose is to enable the audience to enjoy the speech. However, these three purposes can, and often do, overlap. We may have to persuade our audience to listen before we can inform them. We may need to inform them in order to persuade them. And we may have to entertain them to do either.

The major portion of this chapter was devoted to the stages in preparing for a public speech. We focused on the preparation of the speech (we will examine speech delivery in Chapter 9).

There are nine stages of speech preparation. The first stage is choosing a topic. Even if our topic is assigned, we have to select the specific aspect of the topic we will discuss. In choosing a topic, we need to consider what we know about, what we are interested in, and what can be adapted to the audience and the situation.

Stage 2 involves writing the specific speech purpose. We begin by deciding whether our overall purpose is to inform, persuade, or entertain. Then we write one sentence that clearly identifies what we are trying to achieve by speaking. This is similar to writing a goal statement, as we discussed in Chapter 4. By writing a specific purpose, we not only know what we are trying to achieve, but we are also able to narrow down our topic.

The third stage, assessing the listeners and the situation, actually overlaps all the other stages. As we prepare a speech, we must constantly think about whether every aspect of it is appropriate for the audience and the speech situation. To conduct a listener assessment, we need to gather as much information as we can about our audience to try to answer three basic questions. First, we must attempt to determine how much knowledge our audience has about our topic. Second, we should assess how much initial interest the audience has. Finally, we need to analyze their attitude toward our topic. Are they favorable, neutral, or unfavorable? In assessing the speech situation, we need to examine the nature or purpose of the speech or the occasion for the speech. Next, we consider the physical setting and how it might influence our presentation. Finally, we must recognize the influence of time of day on our audience's responses to us and must adapt our speech to compensate for any obstacles created by the time of day.

We write the residual message or main point in stage 4. This is the one idea we want the audience to remember if they forget everything else. This must be compatible with our speech purpose and will also help give focus to our speech.

Stage 5 involves generating the ideas we will use in our speech. We do this by thinking about the knowledge we already have of our topic and by researching the topic. It is important that we do both, because we may have a lot of knowledge about our topic, but additional research will provide us with the most current information as well as supporting materials.

In stage 6 we organize the body of our speech by preparing an outline. There are seven sequences of ideas that we can use to organize our speech: time, space, classification, analogy, contrast, cause-effect, and problem-solution. We choose one of these sequences to organize the main points of the speech. Once the sequence is decided, we can write the actual outline.

We add supporting materials to our outline in stage 7. Supporting materials provide the details that our speech needs to come alive. Supports help clarify, prove, and maintain audience attention. They can take eight forms: examples, illustrations, statistics, quotations, comparisons, definitions, descriptions, and visual aids.

Stage 8 includes the preparation of the introduction and conclusion to the speech. The introduction should consist of an attention-getting device, common ground, attempts to establish speaker credibility, the residual message, and a preview of the body of the speech. The conclusion should restate the residual message and provide a summary of the main points of the speech.

The final stage of speech preparation involves inserting transitions into the outline. Transitions are words, phrases, or sentences that let the audience know when the speaker is moving to a new point and how points are related.

As we discussed the nine stages of speech preparation, we asked you to complete activities to help you prepare for your first speech. In Chapter 9 we will help you prepare to deliver that speech.

chapter *9*

Delivering a Public Speech

CHAPTER OBJECTIVES

1. To practice techniques for improving attitudes and reducing apprehension in the public speaking situation.
2. To understand four types of delivery.
3. To learn to use the voice and the body in delivering the speech.
4. To understand guidelines for effective language use in public speaking.
5. To learn how to use visual aids effectively.
6. To learn how to rehearse the public speech.

INTRODUCTION

In Chapter 8 we took you through the steps of preparing the content of a public speech. How prepared we are to speak can have a tremendous influence on the amount of confidence we feel. And being thoroughly prepared and knowledgeable about our topic can also increase our enthusiasm for speaking. If we are enthusiastic, we are likely to convey that when we deliver the speech. In this chapter we will focus on techniques for delivering the speech. Keep in mind the basic principle that public speaking is nothing more than extended conversation. We advocate that you strive for that conversational quality as you work to develop your own personal style.

We believe that the best delivery is natural. By that we mean that you do not plan each gesture you will use or plan each time you will move; instead, you let your movements and gestures occur as they would in social conversation or group discussion. There are certain aspects of delivery that do need to be planned carefully, such as the use of visual aids, as we will discuss, but overall you should let your delivery be natural and comfortable for you. If what is natural for you involves distracting habits such as gum chewing, pacing, or foot tapping, you will want to try to rid yourself of those habits. But aside from distracting habits, the best delivery is what the speaker is comfortable with.

In this chapter we will begin by discussing techniques for improving attitudes and reducing apprehension about public speaking. We will then examine the steps in preparing to deliver and delivering the speech. As we take you through these steps, continue working on the speech that you started preparing in Chapter 8. By the end of this chapter, we would like you to be ready to present that first speech.

IMPROVING ATTITUDES AND REDUCING APPREHENSION

In Chapter 2 you assessed your beliefs about communication in general and about yourself and others. Now we would like you to think about your attitude toward public speaking and toward yourself as a speaker. Take a minute to list those attitudes here:

1. _____

2. _____

3. _____

4. _____

5. _____

Check those attitudes to determine if they are unreasonable. Do you remember the guidelines for testing beliefs that we discussed in Chapter 3? To determine if your beliefs are reasonable, ask yourself these four questions:

1. *Is the belief true?* For a belief to be true, there must be concrete evidence attesting to its truth. Statements such as "I will bore my audience when I speak" are not true and are unreasonable beliefs. How can you possibly know in advance of the speaking event that you will bore your audience? The belief "I bored my audience when I gave my speech" could be reasonable or unreasonable depending on whether or not the speaker has any observable evidence. However, the speaker who had some evidence that audience members had been bored would still have to question if *all* audience members had been bored for the *entire* speech. The statement "I bored some members of my audience at some points during my

speech" is much more likely to be a reasonable belief than the statement "I bored my audience when I gave my speech." In addition, the speaker should ask, "What is so awful about boring some members of the audience at some points during my speech? Isn't that true of many speeches?"

2. *Is the belief absolutist?* Statements such as "I could never give a good speech" are absolutist. Statements like "I can give a good speech if I am well prepared" represent reasonable beliefs.

3. *Does the belief result in moderate emotion?* Reasonable beliefs tend to stir up moderate emotions, whereas unreasonable beliefs may cause us to have intense feelings. The unreasonable belief "My audience will think I'm stupid if I make a mistake" is likely to produce strong fear in the speaker.

4. *Does the belief help attain goals?* Reasonable beliefs allow the speaker to pursue goals by freeing him or her from the extreme emotions resulting from unreasonable thinking. Thinking, "I will practice using my visual aid so that I can use it effectively," will help you attain your goal. If you think, "I can't use visual aids. I won't be able to handle them well," you will not be helping yourself achieve your goal of presenting visual aids effectively.

If you discover that your attitude about public speaking represents unreasonable thinking, you should rethink your beliefs and turn them into reasonable ones. If any of your beliefs were unreasonable, rewrite them here so that they meet the four guidelines of reasonable thinking.

1. _____

2. _____

3. _____

4. _____

5. _____

Remember that self-acceptance and other-acceptance are also important in having a positive attitude about public communication. Throughout this book we have discussed acceptance of self and others and have emphasized that we can achieve this by making the choice. We must choose to rate our behaviors and the behaviors of others rather than putting ourselves or others down as people. It does no good to say, "If I don't give a good speech, I will be a failure." It is more helpful to look at the behaviors that you did that were ineffective and try to improve those behaviors the next time you give a speech.

In Chapter 8 we asked you to look at your PRCA-24 score for public speaking. If your score was moderate or high, you should practice the relaxation technique that we discussed in Chapter 3. If your score was low, you are rare!

You may want to move ahead to the section on the steps in preparing to deliver a speech.

In Chapter 3 we offered a hierarchy for public speaking. You can use this to practice the relaxation technique, or you may want to write your own hierarchy so that it meets your needs more precisely. By now you have written several hierarchies, so you should find it relatively easy to write one for public speaking. Take some time to compose one, and when you have it complete, write it here:

1. _____

2. _____

3. _____

4. _____

5. _____

6. _____

7. _____

8. _____

9. _____

10. _____

When you have the hierarchy complete, go back to Chapter 3 (pages 63–64) and practice the muscle relaxation procedure we presented. When you have achieved a state of relaxation, look at the first item on your public speaking hierarchy and try to imagine it. If you feel tense, go back to trying to relax by reviewing the muscle relaxation procedure. When you are relaxed, try again to imagine the first item on your hierarchy. When you can imagine it without feeling tense, go to the second item, and so on.

You may prefer to use the shortened version of this relaxation procedure that we presented on page 66. We recommend the complete version if your PRCA-24 score for public speaking is high because it is the complete version that has been found to be effective in reducing apprehension.[1]

As we pointed out in Chapters 6 and 7, a second way to reduce apprehension as well as to improve your skills at public speaking is goal setting. By following the goal-setting procedure, you will have carefully prepared yourself to present a speech and will have divided the goal into small, manageable steps. This procedure can make a task seem much less overwhelming, and the thorough preparation it involves can greatly increase your confidence. At this time you should prepare a goal analysis for your first speech.

1. Goal: _____

   _____

2. Criteria for success:

   a. _____

   b. _____

   c. _____

   d. _____

   e. _____

3. Steps to prepare for the goal:

   a. _____

   b. _____

   c. _____

   d. _____

   e. _____

4. Steps to implement the goal:

   a. _____

   b. _____

   c. _____

   d. _____

   e. _____

By using the relaxation procedure and the method of goal setting, you should find yourself feeling less apprehensive about presenting a speech. Keep in mind, however, that public speaking may be the communication situation for which you have the least amount of experience. Thus it is likely to be the type of situation about which you are most nervous. With practice and experience, you should find that you are less apprehensive. But also keep in mind that your goal is not to be completely relaxed. Not only is that very unlikely, but some tension enhances speech delivery. When we feel tension, it provides extra energy so that we can deliver our speech with greater enthusiasm. Many people think that being nervous detracts from their effectiveness as a speaker, but we believe this is only true if the nervousness is extreme or if it prevents the speaker from thorough preparation. Some people spend their time worrying about the speech rather than preparing the speech. Thus the tension indirectly prevents the speaker from doing an effective speech. When you present your speech, then, you are likely to feel some nervousness even if you have followed our suggestions. Remember that feeling nervous is very normal and may help make your speech lively and dynamic.

PREPARING TO DELIVER AND DELIVERING THE SPEECH

In this section we will be concerned with preparing to deliver the public speech and the actual delivery of it. Remember your listener and situation analysis, however, because you will need to think about making your delivery appropriate to your audience and the speech situation. It is not just the speech content that we adapt; it is also the delivery. And as we deliver a speech, we must always be prepared to do on-the-spot adaptation as we observe the responses of our listeners and occurrences that we did not expect. Keep this in mind as we discuss the six major steps in preparing to deliver and delivering the public speech.

Step 1: Choose the Type of Delivery

There are four types of delivery from which a speaker can choose, although we recommend the extemporaneous type, as we will discuss. The four types of delivery are manuscript, memorized, extemporaneous, and impromptu.[2]

The Manuscript Speech   The manuscript speech is written word for word by the speaker and read to the audience, with little or no deviation from the script. There are times when manuscript speaking is appropriate. You have probably noticed that the President speaks from a manuscript when making a presentation, particularly on television. This is because it is so important that the President not make mistakes in word choice. A wrong word could create quite a scandal or could offend people because there are so many people scrutinizing the President's speech. When we give a speech, it is not likely that listeners will be hanging on every word, although if the situation were such that they might be, we might choose to use manuscript speaking. Also, in speaking on television, people typically use a manuscript speech because they must stick to a very specific time frame.

Beginning speakers often think that they should use a manuscript speech. They feel that their delivery will be more effective that way for three reasons:

1. The message will be presented more accurately since it will be completely written out.
2. The speaker will not make any mistakes of forgetting or confusing the material.
3. The speech can be delivered in an exact amount of time.

There is certainly truth to these ideas, but there are also some disadvantages to using a manuscript style of delivery:

1. The unusual amount of time involved in preparing the speech
2. The inability to speak with a natural speaking style
3. The difficulty of adapting to the audience and the situation

We believe that there is one other major disadvantage of using a manuscript style that is particularly detrimental for the beginning speaker: The speaker does not actually have to think about what he or she is saying. You have probably found when reading chapters in textbooks that your mind wandered. By the end of the chapter, you wondered what you had read. The same can happen when we read a speech to an audience. Because we can read the words without thinking about them, we often put little expression into what we are saying. The result can be a very boring speech. And when we do not have to think much about what we are saying, we are free to focus on ourselves. Focusing on ourselves and how we feel while we are speaking increases our nervousness. If we have to think about what we are saying, we cannot be thinking about ourselves and how nervous we are. This is why we recommend the extemporaneous style of delivery, which we will discuss in detail shortly.

If you are required to speak from a manuscript, here are some suggestions that might improve the quality of your delivery:

1. Use simple sentence structure and wording. Long, complex sentences may make it hard for the speaker to follow the train of thought of the sentence.
2. Practice reading in complete thought units. The more you practice, the better you will be able to present the speech smoothly and naturally.
3. Practice speaking while looking away from the manuscript. The manuscript speaker must practice looking at the audience to try to maximize eye contact.
4. Key the speech for vocal emphasis. Make various marks on the manuscript to indicate when to pause, when to stress a word, and so forth.
5. Type the manuscript so that it can be read easily. End sentences on one page rather than continuing them onto the next page. Have large spaces between lines of the manuscript so that it is easy to follow.
6. Number the manuscript pages in case they get out of order prior to or during the speech.

The Memorized Speech   A second choice of delivery is the memorized speech. This is similar to the manuscript speech in that it is written out, but then it is committed to memory and delivered from memory. Although the memorized speech was once expected and admired, styles of delivery have changed to a much more informal, conversational style of speaking. The memorized speech is the style you are probably least likely to use. This is mostly because of the problems that are involved in using this style:

1. It requires a great deal of preparation time. The speaker must not only write the manuscript but must also memorize it.
2. The speaking style is unnatural.
3. It is essentially impossible to adapt to the audience or situation.
4. If you forget words or lose your place, there is no assistance.

The Extemporaneous Speech   This is the style of delivery we think you should choose for most situations, particularly your classroom speeches (unless you are assigned to use another style). The extemporaneous speech involves careful preparation of the speech, following the steps we described in Chapter 8. The speaker rehearses the speech, but the specific language the speaker uses develops naturally as the speaker delivers the speech. The speaker uses notes, in the form of an outline or note cards, so that the speech remains organized and clear. Your teachers probably use this style of speaking when presenting classroom lectures. They typically have an outline carefully planned, but they do not read a speech or memorize one. Word and phrasing choices are made as the speech is being delivered.

There are some disadvantages to using the extemporaneous style:

1. The length of the speech is difficult to predict. However, this can be overcome by careful rehearsing and on-the-spot adaptation in order to remain within the time limit.
2. The speaker may worry about forgetting ideas because the entire speech is not written out. However, careful preparation and rehearsal can reduce the possibility of this occurring.
3. The speaker's choice of words may not always be the most accurate for expressing his or her ideas.

Although there are these disadvantages to extemporaneous speaking, we believe that they are far outweighed by the advantages:

1. This type of speech combines the carefully prepared speech with natural, conversational delivery.
2. The speaker can easily adapt to the audience and the situation at any time during the speech, without worrying about forgetting what to say (as in the memorized speech) or losing his or her place (as in the manuscript speech).
3. It is easier to maintain the audience's attention with this style than with a manuscript or memorized speech, particularly if the speaker is inexperienced.

The Impromptu Speech   People who are in the limelight are often asked to speak without prior preparation. This can happen on the job as well, where people are asked to talk about something because of their expertise or their position in the organization. The impromptu speech is one in which the speaker has little or no preparation. The speaker must organize his or her thoughts on the spot. Though common, this is a very difficult type of delivery for the inexperienced speaker. Some problems the speaker may encounter include the following:

1. Difficulty in organizing ideas
2. Difficulty in choosing pertinent material and making that material meaningful in a short period of time
3. Audience realization of and response to the lack of preparation by the speaker

Although the impromptu speech puts the speaker at a disadvantage, sometimes it cannot be avoided. The best advice we can give you is to think about whether or not you are likely to be called upon to speak in a given situation so that you can actually do some advance preparation. If, for example, you are attending an awards banquet where you may be the recipient of an award, think about what you would say if you did receive the award. If you are a member of an athletic team and the game is going to be televised, think about what you might say if you were interviewed by a reporter. Whatever the situation, try to do some advance planning to avoid being caught completely off guard:

1. Recognize possible topics of discussion.
2. Be knowledgeable about the topic.
3. Have an opinion formed, with supporting ideas.
4. If called upon, be sure to understand what is expected.

Step 2: Control What the Audience Hears

Once you have decided on the type of delivery you will use, the next step in preparing to deliver a public speech is to think about the language you will use and how you will use your voice to express your ideas. In essence, we are concerned here with thinking about and controlling what the audience hears. We will examine three areas: word choice, speech patterns, and use of voice.

The Words You Choose　Whether you will be writing out your speech or speaking from notes, you must be concerned about the language you use in delivering your speech. We have already discussed the idea that words are interpreted differently by different people because of their experiences, values, beliefs, and so forth. The speaker must be careful in making choices about words to try to minimize misunderstandings and to communicate ideas clearly. White provides several guidelines for using language effectively when delivering a speech.[3]

First, and perhaps most important, language should be adapted to the listeners and the situation as well as to the speaker's own personality. The speaker must consider how the audience is likely to interpret key words, whether or not they are likely to understand technical jargon, and what might offend them. The speaker must consider the nature of the situation and choose language that suits the occasion. If the occasion is a professional convention, for example, the speaker would use more technical language because the audience would be comprised of people in that profession. Using simplified language might offend the audience and be inappropriate for the situation. In addition, a speaker must use language that is comfortable. Trying to use polysyllabic words to impress an audience is not a good idea if the speaker is uncomfortable with them.

Second, the speaker must keep in mind that the language will be heard, not read. As White points out, "Oral language should be personal and direct."[4] We need to use more personal pronouns such as *we, us, you,* and *I* when we are speaking, even though we may not use these when we are writing. Sentence structure for writing can be more complex because the reader can reread material that he or she does not understand. But for the public speaking situation, the speaker must try to keep sentences simple in terms of structure so that the listeners can easily grasp the ideas.

Third, we should strive for clarity in our language choices. White says that we will be more likely to achieve clarity if our language is accurate, simple, and concrete.[5] Language that is accurate is chosen to express a particular meaning. We often hear politicians using words that seem to be deliberately chosen to be vague and confusing. Military spokespersons seem to be particularly adept at using language designed to be unclear. Perhaps you have heard them discuss "neutralizing indigenous forces," which means killing the citizens of a country, or a "preemptive strike," which means attacking the enemy before the enemy can attack us.

Language that is clear is simple language. We might be tempted to use polysyllabic words when a simple one would be more effective or to use jargon that has meaning only to a specific group of people. Simple language is usually the best choice in public speaking.

Language that is clear is also concrete. Language that is not concrete is full of generalities, whereas concrete language presents specifics. "We wish to give the issue our full consideration to determine all possible courses of action prior to presenting the details of our plan" is an abstract way of saying "We don't know what we are going to do yet." As speakers, we need to make our language concrete, being specific in providing details, facts, and figures.

Fourth, we need to try to make our language objective rather than inflammatory. Inflammatory language, such as the expressions "radical feminist" and "male chauvinist pig," tends to produce a strong emotional reaction. Unless our purpose is to generate some strong emotional response in our audience, we should try to select words that are more objective, such as "a supporter of equal rights for women" and "a male with traditional sex-role expectations."

Finally, White suggests that our language needs to be vivid and impressive.[6] We need to try to hold the attention of our audience, and our language can help us do this. If our language can appeal to the senses (smell, taste, touch, sight, hearing), it will be more vivid. If we can describe to our audience through our words how frightened we were when the bear approached our campsite, we will be better able to maintain attention. We can make our language more vivid if we use metaphors, which compare two objects that are different but have something in common. For example, if we say that "the human brain is the most advanced computer ever created," our language is more impressive than if we said, "The brain is complex."

The best way to develop your language skills for public speaking is to read widely to increase your vocabulary and to try to incorporate the words you learn into your speaking and writing when appropriate. The broader your vocabulary, the more choices you have in selecting words to convey your ideas.

Although the speech you will be presenting will use an extemporaneous style of delivery, you have done enough preparation to be able to think about the language you will use even though the speech is not written out. As you think about the language you will use, answer each of the following questions:

1.   Technical terms I'll be using that need to be explained: _____

_____

_____

2.   Metaphors I might use: _____

_____

_____

3.   Words I should avoid that might be vague, inflammatory, or inaccurate in

explaining my main points: _____ _____

_____

_____

4.   Words or phrases I should use to explain my main points simply, accu-

rately, concretely, and vividly: _____

_____

The Patterns of Your Speech

Speech patterns include the way we pronounce words and the rhythm we use in speaking. Speech patterns that are pleasing to hear help the audience enjoy the speech and retain the ideas presented. Patterns that are difficult to understand or are distracting can detract from the speaker's effectiveness.[7]

Cultural and regional influences on pronunciation can present a problem for speakers because their listeners may not be from the same background. Not only may misunderstandings occur, but the audience may also make negative attributions about the speaker. For instance, they may think that the speaker is not very intelligent or is uneducated. As speakers, we need to examine our own patterns of speech to try to determine if they are likely to present any problems. In some regions of the country, for example, people substitute the *t* sound for the *th* sound, so *thought* becomes *taught*. In other regions, the short *i* sound is substituted for the short *e* sound; thus *pen* sounds like *pin*. As speakers, we do not necessarily have to make major changes in our speech patterns, but we do need to be aware of those that are likely to cause the audience to misunderstand our ideas.

A second problem of articulation is distortion due to the speaker's not enunciating words carefully. Endings such as –*s* and –*ed* are omitted, or words are not properly divided into syllables. This kind of sloppiness in speech is more likely to bring negative attributions than cultural and regional influences. The audience may think we are uneducated if our speech is sloppy.

The rhythm with which you deliver the speech is not likely to be noticed by the audience unless there is a problem with it. Sometimes we talk much too quickly, perhaps because of nervousness or a desire to get the speech over with. This problem is not as common as beginning speakers often think, however. Many students have told us that the problem they have when they deliver a speech is that they speak too quickly, but when we listen to them, we disagree. A speaker has to talk very quickly indeed to be too fast for the listeners, because we can listen and understand ideas at an amazing rate. If you think you talk too quickly, tape-record yourself rehearsing your speech and then play it back. If you think you talk too quickly only before an audience, ask your teacher after you have given your speech, and ask a few classmates too.

Talking too slowly can be equally disturbing to an audience, although we rarely encounter a speaker who talks too slowly. We can listen and recognize words at the rate of about 400 to 500 per minute, and the usual speaking rate is about 100 to 125 words per minute. If the speaker drops much below that normal rate, the listeners will have time to let their minds wander.

A third rhythm problem is the unnatural pause. Since we tend to deliver our language with pauses between spoken thoughts, when these patterns are altered, the listener is apt to lose the meaning of the phrase. Perhaps you have noticed this problem when you heard an inexperienced reader read poetry aloud. The person reads the lines of poetry and stops at the end of each one, even though the thought itself continues on to the next line. The listener loses the meaning when the thoughts are chopped up that way. The pause can be a very powerful tool, however. Paul Harvey, the radio commentator, is said to be a master of the dramatic pause. He makes a statement and then pauses to let the audience realize the impact of his message. Well-planned pauses such as those used by Harvey can enhance the delivery of a speech. Again, by listening to yourself practice your speech with a tape recorder, you can try to pick out any speech patterns that are distracting, and you can experiment with using dramatic pauses.

The Sound of Your Voice   The third aspect of controlling what the audience hears concerns the use of our voices. Some famous people are admired for their pleasing voices. Perhaps you know someone who you think has a very nice speaking voice. This can definitely be an asset to a speaker because it enhances the audience's enjoyment of the speech.

Although we are born with physical characteristics that influence the sound of our voice, there are certain things we can do to make our voices more pleasing to listeners. The three voice control areas are volume, pitch, and variety.

Very few problems can be more distracting to an audience than being unable to hear the speaker. But speaking too loudly can also disturb the listeners. We need to speak at the appropriate volume for the particular speech situation. As you know, the larger the room, the louder we must speak, but the problem is in knowing whether we are too soft, too loud, or just right. If you think you have a tendency to talk too softly in presenting a speech, watch your audience's responses as you start your introduction. Do they appear to be leaning forward in their chairs? This may indicate interest in your speech, but it could also be a sign that they cannot hear you. In fact, you may see audience members cup their hands to their ears to indicate that they cannot hear. If you are not sure, however, you can always ask the audience if they can hear you or if you are too loud. You are better off asking them than driving them out of the room with a booming voice or losing them because they cannot hear. Practice your speech standing at the opposite end of the room from your tape recorder. Make sure that your tape recorder has a good microphone, however, or you may assume when you play it back that you need to talk louder when what you need is a better microphone. And you can always ask your teacher after you present a speech in class. That is the beauty of taking a speech class. It gives you a chance to experiment and learn without risking your job or your reputation.

A second area of the voice that we can control is the pitch. When we talk about someone having a high voice or a deep voice, we are probably responding to the pitch at which the person speaks. We all have a natural or optimum pitch level, which is the one we produce with the least amount of effort.[8] The pitch we use habitually, however, may not be our optimum pitch, which can result in damage to the vocal apparatus.[9] Speakers typically strive for a lower pitch because a high-pitched voice may sound shrill and be hard to listen to. Again, your tape recorder can help you determine if your pitch is pleasing. Your teacher can give you feedback, as can your friends and classmates.

A final area we can control is vocal variety—altering the volume and pitch of the voice, as well as the rate of speech, to achieve greater expressiveness. These changes in voice usually come about in conversation as we adapt to the listeners, the situation, the topic of conversation, and our own feelings about what we are saying. When we are enthusiastic, for example, we may tend to talk at a quicker rate, at a higher pitch, and a bit louder. But we also tend to use our voices most expressively when we are excited about what we are saying and when we are concerned about conveying our message. When we present a speech, we need to strive for the same vocal variety that we achieve in conversation. If you think of public speaking as extended conversation and use a conversational style of delivery, you will probably use your voice as you do when talking one to one. That is, you will let your voice reflect how you feel about what you are saying. The one area you may need to be more conscious of, however, is your volume, which must be louder than it is in social conversation. But we have emphasized selecting a topic about which you are enthusiastic, so your delivery is likely to be more exciting and feature greater vocal variety. Practice your speech and then listen to yourself on tape to see if you are using your voice expressively.

One aspect of the voice that we did not discuss is known as vocal quality. This refers to the quality of the sound of the voice—nasal, raspy, breathy, and so on. Although this aspect of our voices can be controlled, it is more difficult to control than volume and pitch. If you are unhappy with the sound of your voice, you can visit a speech therapist, who can assess the quality of your voice. Tests can be done to determine if there is a physical cause for poor voice quality and how the problem can be corrected. If there is no physical problem, you can be trained to use your vocal apparatus (throat, teeth, tongue, lips) differently to produce a different quality of sound. There are also voice trainers, many of whom work with actors, who can help you work on the sound of your voice.

Thus in preparing to deliver and delivering a speech, we need to control what the audience hears. This means making effective language choices, using pleasing speech patterns, and using our voices effectively. To do these things takes practice, so do not be discouraged if you do not like the way you deliver your first speech.

Step 3: Control What the Audience Sees

You have chosen a type of delivery and have thought about your language, speech patterns, and voice. You are ready for the third step in preparing to deliver a speech, which involves controlling what the audience will see. In this section we will discuss body movement and gestures, facial expression and eye contact, and the use of visual aids.

Body Movement and Gestures   "It's harder to hit a moving target," jokes the actor moving about the stage. Old time vaudeville actors knew this adage to be true. They kept moving to avoid being hit by objects thrown at them when they did not satisfy the audience. As speakers today, we do not have to worry about listeners throwing objects at us, but we do have to worry about satisfying the audience. Our body movement and gestures can help satisfy our audience.

An audience can become bored if the speaker stands rooted in one spot. As speakers, we need to move about on the platform, but our movement should be purposeful. We do not want to pace back and forth, which can distract our audience from our message. But we can move forward when we want to emphasize a point or want to create a sense of closeness with the audience. Movement should be natural, though, because if we plan each and every movement we will make, it is likely to appear artificial to the audience. For example, if in the middle of a thought the speaker walked rapidly to one side of the room, stood there for a while, and then two thoughts later walked to the other side of the room, the movements would strike the audience as very unnatural and seemingly without purpose. A speaker certainly may move to the sides of the room to try to involve the listeners who are sitting there, but the movement should be natural. To achieve a natural quality, the speaker would walk slowly to the side of the room, rather than walking quickly to the spot and stopping abruptly.

There are times, however, when we cannot move away from the podium; our situation assessment can help us determine these cases. If, for instance, the room is so large that you will be using a microphone, it is obvious that you cannot move away from the podium unless you can take the microphone with you. If you are presenting a manuscript speech, you cannot move away from the podium because you will have to carry your manuscript with you, and this could be awkward. Finally, there may be no room to move around, so you will be restricted in your movement. In these situations, you may need to rely on your use of gestures to convey a sense of action.

Gestures are the movements we make with the arms and hands, although we often use the complete body, including the head, as we make gestures. Just as body movements need to be natural, so too should our gestures. We can plan gestures, but we need to be careful that they come across as natural. We need to consider the following guidelines in using gestures:

1. *Gestures result from the spoken idea.* We use gestures to emphasize or complement a spoken thought. They can enhance an idea by calling attention to it and visually reinforcing it. With one hand outstretched to the audience, the speaker might say, "Each of you here today is the luckiest person on earth." The outstretched hand pointed toward the audience can emphasize that the speaker means *them*.
2. *Gestures are coordinated with total bodily action.* Our gestures need to complement our facial expressions and body movements so that they appear natural. The speaker who shakes a fist at the audience to illustrate a warning should be frowning, not smiling. If gestures are incongruous with other body movements, they will look planned and artificial.
3. *Gestures are timed appropriately.* In a speech on patriotism, the speaker might say, "What is the essence of democracy? It is freedom." The word *freedom* is being emphasized, and the gesture must accompany that word. Making the gesture too early or too late would look unnatural.
4. *Gestures are made deliberately and forcefully.* If we plan to use a gesture, we should do so forcefully. If the gesture is very slight, it may not come across to the audience or may not match the vocal emphasis we are using.
5. *Gestures are adapted to the audience and the situation.* If the room is large, our gestures need to be bigger in order to be seen by the listeners in the back of the room. If the room is very small, large sweeping gestures might appear melodramatic.

As speakers, there may be some gestures that we plan, and in doing so we should try to follow these five guidelines. Other gestures will not be planned. Most of us use our hands when we speak in conversation. We do the same when we speak before an audience. These movements are natural and usually enhance the speech. But what we want to be careful about are the natural movements of our hands and arms that are repetitive and distracting to the audience. If your teacher videotapes your speeches, you can observe these distracting movements yourself. If you cannot see yourself on videotape, however, you should ask your teacher about this, and perhaps a classmate or two. Chances are that you do not have distracting mannerisms, but if you do, it is best to find out about them and try to correct them.

Eye Contact and Facial Expression   In conversation we usually look the other person in the eyes, and we want them to do the same. In our society eye contact is expected when two people interact. The same is true in the public speaking situation. An audience likes the speaker to talk to them with their eyes as well as their words. As a speaker, you can help make each member of the audience feel involved in your speech by making eye contact with each person. This not only makes the audience member feel involved but can also help maintain his or her attention during the speech. This is because it is hard to look away when a speaker looks at us. If we look away, we might feel that we are being rude to the speaker.

Keeping attention and making listeners feel involved are not the only advantages of eye contact. A very important advantage is that the speaker can observe the audience's responses and adapt his or her behavior. If listeners are frowning, it may mean that they disagree or don't understand. The speaker might want to elaborate the idea further, using additional forms of support.

The speaker's facial expressions are another important aspect of controlling what the audience sees. Generally, our facial expressions vary naturally with the ideas we express and our feelings about those ideas. If you feel very enthusiastic about your topic, your face is likely to display that enthusiasm. It is important that our facial expressions be congruent with our words. We have seen speakers smile as they talked about very serious topics, and the smile seemed inappropriate for the words. The smile may be due to nervousness, but the audience is not likely to know that and may wonder why the speaker is smiling while talking about a grave subject.

When you are not talking about very serious topics, you should smile occasionally as you speak. Your smile is likely to make the audience smile, which will only make you feel better as you speak. A smile when you begin your introduction will let the audience know that you are glad to be speaking to them and that you want them to enjoy the speech. This would be inappropriate only if your initial statement is of a serious nature. It is very difficult to control your facial expressions, so you should let them happen naturally as you speak. If you do, your facial expressions will probably reinforce your thoughts and feelings and will be appropriate for the message you are conveying.

Using Visual Aids   The final aspect of controlling what the audience sees is using visual aids effectively. Visual aids can greatly enhance a speech by maintaining attention, clarifying ideas, and reflecting on the speaker's preparation and professionalism. Poor use of visual aids, however, can distract an audience and make a speaker appear unprepared and incompetent. In this section we will discuss the proper use of visual aids so that they can enhance your speech.

The first point to consider is whether or not to use a visual aid. A visual aid should not be used just for the sake of using it. Ask yourself, "Will a visual aid help me explain this point more clearly or more persuasively?" If the answer is yes, you would want to select an appropriate aid. For example, for the speech on dog grooming mentioned earlier, the speaker might be able to explain the process better by displaying a chart of a dog to point to the parts of the dog that correspond to the steps of grooming. The speaker might also want to show the tools that are involved in grooming the dog, particularly if they would be new to the audience. To help you decide if a visual aid is appropriate and if so what kind of visual aid, consider the following types of visual aids.[10]

1. *Yourself or another model.* In some speeches you may want to use yourself or another person to demonstrate a point you are making. For instance, you may need to demonstrate a dance step or a golf swing to make your point clearer. In this case, your body or that of the model becomes the visual aid. This can be a very effective aid if you are trying to explain how to perform some action or activity. If you are likely to have a difficult time continuing your speech after you have demonstrated the activity (perhaps because you are out of breath), you should use someone else to demonstrate for you. Be sure to practice the speech with that person. Otherwise, you may be nervous about how to work the model in, and he or she is likely to be nervous about exactly what you expect and when.

2. *Objects and props.* Usually, showing an object is more effective than describing one. It is very difficult for an audience to visualize from a verbal description an object they have never seen. They would probably understand it much more quickly if you simply showed the object. In deciding whether or not to show the object, ask yourself if it is large enough that the listeners would be able to see it and if it is feasible to try to bring one to the speech situation.

3. *Inanimate models.* Earlier we mentioned that you could use another person as a model to demonstrate an activity. You can also use inanimate models, such as a model of the teeth for a speech on dental hygiene or the dummy used by teachers of cardiopulmonary resuscitation. Using a model, a speaker can talk about the various parts of the model, how the parts relate to one another, and how the model works. Again, you need to ask yourself if the model is large enough for the audience to see it and if it is accessible and transportable.

4. *Electronic media.* Film strips, slides, videotapes, and the like can be used effectively, but rarely in short speeches. These visual aids use up a lot of time, and a speaker should not rely on a visual aid to give the speech. Showing a filmstrip with a brief introduction and conclusion is not presenting a speech. Overhead projectors and opaque projectors can be used effectively in short speeches. Using an overhead projector, a speaker can display carefully prepared transparencies with diagrams, words, graphs, or numbers. An opaque projector allows a speaker to enlarge a picture or diagram so that the audience can see it. The key to using electronic media in a speech is to be well prepared. You need to know how to use the media and rehearse with them, especially in the actual location where you will be presenting the speech. You need to know where the outlets are, where you'll set up the equipment so that it can be seen by all audience members without blocking the view of some, and so forth. And you must arrive early and set up your equipment and test it on the day you are going to use it. Otherwise, you might discover that a bulb has burned out, a cord is too short, or a table is too

high or too low. It is very embarrassing to be in the middle of a speech only to discover that your equipment doesn't work.

5. *Pictures and diagrams.* You have heard the expression that "one picture is worth a thousand words." It may be a cliché, but there is certainly truth to it. You can more easily convey the magnificence of a mountain or the uniqueness of a piece of art by showing a picture than you can by trying to describe it. The difficulty is in obtaining pictures that are large enough for the audience to see. If you can, however, your speech is likely to be greatly enhanced. Drawings and diagrams can also be very helpful. A diagram of a solar heating system or of an automobile engine can help an audience visualize what you are trying to describe. You need to be careful not to make diagrams so complicated that they confuse your listeners.

6. *Graphs and charts.* Speakers often use graphs and charts to illustrate statistical information. It is hard for the audience to visualize trends or grasp many numbers without the help of a visual aid. A pie chart can show your audience where their tuition dollars go. Bar graphs can show the differences in the cost of two types of energy over time. Organizational charts can help the audience visualize the various divisions of an organization. The speaker must be careful to prepare these accurately and professionally, which can take a great deal of time. However, they are becoming easier to produce with the software that is available for personal computers.

7. *Posters and flip charts.* Posters are one of the most commonly used visual aids. The poster might contain the outline of the main points of your speech or a drawing of an object that you are unable to bring to the situation. You must be sure to have a way to display the poster, however, such as by using an easel. You cannot count on it standing up if you lean it against a chalkboard, and there isn't always one to lean it against. Flip charts are large tablets of paper used in conjunction with a chart stand. As the speaker talks, he or she flips to the next page, revealing the next point. Thus, for example, the steps in learning to ski could be outlined on the first page. As the speaker introduces the first step, he or she would flip to the second page, which might contain the first step, and so on. Suspense can be created in this way as the audience waits to see what comes next. You can also create suspense using a poster by having the poster covered, revealing its content only when you are ready to speak about it.

8. *Maps.* Maps can be used effectively to explain the route you followed on a journey or to discuss a place that people are not likely to be familiar with. In drawing or choosing maps, make sure that they are large enough for the audience to see.

9. *Chalkboard.* Although the classroom chalkboard is one of the most frequently used visual aids in learning, it may not be ideal for the public speaker. When you try to write on the board, it is difficult if not impossible to maintain eye contact with the listeners. As a consequence, you may lose their attention as you write. Also, your writing or drawing will not have the professional look of an aid prepared in advance. And if you don't practice in advance, you may end up discovering that you do not know how to draw the thing you are trying to illustrate.

Once you have decided if you are going to use a visual aid and, if so, the specific aid you will use, there are some points to consider in preparing the aid and using it. Let's begin by looking at three guidelines for preparing our visual aids.

First, you must plan and prepare well in advance. There are two reasons why the speaker should complete the visual aid well in advance of the speech. First, the preparation itself may be very time-consuming, especially when ideas don't work out as planned. It may take you much longer to prepare a visual aid than you had anticipated, and you don't want to stay up all night the night before your speech trying to finish your visual aid. Second, you need to have your visual aid ready as you practice your speech. Beginning speakers often practice without their visual aids and then discover that they are awkward to work with as they deliver their speeches. You need to become familiar with your visuals and know how to handle them, when to display them, when to take them down, and so forth.

Second, you should strive for clarity and simplicity as you prepare your visual aids. You need to make sure that they will be large enough to be seen and that the lines you draw or the words you print are dark enough to be seen by the audience members in the last row. You must try to keep your visual aids simple so that they almost speak for themselves. If they are very complex and cluttered, they will be a distraction and may confuse the audience.

Finally, you need to consider stylistic aspects of your visual aids. You want them to appear attractive and professional. There should be no errors in spelling, and the aid should be neat and uncluttered. It is best to use stencils to draw letters rather than draw them freehand. Use dark colors to draw lines and print words because the audience will be unable to see light colors such as yellow or light blue.

The preparation of your visual aids must be careful, but you must also use them effectively. Perhaps you have seen speakers use their visual aids poorly, even though the aids themselves may have looked very professional. Be sure to consider the following recommendations as you practice with your visual aids and actually deliver your speech.

First, the position of your visual aid is important. You should think about where you will place it so that all members of the audience can see it. It is very distracting to be unable to see the visual aid the speaker is referring to. This also means that you need to consider how you will display the visual aid. Will you need a stand, tape, thumbtacks, or other accessories? If you will need any of these things, bring them yourself. Even if someone else says they will have these available, you are the one who will appear unprepared if the other forgets them.

Second, you should display the visual aid only when you are ready to talk about it. Keep it covered or hidden until you are ready to speak about it, and put it away after you are finished with it. If you display the visual at other times than when you are talking about it, audience members will look at it anyway. And by paying attention to the aid, they may be missing what you are saying.

Prepare your listeners for the visual aid. Tell them what you are about to show them. For example, say to them, "Let's look at a graph that displays the profit increases over the past twenty years." By making a statement like this, you let your audience know what the visual aid is. Just flashing a picture or graph in front of an audience does not ensure that they will know what it is or why you are showing it. You must let them know the point you are trying to make with the visual aid. This also alerts the audience to the fact that they must look as well as listen to understand the point you are making.

Talk about the visual aid. You may have seen speakers hold up posters, say little or nothing about them, and then put them away. This distracts the audience, causing them to wonder why you displayed the visual aid but didn't refer to it. As you talk about the visual aid, be sure to try to maintain some eye contact with your listeners. You do not want to appear as if you are more concerned with your visual aid than you are with your audience.

Finally, avoid using handouts if at all possible. You want the audience's attention focused on you and what you are saying, not on papers or objects being passed around the room or in people's laps. The speaker who passes papers around usually has a difficult time getting or regaining the audience's attention.

Now that we have discussed types of visual aids and guidelines for preparing and using them, we would like you to think about whether or not you should use a visual aid for the speech you have been preparing. Answer the following questions to help you decide if you should use any and what they should be.

1.   Are there any points that I need to make that could be made more clearly

with a visual aid? If so, what are those points? _____

_____

_____

_____

2.   What are some possible visual aids that I could use to make these points?

_____

_____

_____

3.   Of those that are possible, which is or are most appropriate? Why?

_____

_____   _____

_____

4.   The visual aid or aids I will use in my speech: _____

_____   ____   _____

If you have trouble deciding what to use, if anything, for visual aids, be sure to ask your teacher for help. You may decide that you do not need to use any. If there is no need, the speaker should not use visual aids.

In this section we have focused on the third step in preparing to deliver a speech, controlling what the audience sees. As speakers, we need to think about body movement, gestures, eye contact, facial expressions, and visual aids. These are all visual components of the process of delivering a speech, and we want these components to complement and enhance the verbal and vocal elements.

Step 4: Control the Environment

In Chapter 8 we asked you to complete an assessment of the speaking situation in which you would be presenting your first speech. In preparing to deliver a speech, you need to consider how the components of the situation will affect your delivery and which aspects of the environment you can control to enhance that delivery. Let's examine features of the situation that can affect speech delivery and how the speaker might control them. Some of these issues were discussed in Chapter 8, but our emphasis here will be on how to handle them while delivering a speech or controlling them so they work to the speaker's advantage. Whenever possible, you should study the setting in which you'll give a speech in advance of the day of the presentation and again on the day you'll speak. You may need to do some rearranging when you arrive because the room may not look the way it did the first time you observed it.

1. *Podium.* One feature of the situation you will want to observe is whether or not there is a podium, if it is movable, and where you would want it to be. If there is no podium, can you get one? If not, how will you hold your notes? You may need to put your notes on cards because they are easier to work with than sheets of paper when there is no place to put your notes while you speak. If there is a podium and it is movable, place it where you would like it prior to the speech. Do you want it closer to your audience to create a more informal situation and to enable you to make better eye contact? Do you want it farther from the audience to give you room in front of it to move around?

2. *Facilities.* What facilities are available? Are a chalkboard, chalk, and erasers at your disposal? If not and you need them, can you arrange to have them brought in? Are there electrical outlets? If so, where are they? Will you need extension cords? Are there tables or desks to put an overhead projector on? If not, are there carts or chairs you could use? These questions are designed to get you thinking about what you need to look for when you observe the speaking situation. As speakers, we need to make sure the things we need are available, and if not, we need to make arrangements to get them or figure out how to do without them. These are issues to consider in advance, not when you arrive and are about to present your speech.

3. *Audience seating arrangement.* In most classrooms and many other situations, chairs are movable and can be arranged to suit the speaker's purpose. Perhaps you want the audience to sit in a semicircle to create a very informal atmosphere. Or perhaps you would like the audience to sit back from the podium

because you need room in front to conduct a demonstration. If the chairs cannot be moved, you will want to try to move the podium, easel for your visual aids, and equipment so that they serve your needs best. If you are speaking in a large room but your audience is small, you might want to ask the listeners to sit in the front rows. Otherwise, they may sit near the back and be unable to see your visual aids. Also, it will be harder to keep their attention.

4. *Size of the room.* Do you have a choice about where the speech will be held? If so, you want to select a room that is appropriate in size for the audience you expect. It is better to have a room that is nearly full than a large room with a small audience. You don't want audience members to be too crowded either, because they will become uncomfortable during the speech. Thus select a room that is suitable for the size audience you expect. If you overestimate the audience size, ask people to sit in the front rows so that they do not spread out all over the room. If you underestimate the size of the audience and people must stand, try to keep your speech brief and lively. In cases where you cannot choose the room, you may also have to do some of these things, such as ask the audience to move forward.

5. *Distractions.* As you visit the room where you will be speaking, notice if there are any distractions such as uncomfortable chairs, or the like. If there is a way to get someone to take care of these distractions, such as by turning the heat up or down, turning the clock off, and so on, you should do so. Removing distractions may be the best way to deal with them. If you cannot remove them, we have already suggested in Chapter 8 that the speaker should mention them and try to make a humorous remark about the distractions. By acknowledging distractions, the speaker shows the listeners that he or she is aware of them and the effect they are likely to have on the audience. This shows the audience that the speaker is concerned about them.

In Chapter 8, we asked you to assess these aspects of the situation in which you would be speaking. Now we would like you to consider which ones you can control, how you will control them, and how you will handle situational features that you cannot control. Answer each of the following questions as specifically as possible.

1. Is there a podium available in the room? _____

    a. If not, can I get one? Otherwise, how will I handle my notes?

_____

    b. If yes, is it movable? Where will I put it? _____

_____

2. What facilities do I need for my speech? _____

_____

a.   Are they available in the room? _____

b.   If not, can I get them? Where? _____

c.   If I can't get them, what will I do? _____

_____

3.   How would I like the audience seating to be arranged? Why? _____

_____

a.   · Is it possible to arrange it that way? _____

b.   If not, how is it arranged? _____

c.   What will I do to make the situation suit my needs in spite of the fixed

seating arrangement? _____

_____

4.   What is the size of the room in which I'll be speaking? _____

_____

a.   Is the audience likely to be too big, too small, or just about right for

the room size? _____

b.   If it is too big or too small for the size of the room, what will I do?

_____

_____

5.   What distractions are likely to occur? _____

_____

a.   Can I remove any of them? Which ones? _____

_____

b.   If not, how will I handle them? _____

_____

Step 5: Rehearse the Speech

Now that you have selected the type of delivery you will use and have thought about controlling what the audience hears and sees and the speaking environment, you are ready to rehearse your speech. Rehearsing your speech is critical to effective delivery. First, by rehearsing you can increase your confidence. When you actually deliver the speech, you will feel much more familiar with your topic, how you will express ideas, and how you'll move, gesture, and use your visual aids. This familiarity with the speech can greatly enhance your confidence. Second, by practicing your speech, you can make sure that it fits within the time you have been alloted. Finally, through rehearsal, you can discover weaknesses in the speech content, such as an idea with no support, and correct those problems in advance of presenting the speech.

There are several guidelines you should follow in practicing your speech. First, prepare your note cards or an outline, and practice with the actual cards or outline you plan to have with you on the day you speak. These serve to remind you of your ideas, your supports, and the order of your ideas. When you practice with them, you may discover that a particular note card or note on the outline does not jog your memory and leaves you wondering what comes next. You would want to redo that card or that section of the outline so that it better served the purpose of reminding you of what to say.

Second, practice your speech over several days, rather than trying to practice it ten times on the day before the speech. By rehearsing over several days, you will have enough time to make changes, and your speech will have time to "sink in." You are not trying to memorize the speech, as we have already discussed, but it is a good idea to know the order of your main points and what those main points are. That will allow you to adapt to the situation. For example, if you discover that you have two more main points to discuss but you are almost out of time, you will know what two ideas remain and can decide on the spot which one you'll cut.

The third suggestion is to practice your speech as if you were delivering it in the actual speech situation. Stand as you plan to when you present the speech. Use your visual aids as you will when there is an audience there. Try to simulate the speech situation you'll be in. If possible, rehearse in the actual speaking situation. The more your rehearsals simulate the speech situation, the more comfortable you will feel when you deliver your speech to the audience, and you should also be more effective as a speaker. Perhaps you have been in a play of some type. For any type of theater production, there is always a complete dress rehearsal at which the show is rehearsed as if it were an actual performance. That is what we are asking you to do, if possible, because when you get up to speak, the only difference between that and your rehearsal is the audience. You will feel as if you have given the speech before, which can greatly enhance your confidence and effectiveness.

Finally, practice a few times with a tape recorder to check your word choices, speech patterns, and vocal variety. You may also want to rehearse with a roommate, friend, or family member to get an opinion about the speech and how to improve it.

Step 6: Deliver the Speech

The first five steps we have discussed help you prepare to deliver the speech. All that remains is actually to present the speech to your audience!

Some research indicates that it is just before we speak that we feel the most apprehensive.[11] A way to handle this is to refuse to concentrate on your speech after you enter the speech situation. Think about what other people are doing and talking about, and, if possible, volunteer to speak first. The longer you sit there, the more apprehensive you are likely to feel. When you walk up to give your speech, remind yourself that you have a terrific topic, you are well prepared, and the audience will want to hear what you have to say. When you get to your speaking position, pause for a few seconds, take a deep breath, and, if appropriate, smile as you begin. Use eye contact, gestures, and body movement during your introduction. These actions will get you into the swing of your speech and propel you through a lively delivery.

SUMMARY

In this chapter we have examined speech delivery. We believe that the best delivery is whatever is natural for the speaker, as long as the speaker does not have some distracting habits. If we do have mannerisms that may distract our audience, we need to try to correct those habits by monitoring ourselves as we practice and deliver our speeches.

We discussed techniques for improving our attitudes and reducing apprehension in the public speaking situation. To improve attitudes we need to continue to strive for self-acceptance and other-acceptance and to replace unreasonable beliefs with reasonable ones. We can reduce our apprehension about public speaking not only by developing public speaking skills through preparation and practice but also by using the relaxation technique we have described as well as the method of goal setting.

There are six steps in preparing to deliver and delivering a public speech. Step 1 involves choosing the appropriate type of delivery: manuscript, memorized, extemporaneous, or impromptu. We feel that the extemporaneous speech is best for most speaking situations because it combines careful preparation with flexibility to adapt to the listeners.

Step 2 is to control what the audience hears. This means choosing language that is accurate, simple, concrete, vivid, and appropriate for the listeners and the situation. It includes thinking about our speech patterns and using our voice effectively to convey our ideas and maintain attention.

The third step in preparing to deliver a speech is to control what the audience sees. We do this by considering our body movements, gestures, eye contact, and facial expressions and trying to make them reinforce our message.

It also involves preparing visual aids and handling them effectively as we deliver the speech.

In step 4, we control the speaking environment. We must observe features of the speech situation and decide how we will handle them. These features include the availability and location of a podium, other facilities that are available, audience seating arrangement, size of the room, and potential distractions.

Step 5 is to practice the speech. We should rehearse carefully and in a situation that closely approximates the actual speech situation. Practicing our speech can do much to build our confidence.

Finally, we deliver the speech in step 6. By the time we reach step 6, we have thoroughly prepared the content of the speech, decided how we will deliver it, and rehearsed the speech. When we walk up to the front of the room, we can be confident that we are ready to present an effective speech. We may even find ourselves enjoying the experience!

Notes

CHAPTER 1. THE PROCESS OF COMMUNICATION

1. See, for example, Kathleen M. Domenig, *An Examination of Self-reports of Reticent and Non-reticent Students Before and After Instruction* (M.A. thesis, Pennsylvania State University, 1978), and Bruce C. McKinney, *Comparison of Students in Self-selected Speech Options on Four Measures of Reticence and Cognate Problems* (M.A. thesis, Pennsylvania State University, 1980).
2. Frank E. X. Dance and Carl E. Larson, *The Functions of Human Communication* (New York: Holt, Rinehart and Winston, 1976), pp. 171–192.
3. Gerald M. Phillips and Nancy J. Metzger, *Intimate Communication* (Boston: Allyn & Bacon, 1976).
4. Paul Watzlawick, Janet H. Beavin, and Don D. Jackson, *Pragmatics of Human Communication: A Study of Interactional Patterns, Pathologies, and Paradoxes* (New York: Norton, 1967), pp. 48–49.
5. Ibid.
6. Philip G. Zimbardo, *Shyness: What It Is, What to Do About It* (Reading, Mass.: Addison-Wesley, 1977), p. 52.
7. See, for example, Mark L. Knapp, *Interpersonal Communication and Human Relationships* (Boston, Mass.: Allyn & Bacon, 1984).
8. Emanuel M. Berger, "The Relation Between Expressed Acceptance of Self and Expressed Acceptance of Others," *Journal of Abnormal and Social Psychology* 47 (1952): 778–782.
9. See William W. Wilmot, *Dyadic Communication* (Reading, Mass.: Addison-Wesley, 1979) for a review of some of the literature on attraction and similarity.
10. Ibid., pp. 117–118.
11. Timothy Leary, *Interpersonal Diagnosis of Personality* (New York: Ronald Press, 1957).
12. Watzlawick et al., *Pragmatics of Human Communication,* pp. 107–108.

13. Larry A. Steward, *Attitudes Toward Communication: The Content Analysis of Interviews with Eight Reticent and Eight Non-reticent College Students* (M.A. thesis, Pennsylvania State University, 1968).

14. Ibid.

15. Gerald M. Phillips, "Reticence: A Perspective on Social Withdrawal," in *Avoiding Communication: Shyness, Reticence, and Communication Apprehension*, ed. John A. Daly and James C. McCroskey (Beverly Hills, Calif.: Sage, 1984), pp. 51–66.

16. See, for example, William J. Fremouw and Michael D. Scott, "Cognitive Restructuring: An Alternative Method for the Treatment of Communication Apprehension," *Communication Education* 28 (1979): 129–133.

17. James C. McCroskey, "The Communication Apprehension Prespective," in *Avoiding Communication: Shyness, Reticence, and Communication Apprehension*, ed. John A. Daly and James C. McCroskey (Beverly Hills, Calif.: Sage, 1984), pp. 13–38.

18. Ibid., p. 18.

19. Domenig, *Examination of Self-reports.*

20. Lynne Kelly, "Observers' Comparisons of the Interpersonal Communication Skills of Reticent and Nonreticent Students," *Communication* 12 (May 1983): 77–92; Lynne Kelly and Robert L. Duran, *An Investigation of the Relationship of Shyness to Self-, Partner-, Observer-, and Meta-perceptions of Communication Competence* (paper presented at the annual meeting of the Speech Communication Association, Chicago, 1984).

21. Gerald M. Phillips, "On Apples and Oranges: A Reply to Page," *Communication Education* 29 (1980): 105–108.

CHAPTER 2. ASSESSING YOURSELF AS A COMMUNICATOR

1. Emanuel M. Berger, "The Relation Between Expressed Acceptance of Self and Expressed Acceptance of Others," *Journal of Abnormal and Social Psychology* 47 (1952): 778–782.

2. Emanuel M. Berger, "Self-Acceptance Scales," in *Measures of Social Psychological Attitudes,* revised edition, ed. John P. Robinson and Phillip R. Shauer (Ann Arbor, Mich.: Institute for Social Research, the University of Michigan, 1973) pp. 109–111. The scale is included here by permission of Emanuel M. Berger, former professor of psychology, the University of Minnesota.

3. James C. McCroskey, *Oral Communication Apprehension: Reconceptualization and a New Look at Measurement* (paper presented at the Central States Speech Association Convention, Chicago, April 1981).

4. Ibid. The Personal Report of Communication Apprehension (PRCA–24) and scoring instructions were developed by James C. McCroskey, Professor of Speech Communication, West Virginia University. They are included here by permission.

5. Ibid., p. 43.

6. Ibid.

7. Ibid.

8. Ibid., p. 27.

CHAPTER 3. IMPROVING ATTITUDES AND REDUCING APPREHENSION

1. Emanuel M. Berger, "The Relation Between Expressed Acceptance of Self and Expressed Acceptance of Others," *Journal of Abnormal and Social Psychology* 47 (1952): 778–782.

2. D. Stock, "An Investigation into the Interrelationships Between the Self-concept and Feelings Directed Toward Other Persons and Groups," *Journal of Consulting Psychology* 13 (1949): 176–180.

3. R. M. Suinn and H. Hill, "Influence of Anxiety on the Relationship Between Self-acceptance and Acceptance of Others," *Journal of Consulting Psychology* 28 (1964): 116–119.

4. *Hamlet* II.ii. 259.

5. William W. Wilmot, *Dyadic Communication,* 2d ed. (Reading, Mass.: Addison-Wesley, 1979), p. 123.

6. Albert Ellis, *Humanistic Psychotherapy* (New York: McGraw-Hill, 1972).

7. Ibid.; see also S. Walen, R. Guiseppe, and R. Wessler, *A Practitioner's Guide to Rational-Emotive Therapy* (New York: Oxford University Press, 1980).

8. James C. McCroskey, "The Communication Apprehension Perspective," in *Avoiding Communication: Shyness, Reticence, and Communication Apprehension,* ed., John A. Daly and James C. McCroskey (Beverly Hills, Calif.: Sage, 1984), pp. 13–38.

9. For a copy of the tape, contact the Speech Communication Association, 5105-E Backlick Road, Annandale, VA 22003, and ask for "Deep Muscle Relaxation," by James C. McCroskey.

10. We created this sheet based on the procedure utilized by James C. McCroskey in the audio tape he created, "Deep Muscle Relaxation." The sheet is included here by permission. See note 9 to purchase the tape.

11. John A. Daly and Arnold H. Buss, "The Transitory Causes of Audience Anxiety," in *Avoiding Communication: Shyness, Reticence, and Communication Apprehension,* ed. John A. Daly and James C. McCroskey (Beverly Hills, Calif.: Sage, 1984), pp. 67–80.

12. Arnold II. Buss, "A Conception of Shyness," in *Avoiding Communication: Shyness, Reticence, and Communication Apprehension,* ed. John A. Daly and James C. McCroskey (Beverly Hills, Calif.: Sage, 1984), pp. 39–50.

13. Daly and Buss, "Transitory Causes," p. 73.

14. Buss, "Conception of Shyness," p. 41.

15. Daly and Buss, "Transitory Causes," pp. 70–72.

16. Ibid., p. 70.

CHAPTER 4. SETTING PERSONAL COMMUNICATION GOALS

1. Gerald M. Phillips, *Help for Shy People & Anyone Else Who Ever Felt Ill at Ease on Entering a Room Full of Strangers* (Englewood Cliffs, N.J.: Prentice-Hall, 1981), p. 75.

2. Phillips, 1981, p. 83.

3. Phillips, 1981, p. 86.

CHAPTER 5. ASSESSING THE COMMUNICATION SITUATION AND LISTENERS

1. Lloyd Bitzer, "The Rhetorical Situation," *Philosophy and Rhetoric* 1 (January 1968): 1–14.

2. Gerald M. Phillips and Nancy J. Metzger, *Intimate Communication* (Boston: Allyn & Bacon, 1976).

3. Ibid.

4. Abraham Maslow, *Motivation and Personality,* 2d ed. (New York: Harper & Row, 1970).

5. William C. Schutz, *FIRO: A Three-Dimensional Theory of Interpersonal Behavior* (New York: Holt, Rinehart and Winston, 1958); reprint ed., *The Interpersonal Underworld* (Palo Alto, Calif.: Science and Behavior Books, 1966).

CHAPTER 6. COMMUNICATION IN SOCIAL RELATIONSHIPS

1. Robert S. Weiss, "The Fund of Sociability," *Trans-Action* 6 (1969): 36–43.
2. Ibid., p. 38.
3. Gerald M. Phillips and H. Lloyd Goodall, Jr., *Loving and Living* (Englewood Cliffs, N.J.: Prentice-Hall, 1983).
4. Ibid., p. 25.
5. See Gerald R. Miller, "The Current Status of Theory and Research in Interpersonal Communication," *Human Communication Research* 4 (Winter 1978): 164–178.
6. Ibid., p. 168.
7. Ibid., p. 167.
8. Ibid., p. 168.
9. Ibid., p. 169.
10. Irwin Altman and Dalmas Taylor, *Social Penetration: The Development of Interpersonal Relationships* (New York: Holt, Rinehart and Winston, 1973), pp. 15–20.
11. Philip Emmert and William C. Donaghy, *Human Communication: Elements and Contexts* (Reading, Mass.: Addison-Wesley, 1981), p. 78.
12. David W. Johnson, *Reaching Out,* 2d ed. (Englewood Cliffs, N.J.: Prentice-Hall, 1981), pp. 90–94.
13. Johnson, *Reaching Out,* pp. 114–116.
14. See Edward E. Jones et al., *Attribution: Perceiving the Causes of Behavior* (Morristown, N.J.: General Learning Press, 1972).
15. Mark L. Knapp, *Interpersonal Communication and Human Relationships* (Boston: Allyn & Bacon, 1984), pp. 8–13.
16. Ibid., p. 8.
17. Ibid., p. 9.
18. Ibid., p. 12.
19. Ibid., p. 13.
20. Johnson, *Reaching Out,* pp. 6–7.
21. Ibid., p. 51.
22. Ibid., p. 7.
23. Joseph A. DeVito, *The Interpersonal Communication Book,* 3rd ed. (New York: Harper & Row, Publishers, 1983), p. 33.
24. Judy Cornelia Pearson and Paul Edward Nelson, *Understanding and Sharing: An Introduction to Speech Communication,* 3rd ed. (Dubuque, Iowa: Wm. C. Brown, 1985), p. 107.
25. Johnson, *Reaching Out,* p. 80.
26. Ibid., p. 80
27. Philip Emmert and Victoria J. Lukasko Emmert, *Interpersonal Communication,* 3rd ed. (Dubuque, Iowa: Wm. C. Brown, 1984) p. 128.
28. Paul Watzlawick, Janet H. Beavin, and Don D. Jackson, *Pragmatics of Human Communication: A Study of Interactional Patterns, Pathologies, and Paradoxes* (New York: Norton, 1967), pp. 51–52.
29. Stewart L. Tubbs and Sylvia Moss, *Interpersonal Communication* (New York: Random House, 1978), pp. 123–127.

30. Joseph Luft, *Of Human Interaction* (Palo Alto, Calif.: National Press, 1969), pp. 132–133.
31. Dorothy Sarnoff, *Speech Can Change Your Life* (New York: Dell, 1970), pp. 108–126.
32. Philip Zimbardo, *Shyness: What It Is, What to Do About It* (Reading, Mass.: Addison-Wesley, 1977), pp. 176–177.
33. Ibid., pp. 175–186.

CHAPTER 7. GROUP DISCUSSION

1. Marvin E. Shaw, *Group Dynamics: The Psychology of Small Group Behavior,* 2d ed. (New York: McGraw-Hill, 1976), p. 11.
2. Ibid.
3. John K. Brilhart, *Effective Group Discussion,* 4th ed. (Dubuque, Iowa: Brown, 1982), p.25.
4. Stewart L. Tubbs, *A Systems Approach to Small Group Interaction,* 2d ed. (Reading, Mass.: Addison-Wesley, 1984), p. 13.
5. Brilhart, *Effective Group Discussion,* p. 45.
6. For a summary of this research, see Bruce C. McKinney, "The Effects of Reticence on Group Interaction," *Communication Quarterly* 30 (Spring 1982): 124–128.
7. Ibid., p. 126.
8. Brilhart, *Effective Group Discussion,* pp. 51–52.
9. Ibid., p. 56.
10. Ibid., p. 42.
11. Gerald M. Phillips, Douglas J. Pedersen, and Julia T. Wood, *Group Discussion: A Practical Guide to Participation and Leadership* (Boston: Houghton Mifflin, 1979), pp. 136–145.
12. Tubbs, *Systems Approach,* p. 105.
13. Shaw, *Group Dynamics,* p. 158.
14. Ibid., p. 156.
15. Ibid., p. 158.
16. Ibid., pp. 133–137.
17. Tubbs, *Systems Approach,* p. 104.
18. See, for example, Randy Y. Hirokawa, "Group Communication and Problem-solving Effectiveness: A Critical Review of Inconsistent Findings," *Communication Quarterly* 30 (1982): 134–141; and Dale G. Leathers, "Quality of Group Communication as a Determinant of Group Product," *Speech Monographs* 39 (1972): 166–173.
19. Randy Y. Hirokawa and Roger Pace, "A Descriptive Investigation of the Possible Communication-based Reasons for Effective and Ineffective Group Decision Making," *Communication Monographs* 50 (1983): 363–379.
20. Kenneth D. Benne and Paul Sheats, "Functional Roles of Group Members," *Journal of Social Issues* 4 (1948): 41–49.
21. Brilhart, *Effective Group Discussion,* p. 103.
22. Shaw, *Group Dynamics,* p. 247.
23. Ibid., p. 265.
24. Ibid., p. 250.
25. Lynne Kelly and Robert L. Duran, "Interaction and Performance in Small Groups: A Descriptive Report," *International Journal of Small Group Research* 1 (September 1985): p. 189.
26. Ibid., p. 190.

27. Brilhart, *Effective Group Discussion,* p. 180.
28. Ibid.
29. Tubbs, *Systems Approach,* p. 13.
30. Ibid.
31. Susan Sorenson, *Group Hate* (M.A. thesis, Pennsylvania State University, 1981).
32. Phillips et al., *Group Discussion,* pp. 122–241.
33. Tubbs, *Systems Approach,* p. 165.

CHAPTER 8. PREPARING A PUBLIC SPEECH

1. David Wallechinsky, Irving Wallace, and Amy Wallace, *The Book of Lists* (New York: Bantam Books, 1978), p. 469.
2. James Winans, *Speech-Making* (Englewood Cliffs, N.J.: Prentice-Hall, 1938).
3. Rudolph Verderber, *The Challenge of Effective Speaking* (Belmont, Calif.: Wadsworth, 1982), pp. 150–155.
4. Stephen E. Lucas, *The Art of Public Speaking* (New York: Random House, 1983), pp. 258–268.
5. Douglas Ehninger, Alan H. Monroe, and Bruce E. Gronbeck, *Principles and Types of Speech Communication,* 8th ed. (Glenview, Ill.: Scott, Foresman and Company, 1978), p. 307.
6. Ibid.
7. Alan H. Monroe and Douglas Ehninger, *Principles and Types of Speech Communication,* 7th ed. (Glenview, Ill.: Scott, Foresman, 1974), pp. 353–377.
8. J. Jerome Zolten and Gerald M. Phillips, *Speaking to an Audience: A Practical Method of Preparing and Performing* (Indianapolis: Bobbs-Merrill, 1985), p. 41.
9. Gerald M. Phillips and J. Jerome Zolten, *Structuring Speech: A How-to-Do-It Book About Public Speaking* (Indianapolis: Bobbs-Merrill, 1976), pp. 124–165.

CHAPTER 9. DELIVERING A PUBLIC SPEECH

1. See, for example, James C. McCroskey, "The Implementation of a Large-scale Program of Systematic Desensitization," *Speech Teacher* 21 (1972): 255–264.
2. Gordon I. Zimmerman, James L. Owen, and David R. Seibert, *Speech Communication: A Contemporary Introduction,* 2nd ed. (New York: West Publishing, 1980), pp. 205–212.
3. Eugene E. White, *Practical Public Speaking,* 3d ed. (New York: Macmillan, 1978), pp. 322–333.
4. Ibid., p. 322.
5. Ibid., p. 324.
6. Ibid., p. 328.
7. Zimmerman et al., *Speech Communication,* pp. 219–226.
8. Gerald M. Phillips, Kathleen M. Kougl, and Lynne Kelly, *Speaking in Public and Private* (Indianapolis: Bobbs-Merrill, 1985), p. 232.
9. Ibid.
10. Zimmerman et al., *Speech Communication,* pp. 255–258.
11. Rudolph Verderber, *The Challenge of Effective Speaking* (Belmont, Calif.: Wadsworth, 1982), p. 123.

Glossary

ABC model of reasonable thinking   A technique for changing unreasonable beliefs into reasonable ones by identifying unreasonable beliefs and challenging them with logic.

activating event   An occurrence that triggers feelings; the "A" in the ABC model.

attributions   Inferences concerning the causes of one's own or others' behavior.

audience homogeneity (heterogeneity)   How similar (different) a speaker perceives audience members to be in comparison to one another.

breadth of communication   The variety of information or topics one shares with others.

centralized seating arrangement   A seating arrangement for a group of people in which one person is in a position that allows him or her to control the flow of the discussion.

cohesiveness   The degree to which the members of a group like and respect one another, get along, and desire to remain in the group.

common ground   Part of an introduction to a speech designed to show the audience how the speech topic relates to them and why it is important for them to listen.

communication   A process through which people create meaning by exchanging verbal and nonverbal symbols.

communication apprehension   An individual's level of fear or anxiety about communication.

confirmation   The sending of messages that provide another with support and that recognize the other's feelings and ideas as valid.

credibility   The degree of expertise and trustworthiness of a speaker as perceived by audience members.

decentralized seating arrangement   A seating arrangement for a group of people in which members can interact equally, with no individual in a position to direct the flow of discussion; for example, a circular arrangement of group members.

depth of communication   The level of intimacy of the information one shares with others.

destructive spiral A cycle of behaviors in which behavior is enacted that produces undesirable behavior, which produces further undesirable behavior, and so on.

disconfirmation The sending of messages that reject the validity of another's feelings or ideas.

disputing Challenging an unreasonable belief with logic; part of the ABC model of reasonable thinking.

dyadic communication Communication between two participants.

entertainment speech One designed to produce enjoyment in audience members.

example A single instance used to develop a generalization; one of the types of supporting material for a public speech.

extemporaneous speech A speech that has been carefully prepared and rehearsed and is delivered from notes rather than being read word for word.

goal A specific statement of what one is trying to accomplish by talking.

goal setting A step-by-step procedure for formulating communication goals, developing a plan for one's behavior, and identifying concrete indicators of goal achievement.

group Three or more persons who are interacting with one another in such a manner that each influences and is influenced by each other person.

group communication Communication that takes place among a fairly small number of participants who interact both verbally and nonverbally.

group conflict Any disagreement within a group; the conflict may be about personalities or about ideas.

group hate A negative attitude about the group process.

group roles Behaviors consistently performed by group members that come to be expected of those members.

illustration A long example or story; one of the types of supporting materials for a public speech.

impersonal (noninterpersonal) relationship A relationship in which participants relate to one another as social roles and make predictions about one another's behavior on the basis of expectations about people belonging to that group.

impromptu speech One in which the speaker has little or no time for preparation.

inference A guess made on the basis of available information but which is not directly observable.

informative speech One designed to present information in an understandable manner.

internal preview An overview of the points a speaker will be covering embedded within the body of the speech.

internal summary A brief review of the points the speaker has covered before discussing additional ideas.

intimacy A relationship function provided by relationships in which people can express thoughts and feelings freely, trust exists, and the partners are available for one another.

listener assessment The observation of the other participants in a communication situation in order to determine appropriate communication behavior.

maintenance roles Roles enacted to help maintain harmonious relationships among group members.

manuscript speech A speech written out and read to the audience.

memorized speech A manuscript speech committed to and delivered from memory.

Monroe's Motivated Sequence A five-step procedure for organizing a speech.

nonimmediate audience People present in a communication situation but not directly involved in the interaction between two or more participants.

nonverbal communication Any behavior with message value such as facial expressions, gestures, posture, body movements, body positioning, eye contact, and vocal tone.

norms Expectations for behavior operating within a situation.

novelty The newness of a communication situation; one of the major features of a situation producing situational communication apprehension.

other-acceptance The ability to accept other people without any requirements or conditions.

permanent closing A message designed to end a conversation by signaling to the other participants that future interaction is not likely to take place.

perception The process of organizing random stimuli received from the environment, transforming them, and attaching meaning to them.

personal (interpersonal) relationships A relationship in which participants relate to one another as unique individuals and make predictions about one another's behavior on the basis of knowledge of likes, dislikes, values, attitudes, and so forth.

persuasive speech One designed to change or influence the audience's feelings, beliefs, attitudes, or actions.

power The ability to influence the behavior of others.

PRCA-24 A 24-item scale designed to measure traitlike communication apprehension.

preview Part of an introduction to a speech designed to provide an overview of the main points of the speech.

relational conflict Problems and disagreements encountered within a specific interpersonal relationship.

residual message The main point of a speech; the one idea the speaker wants the audience to remember if they forget everything else about the speech.

reticent A term used to describe individuals who avoid and fear communication situations due to their deficient communication skills.

rhetorical (communication) situation A particular time and place in which one feels something can be accomplished by communicating.

self-acceptance The ability to accept ourselves without any requirements or conditions.

self-disclosure Providing another with information about oneself that the other could not obtain otherwise.

self-fulfilling prophecy Bringing about the very outcome one predicted through one's own behavior.

shy A term used to describe individuals who avoid and fear communication situations and who have a tendency to lack self-confidence; similar to the word *reticent* except one who is reticent is presumed to possess inadequate communication skills.

situation A particular time and place in which participants communicate.

situation assessment Observing situational features in order to determine appropriate communication behavior.

situational communication apprehension The occasional experience of fear or anxiety about communication.

small group A group consisting of three to ten members.

social integration A relationship function provided by relationships in which people share ideas, experiences, and small favors.

specific speech purpose A precise statement of what a speaker is trying to accomplish with the audience.

Standard Agenda A six-phase procedure for group problem solving.

status The value attached to one's position in a group.

symbol Something (a word, a nonverbal act, a number, etc.) that represents a thing or idea.

symmetrical escalation   When the behavior produced by a participant is followed by a similar but more intense behavior from another, and so on.

systematic desensitization   A method of relaxation designed to help individuals overcome fears and phobias.

task roles   Those roles that are enacted by group members to help the group achieve its task.

temporary closing   A message designed to end a conversation by signaling a desire to interact with the other at a future date.

traitlike communication apprehension   An individual's generalized level of fear or anxiety about communication; the experience of fear or anxiety across communication contexts.

transitions   Words, phrases, or sentences used in a speech to show the audience when the speaker is moving from one idea to the next and how those points are related.

unreasonable beliefs   Beliefs that require speakers to be perfect or to do the impossible; beliefs that are unrealistic.

Index

ABC model of reasonable thinking, 58–61, 70, 125, 231–232
Activating event, 59–61, 231. *See also* ABC model of reasonable thinking
Anxiety, 15–17, 23, 37, 62, 64–65, 126, 130, 155, 227, 231, 233. *See also* Communication apprehension; Fear; Nervousness
audience, 227
situational, 65–70
traitlike, 45
Apprehension. *See* Communication apprehension
Attitudes, 12–15, 27. *See also* Beliefs
assessing, 28–33
improving, 52–62, 69–70, 120–126, 153–154, 168, 200–202, 223
reasonable, 55, 70
toward communication, 17–19, 21–22, 25, 28, 31, 47, 51, 92, 122, 153, 200, 226
toward others, 17–19, 21–22, 25, 28, 51, 54, 122–123, 153, 200. *See also* Other-acceptance
toward self, 17–19, 21, 25, 28, 46–47, 51, 54, 122–123, 153, 200. *See also* Self-acceptance
unreasonable, 55, 70, 200
Attribution, 124–126, 209–210, 228, 231. *See also* Meaning
checking, 124
Audience. *See also* Listener
analysis, 170–173, 175, 178, 183
attitudes of, 179–181, 197
characteristics of, 67–70
defined, 67
expectations, 181
goals of, 170
homogeneity (heterogeneity), 67–68, 70, 231
interests of, 170, 179–181, 197
knowledge level of, 179–181, 183, 197
needs of, 170
nonimmediate, 98–99, 102, 232
novelty of, 67, 70
position, 172–173
size of, 96
Authority figures, 27, 72–73, 79, 102–105, 127. *See also* Communication, dyadic

Beavin, J. H., 9, 11, 14, 225, 228
Beliefs. *See also* Attitudes
consequences of, 59–61

guides for testing, 57–58, 70, 200–201
realistic, 54
reasonable, 26, 32, 58–59, 61, 70, 92, 200–201, 223, 231
scale, 31–32
unrealistic, 56
unreasonable, 21–22, 28, 31, 33, 46–47, 56–62, 70, 92, 121, 125–126, 200–201, 223, 231, 234
Bitzer, L., 90, 227
Brilhart, J. K., 145, 152, 229–230
Buss, A. H., 66–67, 69, 227

Class participation, 23, 25, 47
Communication
breadth, 120, 136, 142, 231
components of, 6–9, 17
defined, 5–6, 17, 231
depth, 120, 136, 142, 231
dyadic, 4, 10, 16–18, 38–40, 45, 47, 117–142, 227, 232. *See also* Authority figures
nonverbal, 5–6, 10, 17–18, 54, 96, 111, 139, 232
process of, 4–9, 145
public, 4, 10–11, 16–18. *See also* Public speaking; Public speech
value of, 11–12
Communication apprehension, 12, 15–19, 23, 25, 27, 33, 35–37, 47, 51, 53, 56, 62, 64–66, 69, 123, 127, 154, 175, 201–204, 223, 226–227. *See also* Anxiety; Fear; Nervousness
assessing, 33–37
controlling, 53, 62–66, 70, 127–129, 153–155, 168, 202–204, 223
defined, 231
situational, 37, 46, 62, 65–70, 223
traitlike, 37, 46, 62, 65, 233–234
Comparisons, 191, 198. *See also* Public speech, supporting materials
Confirmation, 132–133, 142, 231. *See also* Disconfirmation

Daly, J. A., 66–67, 69, 226–227
Dance, F. E. X., 4, 225
Definitions, 191, 198. *See also* Public speech, supporting materials
Delivery. *See also* Public speaking
adapting, 204–207, 213–214, 222
environment for, 219–222, 224. *See also* Physical setting

Delivery (*Continued*)
  eye contact, 212, 214, 219, 223
  facial expression, 214, 219, 223
  gestures, 212–214, 219, 223
  language, 206–209, 212, 223
  speech patterns, 209–210, 212, 223
  steps in preparation for, 204–224
  types of, 204–207, 222–223
  use of body, 141, 168, 212–214, 219, 223
  use of notes, 169, 206, 219, 222
  use of voice, 141, 168, 207, 210–212, 223.
    See also Voice
Descriptions, 191, 198. *See also* Public
  speech, supporting materials
Destructive spiral, 55
  defined, 232
Disconfirmation, 130, 132–133, 232. *See also*
  Confirmation
Disputing, 59–61, 232. *See also* ABC model
  of reasonable thinking
  effect of, 61
Donaghy, W. C., 121, 228
Dyad. *See* Communication, dyadic

Ehninger, D., 173, 230
Ellis, A., 55–56, 59, 227
Emmert, P., 121, 228
Entertainment speech, 170–175, 177, 197,
  232. *See also* Public speech, types of
Examples, 185, 190, 198, 232. *See also*
  Public speech, supporting materials
Extemporaneous speech, 24, 80, 204–206,
  209, 223, 232. *See also* Delivery, types
  of

Fear, 15, 56, 62, 66, 68, 70, 92. *See also*
  Anxiety; Communication apprehension;
  Nervousness
  of public speaking, 168

Goals, 44, 73–75, 90, 92–93, 97–99, 101,
  105–106, 108, 112, 155, 162, 203
  defined, 72, 232
  defining goal areas, 76–77
  formulating goal statements, 77–80
  preparation for, 83–87, 128–129
  realistic, 79
  unrealistic, 79
Goal setting, 4, 17, 89–90, 106, 128–129,
  142, 154–155, 157, 202–203, 223
  defined, 72–73, 166, 232
  steps of, 75–87
  value of, 73–75
Goodall, H. L., 119, 228
Gronbeck, B. E., 173, 230
Group, 10, 57. *See also* Small group
  agenda, 147
  apprehension about, 143–144, 146–147,
    153–155, 165–166. *See also*
    Communication apprehension
  attitudes about, 143–144, 146, 153–154,
    165–166. *See also* Attitudes; Beliefs

cohesiveness, 151, 166, 231
communication, 16–18, 149, 166, 229, 232
conflict, 151–153, 164, 166, 232
defined, 144, 232
discussion, 23, 25, 40–42, 47, 78–79, 200,
  229–230
environment, 147–149, 165
leader, 146–148, 163. *See also* Leadership
members, 146–149, 165
norms, 41. *See also* Norms, group
outcomes, 149, 151–152, 156, 162, 166
problem-solving, 149, 152, 156–161,
  229
procedures, 149, 166
process, 144–152
purpose, 147–149, 165
size, 147–149, 165
skills for, 143–144, 149, 155–166
task, 147, 162, 165
Group-hate, 153, 230, 232

Hirokawa, R. Y., 149, 229

Illustrations, 190, 198, 232. *See also* Public
  speech, supporting materials
Impromptu speech, 204, 206–207, 223, 232.
  See also Delivery, types of
Inferences, 107–108, 110, 112, 179, 232
Informative speech, 170–172, 174–175,
  177–179, 181–182, 197, 232. *See also*
  Public speech, types of

Jackson, D. D., 9, 11, 14, 225, 228
Johnson, D. W., 130, 228

Knapp, M. L., 125–126, 225, 228

Larson, C. E., 4, 225
Leadership, 25, 40, 150, 163–164, 166, 229.
  See also Group, leader
Leary, T., 14, 225
Listener, 21. *See also* Audience; Listening
  adaptation, 141–142, 165, 170, 172
  analysis, 134–135, 155, 180, 204
  assessment, 89, 91–92, 100–113, 120, 135,
    139, 162, 164–166, 176, 178–183, 192,
    197, 232
  defined, 91
  goals of, 106–111, 113
  motivating, 170–171
  needs, interests, values of, 109–113
  relationship with, 103–106, 108, 113. *See
    also* Relationships
Listening, 17, 38, 40, 136, 179, 181, 186,
  210. *See also* Listener
Luft, J., 133, 229

McCroskey, J. C., 33, 35–37, 63, 226–227,
  230
Manuscript speech, 204–205, 213, 223, 232.
  See also Delivery, types of
Maslow, A., 110, 227

Meaning, 5–6, 17, 121–125, 208, 210. *See also* Attribution
Memorized speech, 204–206, 223, 232. *See also* Delivery, types of
Message, 9, 18, 169. *See also* Communication, components of
confirming, 132–133
disconfirming, 132–133
Monroe, A. H., 173–174, 230
Monroe's motivated sequence, 173–174, 232

Nervousness, 15, 18, 22, 33, 64, 203–205, 210, 214. *See also* Anxiety; Communication apprehension; Fear
Norms, 8, 90–91, 93–96, 98–99, 101, 103–105, 107, 112, 120, 136–137, 139, 141–142, 233
group, 150–151, 165–166. *See also* Group, norms

Oral presentations. *See* Public speech
Oral reports. *See* Public speech
Other-acceptance, 14, 53–54, 61, 70, 121, 130, 142, 153, 201, 223, 227, 233. *See also* Attitudes, toward others
Outline, 169, 184–193, 196, 198, 206, 216, 222. *See also* Outlining; Public speech, organization of
transitions, 170, 172, 195–196, 198, 234
Outlining, 42, 84, 185–190. *See also* Outline; Public speech, organization of

Pace, R., 149, 229
Participants, 6–7, 9, 17–18. *See also* Communication, components of
Pedersen, D. J., 147, 156, 229
Perception, 5–6, 68
checking, 123–124
defined, 121–122, 233
influences on, 123
mistakes of, 123
process of, 121–125, 142
Personal communicator profile, 44–45, 47, 51, 62
Personal improvement program, 45–46
Persuasive speech, 170–175, 177–179, 184, 190, 197, 233. *See also* Public speech, types of
Phillips, G. M., 119, 147, 156, 225–230
Physical setting, 96–98, 102, 113. *See also* Situation, assessment; Situational features
comfort of, 182–183
distractions in, 96–97, 145, 147–148, 182, 220–221, 224
organization of, 97, 147–148, 181–183
size of, 96–97, 147–148, 220–221, 224
Power, 233. *See also* Status
in groups, 150, 153, 166
PRCA-24, 33, 36–37, 47, 62, 65–66, 126, 143, 146, 154, 168, 201–202, 226, 233
scale, 33–35

Public speaking, 21–23, 25–26, 42–47, 56, 92, 168, 230. *See also* Delivery; Public speech
apprehension, 168, 175, 192, 201–204. *See also* Communication apprehension
attitudes about, 168, 200–201. *See also* Attitudes; Beliefs
as extended conversation, 167–170, 174, 196, 211
hierarchy, 64, 202
skills of, 167–168
Public speech, 17, 21–23, 42, 47, 67–68, 96, 168–169. *See also* Delivery; Public speaking
attention-getting devices, 23–24, 135, 179, 190, 192, 195, 198, 208–209
conclusions, 43, 171, 185, 189, 192–196, 198
delivery. *See* Delivery
generating ideas for, 184–185, 190, 197
introductions, 23–24, 42, 171, 185, 189, 192–196, 198, 214, 231, 233
notes. *See* Delivery, use of notes
occasion, 174, 181–182, 197, 207
organization of, 169–170, 172–174, 178, 185–190, 198. *See also* Outline; Outlining
preparation, 23–24, 84, 167–168, 175–198
purpose, 170, 174, 177–178, 180–184, 187, 197
rehearsal, 42, 84, 205–206, 210–212, 215, 217, 222–223
research, 184–185, 197
supporting materials, 185, 190–192, 195–198, 214
topics, 170–172, 175–178, 180–181, 197, 212
types of, 167–168, 170–174, 179

Quotations, 185, 191, 195, 198. *See also* Public speech, supporting materials

Reasonable thinking, 54, 56–61, 201. *See also* ABC model of reasonable thinking
Relational conflict, 8, 233
Relationships, 11–12, 54. *See also* Communication, components of
apprehension about, 126–128, 142. *See also* Communication apprehension
attitudes about, 120–126, 142. *See also* Attitudes; Beliefs
impersonal, 232
functions of, 118–119, 142
with listeners, 103–106. *See also* Listener, relationship with
misconceptions about, 125–126, 142
personal, 233
skills for developing, 130–142
stages of, 12
types of, 8, 103–106, 118–120, 142

Relaxation techniques, 37, 46, 65–66, 70, 127, 154, 166, 201–203, 223. *See also* Systematic desensitization
muscle procedure, 63–64, 202
short version, 65–66, 128, 154
Residual message, 184, 186, 189, 193–194, 197–198
defined, 183, 233
Reticence, 225–227, 229. *See also* Reticent; Shy; Shyness
Reticent, 14, 223, 225–226. *See also* Reticence; Shy; Shyness
Roles
group, 149–150, 166, 229, 232
maintenance, 150, 163–164, 232
novelty of, 67
task, 150, 163–164, 234
Rules. *See also* Norms
in groups, 165
private, 8, 105, 120, 142, 165

Sarnoff, D., 135, 229
Schutz, W. C., 110, 228
Self-acceptance, 13, 15, 21, 26, 28, 31, 45, 51–53, 61, 69–70, 121, 130, 142, 201, 226–227. *See also* Attitudes, toward self
defined, 13, 52, 233
scale, 28–30, 47, 153, 223
Self-assessment, 26, 45, 51
guide to, 27–44
Self-disclosure, 133–134, 142
defined, 233
Self-fulfilling prophecy, 13–14, 55
defined, 233
Shaw, M. E., 144, 150, 229
Shy, 11, 14–17, 22, 29, 227. *See also* Reticence; Reticent; Shyness
defined, 233
Shyness, 11, 140, 225, 227, 229. *See also* Reticence; Reticent; Shy
Situation, 7–9, 18. *See also* Communication, components of; Physical setting; Situational features; Time
adaptation to, 141–142, 165
analysis of, 24, 105, 112, 134, 155, 170–171, 175, 182, 192, 204
assessment, 25, 89–92, 102, 105, 135, 139, 164–166, 176, 178–183, 192, 197, 213, 233
defined, 90, 233
novelty of, 66–67, 70
presence of others in, 98–100, 102, 113
purpose of, 94–95, 102, 107, 113
rhetorical, 90, 227, 233
types of, 9–11, 18
Situational features, 93–102, 136–138, 147. *See also* Physical setting; Situation; Time
provoking apprehension, 66–70

Skill level, 16–19, 51, 126, 144, 168
assessing, 37–44
Small group, 26, 229. *See also* Group
definition of, 144, 233
discussion, 22, 24–25, 27, 47
problem-solving, 152
task-oriented, 144
Social conversation, 22–23, 25, 37–38, 47, 78, 81–82, 84, 111, 134–136, 140–142, 168–170, 200
ending, 38, 139–140, 233–234
initiating, 38, 136–137, 211
maintaining, 38, 137–139
Speaker credibility, 194, 198, 231
defined, 193
Standard Agenda, 152, 233
phases of, 156–161
Statistics, 185, 190–191, 198, 216. *See also* Public speech, supporting materials
Status, 233. *See also* Power
in groups, 150, 166
Stock, D., 53, 227
Symbol, 5
defined, 6, 233
nonverbal, 5–6, 9, 18, 125, 231
verbal, 5–6, 9, 18, 125, 231
Symmetrical escalation, 14
defined, 234
Systematic desensitization, 62–66, 70, 127–128, 142, 230, 234. *See also* Relaxation techniques
hierarchy, 70
hierarchy for group discussion, 154–155
hierarchy for public speaking, 64, 202
hierarchy for relating, 127

Time, 102, 113. *See also* Situation; Situational features
available, 100–101, 182–183
of day, 100–101, 182–183, 197
of week, 100–101
Trust, 130, 134, 136, 142, 146
Tubbs, S. L., 145, 228–230

Verderber, R., 171, 230
Visual aids, 17, 84–85, 181, 191–192, 198, 200–201, 212, 220, 222, 224
use of, 214–219
Voice. *See also* Delivery
effective use of, 38, 41–42, 140–141, 168–169
sound of, 210–212

Watzlawick, P., 9, 11, 14, 225, 228
Weiss, R. S., 118, 228
White, E. E., 207–208, 230
Winans, J., 168, 230
Wood, J. T., 147, 156, 229

Zimbardo, P. G., 11, 140, 225, 229

CPSIA information can be obtained at www.ICGtesting.com
Printed in the USA
LVOW11s2130020715

444839LV00001B/142/P